Sing Before Breakfast

A Story of Gettysburg

By George Stein

Art and illustrations by Doug Stein

ISBN: 0615605214
ISBN 13: 9780615605210

To the memory of my wonderful old fighter-pilot friend,
Vincent T. Ford,
for his grace, his decency and his love of history;
He was always a joy to be with.

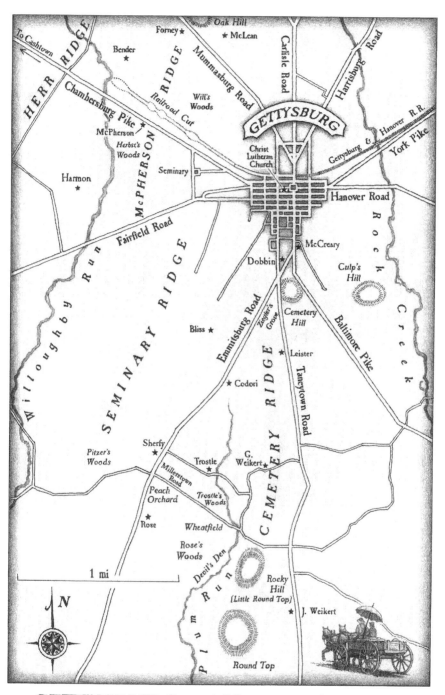

GETTYSBURG and Vicinity - June 1863

Contents

Illustrations

Title Page

Full Page

Chapter Endings

PREFACE

History is after all the story of everything. This story is about events that happened at one small place on the map in mostly three days, a mere speck in historic time and place but a very significant speck that would have extraordinary effect on the future of the United States and the world as well. This story is an allegory for the renewal and coming out of the United States as a nation and the major changes brought about by the American Civil War.

The four years of the Civil War were arguably the most consequential in American history. We often hear that the war ended slavery and that more American lives were lost* than in all the other wars combined. These facts are essentially true. But also of great impact and enduring consequence is the fact that the nation itself came into being then as well. In an incredible surge of growth, what had existed before that time as a loose federation of individual states was transformed into a world power in such fields as invention, medicine, manufacturing, transportation, communication and military superiority.

Out of the ashes of the Civil War, the United States *became*.

*During the Vietnam War, 58,000 Americans died and are memorialized on black granite panels in Washington, DC. It would require eleven such monuments stretching over a mile to contain the names of those who died in the Civil War.

INTRODUCTION

I am a handsome soldier boy;
Now, don't you think I'm grand?
I wear a pretty uniform
And strut to beat the band
I march along to drum and fife
As off we go to war.
I'd never trade the army life
For what I had before

THERE ARE A FEW THINGS I should tell you about before we get on with the story.

We were all as innocent as newborn lambs here in Adams County before the rebel army came through. We thought we knew all about war, but we knew next to nothing, and when it came, it came down on us hard.

In late June of 1863, the armies of both north and south converged on Gettysburg with 170,000 men and 80,000 animals. In twenty hours of combat spread over the first three days of July, almost a third of those engaged, lay dead, wounded or were missing or captured. Besides the enormous task of disposing of the 7,000 bodies dead on the field, another 4,000 of the 21,000 wounded would later die, and five thousand dead horses were left to rot in the July sun for the citizens of Gettysburg to deal with. In the course of that monstrous event, much of our quiet, beautiful countryside was savaged and destroyed. Eventually, nature would take over to heal the land, but some things would never come back as they once were.

I wrote this book over most of my life. It has lain fallow for long stretches, years even, like an old, neglected friendship, separated by allowed distractions and by the beguiling daydream that a lifetime is forever. I began seventy years ago from notes I wrote down when I was twelve years old. Therefore, parts of this book will speak to you in the childhood eloquence of simpler times. Other parts will be drawn from across the spectrum of my life's experience. The opportunities of the passing years have enabled me to fill in and clarify things unknown or not understood by me at the time of the battle. I hope you will find this passing from one voice to the other rather seamless and not confusing.

If anyone else had told me all he had seen and done, I guess I would have found it hard to believe, but I have never had to stretch the truth. It came already stretched to the limit that sane and ordinary men could do to one another such things as they did.

I have always striven to be accurate as well as truthful, unlike others who plump up a story to make it more interesting or dramatic, or to fill gaps in their knowledge, often with a seriously flawed imagination. My real life experiences were dramatic enough to stand on their own and were more far-fetched than anything my limited imagination could put up in competition. I saw horrors enough, and less often, acts of sublime courage and gallantry, but I never saw the need to fiddle with the truth about any of it. If there are inaccuracies in my report, they are likely due to the following reasons.

First, the passing of time will fog the memory to some degree and, what's worse, will reinforce perceptions wrong from the start. Furthermore, after so many years, it is next to impossible to make all the pieces fit as well as they once did. Yet other things remain as fresh and clear to me now as if they had happened yesterday.

Second, in the extreme excitement of the battlefield, the mind can play strange tricks on itself. There were times I was so scared I felt my heart would pop out through my mouth. Other times, in the thick of the fight swirling around me, enthralled by extreme terror, a strange calm would descend about me. All fear would dissipate and give way to fateful, even peaceful, resignation. The scene before me would become crystal clear. The din of battle would go silent, and I would be suspended as if in a dream. In those instances, I'm not sure how well I separated what truly was from what appeared to be, but I've tried to do so here.

Third, no matter how wise in the ways of war and how high a rank a man attains, in most cases, he only can see what's going on for maybe fifty yards. Most actions are obscured by terrain or smoke or trees and brush, or may be out of range of vision and out of control ... or beyond comprehension altogether. Further, once a battle gets going, it quickly develops into a savage, indescribable free-for-all.

And no one person ever sees or knows it all.

As I review what I wrote so many years ago, I realize that some memories remain undimmed: the sharp *spangs* and dull *whumps* of the guns, the *fitz!* and *crack!* and concussion of bursting shells, the acrid smell of gunpowder, the deafening crash and roar of massed musketry, the obscene wreckage of the battlefield, the haunting cries of the wounded and the pale faces of resignation on men reaching out to take the hand of death.

Other memories are more elusive: the overriding private fear that I would never see home again, the sinking fear that we would not prevail against such a terrible and determined adversary, and the piercing, disorienting terror brought on by the chaos of the moment. These hang somewhere in a mist between knowing and forgetting, made gentler by a blessed clemency to survive such things and move on with life.

All the thousands of books about Gettysburg disagree to some extent. Certainly, none are the same. But this much is true and immutable: you cannot set foot upon this hallowed ground but that you feel a sense of drama with every step. These fields and pathways abound in gentle quietude now, yet here you feel the encompassing tension of history yearning to come forth and speak to you. The names of ordinary and anonymous country swatches of land have rung out with emotion down through the ages: Willoughby Run, The Railroad Cut, McPherson's Farm, Culp's Hill, Cemetery Ridge, Seminary Ridge, Little Round Top, Devil's Den, The Peach Orchard, The Wheatfield, The Valley of Death, The Little Copse of Trees, The Low Stone Wall.

People by the millions from all over the world come to the stillness of this place and let its mystery descend about them and try to comprehend the enormity of what happened here.

Now for me, the writing is finally done, on this my eighty-second birthday, an age when old men rub their elbows, complain about the cold, and appreciate a comforting fire and a good cup of sassafras tea to thin the blood. The many years of my life have slipped quietly away, and it seems as though one day I just looked up and noticed they were gone. I know too well the sands are running out for me now, and I have no idea how many days I have left but not many, I think. Sometimes I feel finality rushing toward me like winter twilight.

So, I leave you these words to reflect upon ... and to ponder.

C.R.B., November 6, 1932 — Fairfield, Pennsylvania

Chapter One - In for a Blow

Old times done be passin',
Yonder come de dawn;
Armies be a-massin',
Old times soon be gone.

I GUESS I SHOULD START with what we knew of the whereabouts of the rebel army, which is to say, not very much at first. We did know that Robert E. Lee and an army some said was 100,000 strong had crossed into southern Pennsylvania somewhere southwest of Chambersburg and now lay stretched out all the way to the Susquehanna River.

Everybody read the newspapers and gossiped constantly about the war. There had been a lot of talk about what would happen if the war came into Pennsylvania. Mostly people didn't believe that it would and hoped that it wouldn't, but the thought persisted and hung over everything.

We were all aware for the past year that General Lee, a modest Virginia gentleman career soldier, had bested every general and army the Federal government had thrown at him. Only two months ago, and against all odds, he had whipped a Union army at least twice his size at Chancellorsville, Virginia. But he had done it all at a terrible cost to the South. Virginia was being torn apart, and every battle depleted his army of irreplaceable men, materials and provisions. And all his efforts and success had carried the Confederacy not one inch closer to independence.

Now, in late June of 1863, he invaded Pennsylvania, and our worst fears were realized. General Lee intended to bring his war into the North and gather supplies and try to force a settlement that would lead to southern independence. He had total confidence that his army could pull it off. And those of us in his path were made to suffer for it.

A division of rebels came through town and scared the dickens out of everyone. Some of them shot a local young man off his horse and killed him before moving on towards Harrisburg. Others had come down the pike from Cashtown a few days later for a look around. By dawn on Wednesday, the first of July, the whole town was running around and full of anxiety about what might happen next.

I had pretty much finished morning chores before six o'clock and was all set to go fishing for the rest of the day, rebels or not.

THE DAY WAS ALREADY as heavy as hot breath. Gramma said it was so close she could hardly breathe. She wiped her hands on the dishrag, went out onto the porch, cupped her hands around her mouth and cried out to the heavens like she was calling hogs:

"*Raaaaa-EEES . . .!*

"If he doesn't get in here in the next ten seconds, I'm going to put everything away." She walked to the end of the porch, put her hands on her hips and glowered at the barn.

"'*Reis!*' Such a name as that is anyway!" she muttered. "I always said don't name your youngins anything that don't holler well! That's why I named mine, John, Tom, Don, Rob and Molly . . . I could give one big long bellow and get them all with just one syllable."

Gramma, like she always did, commenced thrashing the big iron triangle that hung from the porch. A wonder she wasn't deaf. It always made her body do a funny little wiggle, which she did not like brought to her attention one bit, and heaven protect you if she ever caught you doing an imitation of it.

Around the farm, men came running when called to eat, because they worked themselves into a state of near starvation every day. Food preparation in those days was such a task, the women scarcely had time to breathe between one meal and the next. Everyone was always under pressure to sit down and eat on time so the women could clean up and clear the table.

My mother knew how to make the things that were common around a farm taste better than anyone else ever could. The men would get up way before dawn, do the feeding, milking, gathering eggs, cleaning stables and be in for breakfast by six o'clock. After eggs, bacon, ham, fried potatoes, biscuits and gravy, or homemade bread with butter and jelly, milk and coffee, they were ready to hitch up the team and go fight the plow for five or six hours. In the kitchen, the daily baking would be in progress, and preparations under way for the midday meal, which everyone called "dinner."

About noon, when Gramma would go beat the daylights out of the triangle again, the men and hired hands would come in from the fields, wash up and sit down ready to eat everything in sight. As the field work concluded in the fading light of evening, everybody would return home exhausted to another meat-and-potatoes supper topped off either with pie – apple, pumpkin, berry, peach or cherry with whipped cream – or buns, cakes, cobblers or strudels.

The demands of make-ready and put-away in the massive enterprise of feeding the family plus raising the children comprised the lifelong career of most farmwomen. They became experts at those two essential elements of life on the farm and had time for little else, except for laundry, working a garden patch and sewing, quilting and repairing garments.

ON THIS DAY, I WAS TRYING, BETWEEN FINISHING CHORES and dashing off to breakfast, to get my fishing tackle ready, as I was all fired up to go after speckled trout up on South Mountain one last time before the streams got too low and clear.

Gramma was still shrieking and clanging for dear life when I bounded up on the porch behind her, whistling away at *Garry Owen* and dancing around her like a fool. She stopped and glowered into my face. I whistled at her all the harder: *"Tweedle deedle de deedle de deedle de dee ...."*

"'Sing before breakfast; cry before night,' Mom always said!" she snapped at me.

"I ain't singin', Grannie, I'm *whistlin'!*" I pulled her apron strings loose. She grabbed at her apron and made two unsuccessful swipes at me with a big wooden spoon she carried around like a scepter.

"Mind your mouth, smarty! And don't you call *me* Grannie, you briggety youngin, you! Go wash your hands!"

Which I sort of did and wiped them on my pants as I slid into my seat with a bump and a bang and started loading up on fried eggs, potatoes, ham, fresh bread with butter and apple butter, and a big white cup of milk.

THERE'S A FLAW IN OUR NATURE that causes us to look back and miss the good old days, yet we pay them so little mind while we're living them. Time comes when we look back and long for the good things of times gone by. But for the most part, we fill our days doing things we don't remember at all later on and fail to see the miracles in an ordinary day. I guess we get so busy looking after what we need to, we forget to stop and savor the things around us that matter most – like children while they're young and still sparkle, and all our loved ones while they're alive and to-gether. Gramma says the Good Book says, "*. . . to them that hath, it shall be given. And from them that hath not, even that which they have shall be taken away.*" Actually, Gramma's version was more like, "Them that has, *gits!*"

I always thought this seemed powerfully unfair of God until it came to me a long time later that maybe He wasn't talking about what you had but how you thought about it. If you can see the wonders present in every day and be grateful for them, they will be there forever and may even multiply. But if you wander through life unaware of the treasures all around you – your health, your freedom, your good senses or, outside yourself, a brilliant white full moon, God's promise in a rainbow, a twilight cloud bathed in the fading soft red glow of sunset . . . or the smell of fresh turned earth hungry for the seed, or just a warm home with food on the table and a loving fam-ily – the day may come when you will no longer see them at all. If you fall out of the habit of being mindful of such things, they may disappear before your very eyes, even though they are still right there in front of you.

For me, at least, there really was a time back then when I saw that everything *was* good and counted my blessings every day. I knew I never had to give a passing thought about where my next meal was coming from or what joy there might be in a drink of cool water. We lived by a principle that friendliness, cleanliness, hard work and prayer would meet the needs of the day and keep us on course for eternal life. Other than a vague ap-prehension about how, or even *if*, we might fit into the Hereafter, we had suffered no real fears about anything before the war. Even then, war had always seemed far away and 'down there.' As little as a week ago, I had no idea our notions of quiet and peaceful prosperity would change forever, or that I would soon add to the list of things to be thankful for a few I had overlooked heretofore.

BEFORE WAR CAME TO PENNSYLVANIA, I guess I had the best life any boy could want. It was a life full of hard work, but it was a good life. Our farm was blessed with rich soil and plenty of cold, clear water. Most years it rained enough to bring in crops full and sturdy at harvest time. We had stock and animals of all kinds you'd expect to find on a farm, and I loved caring for all of them, from our big workhorses, Sport and Nell, down to the biddies, peeps and ducklings for which I had, and still have, a tender heart. I hated the hogs when they got loose, though. I was usually delegated to fetch them home, and they were stronger than I was and just as smart. They were absolutely without conscience and would tear up anything in their path. Turkeys weren't a whole lot of fun either.

I used to like to stroke a hen's comb gently while I stole the warm egg out from under her without scaring her off the nest. If you caught the egg as it dropped, the shell would still be soft for a moment until the air hit it. The secret in being friends with hens is to talk to them and gain their friendship before you take liberties, as a hen will get all flustered if anyone comes clomping and banging into the henhouse without proper introductions. The hens were, as were all the others, my special friends.

The laying hens were allowed to run free to scratch up all manner of bugs and worms along with whatever else they could find. Gramma said the bugs and worms were what gave eggs their good taste and made the yolks show up a deep yellow-orange. The yolk of a fresh egg from an old hen that's been let loose to scratch all day sits up high on a plate like half a peach.

OUR PLACE WAS AS GRAND A PLACE TO LIVE and witness the changing seasons as God ever created. My favorite season was spring, mainly because that was when trout were active, and I had such a shameful passion for trout. There was good reason for it. Trout are the most beautiful of all fish. The ones I caught in the cold mountain streams were charcoal overlaid with bright silver wiggle-worms around to the color of sunset on their bellies. On their sides, they had these brilliant red spots with silver circles around them. I used to love bringing home enough for everyone. Ma said they looked like little jewel boxes. Mainly I guess I liked to fish for trout because you had to go after them and work the stream to find them, unlike other fish where you mostly sat and waited for them to come to you. You never got bored fishing for trout.

And I loved the fresh newness of spring. There is no greater glory than to be alive in early spring and witness the whole countryside bursting with new life, with newborn lambs romping among the bright yellow dandelions in the dark green grass.

I liked summer almost as much. Summer was a stretch of relief from schooling for one thing. It's hard to find time to do fun things when you have go off to the schoolhouse every time you turn around and still have all the farm chores to do. Summer was a time to go swimming until your fingers got all wrinkled, to eat watermelons, fresh corn and ripe tomatoes right off the vine. Pa always tried to have a ripe tomato by the Fourth of July, but he was never successful at it, unlike Grampap Reis down in Maryland who almost always did. "Too far north," claimed Pa, although it was a difference of only about thirty miles north and south. I think there was more to it than that.

Summer was also a time to sit under the old sycamore down by Marsh Creek with a line in the water and watch water spiders rowing in the gentle current ... and daydream. Pa says a daydream is imagination without results, but I think you need daydreams to set the mind to work on things. I think old Columbus probably started off with a daydream. And how about that fellow who invented the telegraph — a thing we couldn't do without these days? I doubt he just sat down and did it without forethought. You have to let your mind wander a spell if you want to come up with something no one else ever thought of before. But I'd usually work at something only until the mystery was out of it, and then I'd go on to something else. Pa allowed I never would stay at anything long enough to get really good at it.

And what could be lovelier than to sit on the porch of a summer evening with a glass of lemonade and hear the whippoorwills come out and to watch a million fairy fireflies all a-glitter down in the meadow? There was one place with a little marsh in the bend of the road where now and then the fireflies would come out so thick you could have gone down there at night and read a book by them. I used to stare at that big magic bundle of shimmering light and feel closer to God for it than I ever did in church, but I never said so to anyone.

Come August, we'd offer a couple shoats or some chickens or geese to the family that owned a tract of timber where we could go cut wood so it would be seasoned right by time to use it. If you cut too early, it would dry out and burn too fast; but if you cut too late, it'd be so green it wouldn't burn smooth and steady. We'd bring the wood home in logs on a sledge, stack it up like a teepee to keep dry and out of the dirt, and then we'd cut it up and split it as we needed it. One thing sure: making wood is hard work.

We had lots of maples, and in the fall they would come in like fire in every shade of yellow and red and everything in between. We'd tap the sugar maples toward the end of winter when the sap was rising to make syrup and sugar. We'd spend days cooking it down, and the breezes would spread the smoke and smells of sweet maple syrup and burning oak for miles around. You had to cook down forty gallons of sap to make just one gallon of syrup.

Fall was a gentle time of year, and I always loved the smell and feel of it. There was something warm and rich and homey about the smells of autumn that the other seasons lacked. Fall always made you a little homesick for something you missed, but you never quite knew what it was. Gramma never much liked fall because it reminded her that winter would soon be coming on, when she would be cold all the time and have to heat a brick to take to bed for her feet at night. I was sorry to see autumn give way to cold weather, too, but I also loved the sweet smell of oak ablaze, a big cup of crisp cider and Ma's mincemeat and pumpkin pies and roast turkey dinners that showed up with the cold weather.

We butchered when it got cold enough to hang meat. Hog butchering was always a big to-do, and relatives and neighbors all pitched in to help one another. Old Joe Stegmaier had the job of shooting the hogs in the forehead. Then he'd stick them in the throat with his 'pig sticker' so's they'd bleed proper. Then we'd hang them up and gut them and dip them in barrels of scalding water to soften the bristles for scraping. Us kids were given the job. We'd use the zinc lids from Mason jars with the sharp edges and go over their hides in little circles, and the hair would come right off. Gramma said we were giving them a shave. One year, a young cousin, a girl of eight or nine, was visiting from Pittsburgh, and the whole thing made her run off sick. The rest of us had been used to it from the time we could remember and didn't notice anything to get sick over. Mainly, I thought about the good things coming, like fresh ham and souse and puddin' and of course scrapple – or ponhaus as some folks called it. Crisp fried scrapple with fresh maple syrup was always a welcome treat on cold mornings – or any other morning.

We made use of everything we could. We rendered the fat for lard and pressed out cracklings that us kids were wild about. The women ground and seasoned the leftover scraps, stuffed the guts and twisted them off into sausages. They would cut out the hams and shoulders to cure, and cut the back meat into pork chops and such. And there was no meat so sweet as hog jowls, folks said. The hog jowls always went to the hog's owner.

It got plenty cold in the wintertime back then. One winter it was so cold they said the ice was twenty-seven inches thick over on the Susquehanna. Men would go there and cut out big blocks of ice to bury in sawdust, and some of it would keep almost the whole year that way. I worried about how fish would survive in the small streams when it got so cold.

Most winters got cold enough for the thundermugs to freeze over at night, and in the morning you held off as long as you could to come out from under the warm covers to pee. When he could get away with it, my dog, Old Jack, would sneak slowly up the stairs to my room at night, his toenails softly going *tfit, tfit, tfit* on the steps. He would stand there in the dark a few seconds to test his welcome and then leap onto the bed and burrow down deep under the pile of blankets. After a little while, he would come crawling back out gasping for air and spend the rest of the night there with his nose out.

I always thought the place looked so majestic the day after a big snowfall when the sky was such a deep blue and the snow so bright you couldn't look right at it for more than a few seconds. Gramma said it could make you go blind, but folks were always coming up with things they said could make you go blind, some of which I didn't understand even a little bit.

One of my favorite memories is how we used to hitch Nell to the sleigh and hang on it all the brass sleigh bells we had, and then head out to flit all over the countryside visiting people and showing off, old Nell prancing along, snorting out white puffs and tossing her head up and down like she was loving every minute. I can close my eyes and still feel that cold breeze on my cheek and smell the smells of wet wool and leather and horse.

GENERALLY, I WAS PRETTY SATISFIED with how I had lived out my first twelve years. I knew how to catch, scale, gut and clean all kinds of fish: trout, bass, sunfish, perch, pike, catfish, eels and frogs. We threw everything else back. I learned how to shoot and became a good shot. I learned to skin and dress deer, squirrels, rabbits, muskrats, coons, possums and even snakes. I had plenty of experience picking, stringing and snapping beans, shelling peas, thinning beets, digging potatoes and knowing how to tell when melons were ready. I planted corn, hoed corn, harvested corn, shucked corn, shelled corn, cut cornstalks for silage and made hay besides.

I discovered a thousand secrets of hill, stream and meadow. I knew where to find delicious spring mushrooms in late April. I knew the best places to look for wild strawberries in early June, raspberries in mid-June, blackberries in July and huckleberries in early August and brought all of them home to Ma by the bucketful.

I brought my mother bouquets of violets, johnny-jump-ups, bluebells, wild geraniums, butterfly bush, black-eyed susans, pinks, daisies and glorious other species whose names were unknown to me. Sometimes, I brought her mullein leaves for poultices or dittany for tea.

I could identify all the local fowl and songbirds and knew the calls of most. I could tolerably imitate many of them.

I learned how to run a forge, shape iron on an anvil, make nails and shoe a horse. Pa taught me to hitch and drive our workhorses — and, on occasion, mules, which we borrowed sometimes. Mules had their own ideas about things.

AMONG MY MANY BLESSINGS was an abundance of advice wanted or not on all matters and from all quarters. Take religion. There was always a lot of caution about avoiding the temptations of the Devil, which I never viewed as much of a contest. It seemed like the older people got, the more

they felt they needed to press me about just where the state of my salvation stood, and did I realize that time was running out? Maybe the older
ones were after me so much because they could feel the closeness of that
eleventh hour bearing down on them.

All I ever seemed to hear about in church was fear of punishment
or hope for reward, but, heck, if it was as simple as all that, why wouldn't
everybody be afraid to be bad? And wouldn't God in all His wisdom see
through the hypocrisy of being good just for profit? I believed it meant
more to God if you came to Him from inside yourself because you wanted
to, no matter how long it took, and that genuine repentance had it all over
obligation – or else I missed the point entirely of The Lost Lamb … or
The Prodigal Son.

The instincts of my young heart told me that God just didn't work
in the ways most people said He did. I was neither afraid of the fires of
Hell, nor did I ask anything special from Him except maybe a day to go
fishing now and then, and otherwise I'd be thankful if He would leave
things just about where they were. I tried to do good mainly without expectation, because I felt I was supposed to love God and Jesus and anybody
else with halos.

Jesus said we were to love God with all our hearts and our neighbors
as ourselves and everything else would follow. He didn't say we should love
the good ones but not the bad ones. He meant we should love whoever it
was that Providence sat down beside us – whatever their color or station
in life – and it seems to me that that's lesson number one in understanding what Christian love is. The fact that life seems a lot more complicated
than that is mainly our own doing, with some help from the Devil, maybe.
Everyone seems to be running around looking for God, but I don't think
you go look for Him, you just let Him come in.

I was often cautioned about the pitfalls of having impure thoughts
about girls. In those early years, I was confused about what they had in
mind, because mostly I thought I *was* having good thoughts about girls. I
loved to sing *Jeannie with the Light Brown Hair* when I was all by myself, and
I'd imagine some longhaired girl whose hand I'd hold down by the creek. I
never knew exactly what "borne like a vapor," meant, though, and was half
afraid to ask lest it might be something I was too young to be asking about.

Then I was forever being counseled by first one and then the other about making the most of my life. This, of course, more often than not, was offered up by those without a whole lot of room to talk themselves, unless they figured they were experts about the right path because they had tried all the others. Mostly, I let all of it in one ear and out the other and just grew up as I saw fit. But of course that didn't slow down the flow of advice.

Take this morning. I was all worked up and chafing at the bit to go fishing. Now, if there was anything I'd rather do in this world than go fishing, I wish somebody'd a-told me what. On this particular morning, everybody was up early as usual. I was rarin' to get on the road before the heat of the day when I began getting advice right and left with none of it asked for — and none of it of any help at all.

"Go fishing? Today? Well you just will in a pig's eye! I should say not! What on earth do you want to go off fishing for when it's going to be hot as blue blazes here on the first of July?" Gramma took a breath. "And with those awful rebels around Lord knows where. Why, they could come through here any minute!" said Gramma, flapping her apron up and down. "Whew! It's so close already again today, I can hardly breathe! How much do they think a body can stand?" Without giving it much thought, Gramma always had a notion that somewhere there must be some authority responsible for making sure everything — even the weather — was under control. "And Reis, go draw us a fresh pail of water. I swow this one's turned warm already here this morning."

"Why don't you write a letter to the man in charge, Grannie?" This sort of making fun of her always got her dander up, and made her high on threats if short on execution. "I always thought the Lord was in charge of the weather."

"Shush! Don't talk like that!"

"But, Grannie, you're the one doing the complaining."

"Deed and double! You *are* an exasperation! I swow, youngin, you'd better not cross my path any more today, or you're gonna get what *for!*" I knew her threats didn't have any real danger of being carried out, but every now and then, I'd hurt her feelings, and she would kind of go off to be by herself a while, and then I would feel so bad, I would much rather that she had laid into me.

I loved my grandmother, but she had strange notions sometimes. Pa said she had some oddities, "quirks," he called them. Like, she claimed God knew every time somebody killed a sparrow and that He even counted every hair on your head. I felt God must have more to do than wondering how many hairs everybody had, or how would He ever get anything else done? Gramma claimed that everything that happened was part of God's plan. I wasn't so sure, myself.

TAKE BUM PILES, FOR INSTANCE. If ever I saw a person the world couldn't figure out what to do with, it would be Bum Piles, and if he was part of God's master plan, I sure as heck couldn't wait to see how He planned to use him, because nobody else had figured it out to date. Bum usually had the same clothes on he did when you saw him last no matter how long ago it was. Wherever he went, a small cloud of smells went with him. He had that blend of wood ashes, fried ham, horse, dog, sweat, chaw tobacco, dirt, straw, barnyard and chickens peculiar to older country men. You could tell ahead of time when he was in the neighborhood.

Bum rode a poor old horse named "Rip" (everyone said it stood for 'Rest in Peace') that was on the short end of his better days. Bum would stop by and sit a spell, and he always seemed to pick a time when everybody had more important things to do than entertain, but Ma and Pa always tried to make him feel welcome and never turned him away. He invited us all over to his place a few times, but we never went, because Gramma wouldn't hear to it. "Oh, they say it's such an awful place. It's so filthy, I'd be afraid to sit down anywhere," she said.

"He said if he knew you were coming, Mother, he'd redd up first," said Pa, like as if that was going to cut any ice with Gramma.

"Well, I'll be switched if I'll go over there! Redd up my foot! You couldn't clean that place in a month o' Sundays."

Bum had this hearing defect that would come and go with the weather, he said. Sometimes, you had to yell for all you were worth to make him hear, and he usually couldn't hear anything beyond a few feet. Gramma allowed he could hear "when he wanted to." When us kids saw he was fixing to leave, we'd run off down the road a piece and hide in the woods. When Bum's horse came along side, we'd call, "Whoa!" just loud enough for Rip to hear but not loud enough for Bum. Poor old Rip would stop all of a sudden and haul Bum up short. Bum would cuss and kick him in the ribs and get him started up again, and we'd call "Whoa!" again, and the whole thing would happen all over, with us rolling around in the brush peeing our pants and slapping our sides off. Bum got so exasperated he swore he was going to shoot old Rip. One day he stopped and sat a spell, and when he was leaving, we noticed his old blunderbuss stuck alongside his saddle. He declared the time had come for the dreaded deed to be done, and now us kids felt bad for our part in it.

The next time Bum stopped by, he was still up on Rip. We felt relief but we yelled up that we thought he was going to shoot him last time he was here.

"Well, that's right I was, by cracky, and I would have, too." Bum paused to pinch his nose above the nostrils, turned to the side and blew the contents in a double-barreled blast to the dust below and relieved his face with the help an old red bandanna. "I got out there in the woods fur enough so the smell wouldn't come back on the place, y'unnerstansee, and it hit me then that the way back was a right fur piece to walk. So I thought on it some more until I lost interest in the whole idea."

Anyways, back to my grandmother. She came from a line of folks who were good people and strong people but in some ways strangely set. They never failed to remind you that every good thing would sooner or later have to be followed by something bad, so none of them ever fully enjoyed life for worrying about what might be coming next. They always ate the apples that were going bad first, but they never caught up with the good ones and spent their whole lives eating half-rotten apples.

Now Pa, he puts *his* two cents on the table this morning. "This is hardly a time to go fishing when there's still plenty of chores to be done." Now on a farm, mind you, there is *never* a time without chores to be done. I wanted to remind Pa how truly this was so and to tell him that the best time to go fishing is whenever you can, thank you. But I thought about it and decided the best course was to keep my trap shut.

Of a sudden, we caught the shadow of someone outside hitching up his horse. Gramma went to the window and peered out between the curtains.

"Oh, for Lord sake! It's that old Bum Piles. What in heaven's name is he poking around here for this morning? Here it is hardly daylight yet!"

"Now, Mother," said Pa. "Don't say anything to hurt his feelings."

Gramma chose to make herself scarce and headed for upstairs. "What feelings?" I heard her mutter just as Bum opened the door and let himself in.

"Howdy!" Bum grinned from ear to ear like he always did. "Miz Bramble," he nodded to Ma.

"Come on in, Bum. What are you doing calling so early?" asked Pa.

"Howdy, Miz Bramble," he nodded up at Gramma. Gramma didn't so much as give him a flicker.

"I come to warn yins that all them rebels camped over at Cashtown is on the way here, and they takin' away with 'em anything edible or rideable. Better hide yer food, yer valables, yer stock and yer horses afore they git here, or you won't have 'em very long!" Bum sought out a place to spit and did so into the slop bucket. I wondered if the hogs would notice their meal was a bit spicy today. "They sent a company of infantry down to Fairfield night before last and got into a scrap with some cavalry. They mighta killed one or two and wounded a few others, but other than that, it wasn't much of a fight. But they was a *big* cavalry fight over to Hanover that same day."

"I thought they all went on to York." Gramma had come sidling back down to hear what was going on.

Bum spit again; Gramma winced. "The ones that come through here last Friday was just the advance. Even then, they sent that milishy of our'n high-tailin' it north. Jennings had seven hundred an' fifty men camped out a mile or two west of town and they skedaddled without a shot bein' fired. Old Jubal Early captured a hundred and seventy-five! What the hell kinda soldierin' do you call that?" Gramma really winced this time, and Bum nodded an apology for the profanity.

"Old Jube marched 'em down to the diamond and told them they shoulda stayed home safe with they mommas." Bum chuckled. "Then he made 'em promise to go home, and he let 'em all go. Not a blamed shot was fired. Not a man was hurt, 'cept some fat captain what got run over by a horse, and he wasn't hurt all that much. I tell you, I wouldn't feel very snug if that raggedy-ass milishy was all we had between us and maybe a hunnert thousand mean, hungry rebels. I tell you this thing is a-buildin' up, and a day of reckoning ain't far off. They been easy on us for the most part, but they killed that Sandoe boy over on Baltimore Pike on Friday out of pure meanness. They's some uvvum that would as soon shoot you as look at you. Both sides is a hankerin' to git at each other, and it won't be long before one or t'other starts the dance."

Well, there just went any chance of me going off fishing today – and certainly not up on South Mountain!

Then Ma, she speaks up. "Reis, I do think you should stay close to home with all the rebels flittin' about all over creation and heaven knows where next, snapping up everybody's hard-earned livelihood ... and animals! Doing such awful things! I'm scared to death they'll come around here yet, and I don't think this is any time for you to be out gallyvantin' around, you mind me? Davey Snook was out to Herr Tavern yesterday, and he said a whole flock of them came down the pike – must have been a thousand – and then about a mile from town, they up and went back towards Cashtown again. Lord knows what they're up to. No good, I can tell you that much. They could come along and whisk you up and take you back south along with everything else. And then where would we be? What would we do if we never heard anything about you ever again? I get so worked up just thinking about it! I hope to the Good Lord they don't come anywhere near here."

"No, Miz Bramble," said Bum. "The rebs didn't turn around a mile from town. They come clean down to the Seminary and some uvvum went all the way down into town to look for *shoes*, for Pete's sake! When they seen Buford's cavalry coming up the Emmitsburg Road, that's when they high-tailed it back out the pike."

Bum didn't seem to have a whole lot of trouble hearing this morning. "Bum, how come you know so much about what's going on?" asked Pa.

"Oh, I just wander around all over and keep my eyes open and my mouth shut. Nobody pays no mind to an old cuss like me. Hee, hee, hee! Would *you*, now?"

Pa smiled. "Well, there're rebels just about everywhere around, it seems, and all roads lead to Gettysburg. I don't think it's a matter of *if* they come here, but *when* they come here."

"Old Pap Settles was six years old when they signed the Declaration of Independence. Like he says, he's lived through the whole blamed thing," said Bum. "He says 'them rebs didn't come all the way up here for funsies, and they ain't gonna let us off light, nither.'"

I must admit, while I wouldn't say so, some of the things I was hearing about what the rebels were doing weren't exactly reassuring, and there was a little part of me that held a certain amount of trepidation about being out and around these days. On the other hand, it was exciting, too. I was profoundly curious to see the rebel army on the move – preferably without them seeing me, of course.

We had heard all sorts of things about them –– everything from some behaving with considerable restraint, even kindness, to others committing all sorts of mischief. They say General Lee is like some sort of god to them, pardon the expression, and that they toe the line for him. He told the whole army to conduct themselves as gentlemen while they were in Pennsylvania, and that they should pay for anything they took. Bum says it takes a strong and wise leader to control an invading army. If you don't control them, they'll tear the land apart, and these rebels are ragged and hungry to start with. I think it would be pretty hard for a man with no money who hasn't eaten all week to look an enemy chicken in the eye with any objectivity whatsoever. And as far as payment, the only thing like money they have is what they stole or their Confederate notes. You'd have to go down south to spend it, and who would ever want to do that?

"Well," said Pa, "Seeb Carter was here yesterday and said the bunch that came through here last week on their way to Harrisburg tore down and burned Thad Stevens's iron works out at Caledonia Furnace. Now, dagged if *that* ain't like lighting a fire under the Devil himself. Thad hates rebels with a vengeance to start with, and he's certainly not a man to anger. They'll pay for that after this war's over, mark my words. Old Thad is sure to have his revenge."

Pa continued. "Seeb also told me that some of that same bunch was camped over near Hanover, and he heard the men wanted to tear down the fences for their campfires, like they always do, and asked their general for permission. He, being something of a gentleman, told them 'all right but only take the top rail.' Next morning, the fence was gone and the general mustered them out and demanded to know what happened to the fence after his express orders to take only the top rail. Each man said, 'Why, I didn't take any but the top rail,' and turning to his neighbor, 'Did you take more than the top rail?' Each man said, 'Why no, I only took the top rail,' and each one allowed as how he only took the top rail, which of course they did until the whole fence was gone."

Bum hee-heed all over himself at that one. "I heerd tell last Friday that one of the local belles, and I ain't sayin' who, stepped out in front of a bunch o' rebels comin' up the street with a big scowl on her face, her hands on her hips with the Stars and Stripes pinned across her chest and defied 'em to just *dare* touch her. With that, a rebel officer ridin' on ahead tipped his hat and declared, 'I should warn you madam, these boys are in the habit of storming any breastworks that flies that flag!' Ever'body laughed, and the lady turned red and stepped back into the crowd."

Pa went on. "They say there's some a lot worse, and they just take whatever they want. They all look just desperate. Their clothes are in tatters, they've worn their shoes out, those that have shoes at all, 'cause a lot of them don't, and, as Mother says, they're skinny as a small cake of soap after a hard day's wash. Well, Seeb said don't have no pity on them. They're all savages and they show no mercy to anyone or anything that stands in their way. If they say halt, and you don't, they'll blast you right then and there."

"I hear the militia got themselves up in arms," said Gramma. "Maybe they'll turn them away."

"Now, Mother, what did Bum just tell us about? Seven hundred militia volunteers ran away at the first sight of the enemy and never fired a shot. Now I'm sure *that's* going to keep away a whole lot of rebels. Oh, they're 'up in arms,' all right," said Pa. "This militia thing is a whole lot o' nothin'. They'll get swept away, some of them killed, and we'd all be better off if they just stayed home like General Early said."

"Well, they're not all that bad, and they do it because they have to," said Gramma, getting herself worked up. "They have to do *something*. They can't just sit, and they can't just up and run without first they do something to at least make 'em look like men. I think *you* should run, John," she said to Pa. "I hear the rebels are taking all able-bodied men prisoner. Even if they are civilians. Land sakes! All of it just upsets <u>me</u> ... <u>to</u> ... <u>death</u>!"

"The only reason I made that crack about the militia is this," says Pa. "When the rebels met the ones out the pike all they had to do was yell 'boo' at 'em and chased them all home. They never hurt any of 'em because they probably couldn't stop laughing long enough. But those that have survived to this point are veteran killers and have an awful lot of war under their belts. It would take just once for our local boys to show a little backbone and the rebels'll sweep those greenhorns away, and a lot of them will die to no purpose. It'll be a terrible tragedy that could have been avoided. Leave the dirty work up to the army and stay the devil out of the way is what I say."

"I'm tellin' you, John," said Bum, "If I was you, I'd hitch up y' two horses to the biggest wagon you got, load it up with ever'thing you hold dear and valable and all the foodstuff you can carry and head out southeast somewhere until this thing blows over."

GRAMMA ALWAYS SAID I could talk a body's leg off, but when that didn't work, I used another device to get what I wanted. Ever since Bum got everybody all worked up here this morning, I had been practicing what Pa calls The Master of the Long Face. I've used it ever since I discovered that Ma and Gramma have very little resistance to it, and if I can keep the pressure on long enough and don't crack a smile (a smile will let all the air right out of it, and you'd just as well forget about it and go on home), it usually works.

"You can just forget the long face," said Gramma. "It's not going to do you any good this time." I tried to let my face hang right down to the floor. "Just to look at him now," she said ruefully, "His face is so long, he could eat out of the churn!"

Then Pa's voice took on that serious tone he uses when he's about to make some sort of pronouncement, and we all know it's time to pay attention. "I'd like to speak my mind here, and I want everyone to listen to what I have to say." He looked around at each of us. "We are living in a time and place where great history is passing before our very eyes. Lord knows what the days just ahead will bring. This boy is coming up on the edge of his manhood and appears to be handling it about right so far, I'm pleased to say." He looked me clean in the eye. "Whatever happens, he ought not to miss it entirely. When his grandchildren ask him to tell them about it, I don't want him to have to say he don't know because he spent the time in the kitchen with his Ma and his Gramma." (God bless you, Pa!) "On the other hand, boy, I don't want you to do something so foolish that you won't be around to *have* any grandchildren either. Do you understand me?"

"Yes, Pa." I gave the only answer I could.

"Go ahead and go fishing, and keep your eyes peeled. And don't go looking for trouble, but if you see it coming, or if you find yourself in a spot, or about to get in one, I want you to promise me you'll head home by the most direct way you know how, and I know you know all of them. Is that understood?"

"Yes, Pa."

"At the sound of firing – anywhere – you break off and come home right then. Understood?"

"Yes, Pa." I could feel the excitement of his permission still hanging in the air.

"And whatever you do, don't let the rebs get their hands on old Sport, or they'll have him pulling cannons around, and he'll make a nice big target. If you find yourself drifting from your better judgment, remember that you are responsible for Sport's safety, too, and if necessary, bring him straight home. Promise me that."

"I promise, Pa."

I looked over at Ma, who was twisting her hands in her lap. "I was only going to take Sport and Old Jack and go down to Marsh Creek, Ma," I whined. Now, that wasn't completely true. I had originally planned to take the whole day and seek out that little cold water stream up on South Mountain I'd heard was full of speckled trout, but I knew that would be pushing my luck now. Besides, the streams were probably too low and clear for trout this late. Anyways, as usual, I got my way.

"Go on and go fishing," sniffed Ma, "But you stay close to home, now. Hear me?" I felt a little guilty to see her worried like that, but it wasn't quite enough to stay home over. And that wasn't the only reason for a guilty conscience. I had made a promise to Pa, but deep down, I found myself fighting with a decision to go find Bill Bayly and see if he wanted to go with me.

BILL BAYLY LIVED IN THE OTHER DIRECTION from where I planned to fish, but in my heart of hearts, I knew the *real* reason I was going his way was that he lived a couple miles north of Gettysburg, and I was terribly tempted to saunter up that way to see what I could of what was going on. From what I could piece together, and from what Pa said about all roads leading to Gettysburg, and what with the rebel army on its way from Cashtown according to Bum, I figured they were likely to come in on the Chambersburg Pike, which enters town from the northwest a couple miles this side of the Bayly's.

My promise was losing out to the great temptation of curiosity, and this pestered my conscience considerably, but I took some comfort in the notion that folks surely outgrew their childhood transgressions of telling falsehoods as they got older and wiser and closer to the Day of Judgment.

It was still early, and my heart was full as I swung the big saddle across Sport's curving backbone with a mighty heave. At the ends of his shaggy legs, his hooves were big as pie pans, and everyone wanted his old shoes to play horseshoes with. He was so wide he spread me like a wishbone, and his back was so high off the ground Pa used to bring him alongside the smokehouse landing from where I could mount up when I was smaller. When I got bigger, I was able to get a running start and leap high enough to grab the saddle horn and pull myself up the rest of the way and kick a leg over. My body would smack against him so hard you'd think it would offend him at least some, but he was so strong, he never flinched a muscle. Trouble was that he had this trick where he would take in air when he sensed you were about to cinch him up, so then the saddle would be loose when he exhaled. It was more comfortable for him like that, but I learned the hard way when I leaped up and grabbed the saddle horn that the saddle would swing around underneath and dump me in the dirt. Then everybody would stand back and guffaw at my humiliation, but I guess that's how you learn things: the hard way. But don't tell me horses ain't smart. I pretty much still mount the same way. Even as tall as Pa is, it's about all he can do to stretch his foot up to the stirrup. Keeps him supple, Ma says.

Old Jack sensed adventure in the air and dang near wagged his whole back end off while I finished putting the saddle and bridle on Sport and got my fishing stuff on board. We got Old Jack from a fellow passing through who was looking for a good home to drop off this pup. I was just a pup myself back then, and he and I have been good friends ever since.

Old Jack was a breed like nobody had ever quite seen before. He had one brown eye and one yellow eye. From the brown-eyed side, he was just a good boy, but from the yellow side, he had a kind of crazy look to him, and when you saw him straight on, the effect was downright scary the first time. "Looks like 'Old Jack' to me," Gramma said, which was one of her many names for the Devil. Old Jack may have been a fright to look at, but he served important picket duty keeping deer, coons, whistle pigs, rabbits and any other varmints out of the crops and garden, as well as foxes, skunks, possums and weasels out of the henhouse, all of which duties he applied with equal seriousness and consistency. Anyways, Old Jack was what we called him, and his blood was up now for adventure and so was mine.

Was there ever a man so rich as a boy who has youth, health and happiness on his side and a perfect day all to himself to go fishing? I was putting as much whistle into *Jeannie with the Light Brown Hair* as I had wind for when Gramma's voice crackled from the kitchen doorway.

"Sing before breakfast, cry before night!" she reminded me. I just grinned.

"But Gramma, I already had breakfast! Beautiful day, isn't it?"

"Yes, well, it won't last." She peered up at the sky. "It looks like we're in for a blow before long."

"Well, of course it won't last. I'm talking about the day, not some kind of *rock*, Gramma," I said, grinning at my own wit.

"You mind your mouth, smarty."

I mounted up and puckered a kiss in her direction as I swung Sport around toward the open gate. Gramma responded. "Oh my, ain't we peert, now — now that we got our way today?"

"Let's see, I got my pole, my canteen, my pack of hooks and sinkers and things," I patted my pocket to make sure, "a little poke of worms and a poke with my lunch in it," I announced.

"Look out you don't get them mixed up," cautioned Gramma wryly.

I let my mind wander to how good it felt to be born unto this land with a day of my own. I began to hum *Jeannie* all over again, and, by the time I had passed the last fence line, I have to admit, I had pretty much made the decision to ride to Billy's house and see if he was free to go fishing with me. That's kind of where my mind had been going all along anyway, but I had turned my back on those thoughts back at the house so I could answer Ma and Pa with what they wanted to hear without fibbing – directly.

The thing that could hurt most of all and the thing you had to be careful to avoid was if Pa showed his silent disapproval about something you did or didn't do. When he did that, he got way down to where you began to doubt the quality of your own character, which served as a powerful deterrent to misbehavior. He said that any boy that disobeyed his Pa was flirting with breaking a commandment.

I turned in the saddle and looked back for a moment at our place, which I always loved to do. The farmhouse was built of native dark red sandstone pulled from the fields and cut long ago by Pa's people, the Brambles, who were English. Ma's people's name was Reis, which means "rice" in German, so I guess that made me half and half. About half the folks around were English, Scottish or Irish and the other half were mostly German, popularly called "Pennsylvania Dutch." "German" in German is spelled "Deutsch," and pronounced "Doytsh," which most Americans pronounced "Dutch."

THEY NAMED ME CHESTER REIS BRAMBLE, although I never liked the Chester part and never used it. Ma said it was derived from "Caesar," but that didn't help it much. Gramma fussed about my name because Chester "hollered without much success." Ma disagreed and said she had no trouble at all with it, particularly if she was fired up at me about something. "Reis" was almost as bad, Gramma allowed, but "at least it's only one syllable," even though she hollered it in two every time she called me. So Reis won out over Chester, and they took to yelling it to summon my presence whenever required, and I was not readily available.

They spelled my name "Rice" at school, as they did just about every-where else over the years. Like many young people, I disliked my name and was self-conscious about it. I got teased about it at school. "Better watch out for them Chinamen! They *eat* rice!" In time, as I became more mature and confident, I changed my view of my name and came to like it and see it as special and dignified.

Anyways, the red sandstone of the old house was all cut to fit so nice. The mortar in between the stones was almost white, as were the window frames and trimmings. It had a wide porch, and there, in good weather, family and visitors passed the time with each other over a glass of lemon-ade. The house, barn and outbuildings sat tucked in among a dozen or so old towering chestnut and white oak shade trees. Everyone said it was the most homey and inviting place for miles around.

Ma had a garden patch which she planted, hoed and weeded with great care. It was a thing of beauty, and we all respected it. Ma always said a garden grew better if it was made to look right. Pa said the quality of her garden made her proud to visit it more often, so it was apt to benefit from the attention as a result of her being there and fussing over it.

About two weeks from now, the sweet corn would be in (Ma always swore by Stowell's Evergreen) and there'd be big red tomatoes you had to wait ten months to come around again, but they sure were worth waiting for. And Ma had all these flowers she put in around the place – holly-hocks, pineys, flags, lilies and such – and add to that lilacs and rose bushes, and you had color enough to be proud of, as indeed we were. She also had these clumps of oxalis that she would take up in the wintertime. She said they had been in the family "for generations." The whole thing was a testimony to Ma's caring hands. Over the years, I never saw irises or lilies or peonies all a-bloom in a country yard that I didn't think of Ma. And a pot of oxalis in a sunny windowsill still makes my eyes mist up after a passage of seventy years.

The land and its treasures were our livelihood and our welfare, and our elders demonstrated respect and reverence for all of it. We exploited the land but respected it as if it were on loan from God. We were taught to make use of animals sparingly and with love and compassion. Pa allowed as how there was no nobler profession than for one to make his living from the earth and that God smiled with favor on the 'husbandman.' The magic of the seed, the soil and the seasons were God's other gifts, and man was the instrument by which the whole was wrought.

My older brother, Jed, had been sent north to stay with Aunt Effie and Uncle Reb at Milton until the dark clouds of war went back south (*Reb* was a nickname for *Reverdy*, his real name, and I always thought it a hoot that he, a dyed-in-the-wool Yankee, would be called "Reb"). Pa took on local boys from time to time to help as needed. Hard work was required of me, too, in the harvest season, but there was always a little time left for fun and mischief, and I never felt too put upon.

On the near end of the cornfield, Pa put in a couple acres of vegetables to sell. We had peas and green onions in May and string beans in June. Then we pulled beets and picked squash. By July, we were picking cherries and pulling carrots, parsnips, turnips, more beets and more onions; then the tomatoes and sweet corn came in, then cabbage. By August, we were pulling the big onions and digging potatoes. Then all of a sudden we'd be awash in more watermelons and cucumbers and everything else than you could shake a stick at. And all the fruit trees would come in so fast, we'd hire darkies as pickers. There was one I remember that was so dark they called him "Silhouette." Sometimes, they'd sing deep and soft while they worked. They sounded so lovely and beautiful, I'd linger among them as long as I could.

Whenever we had accumulated a load of whatever was in, which was most days from mid-June to mid-August, Pa would hitch Sport and Nell to the buckboard and put on the big yellow umbrella that shaded the whole seat, and we would set out and deliver our bounty far and wide. People came to favor our produce, and we never had any trouble selling it off. Pa divided the area around Gettysburg into six regions for the days of the week, minus Sunday, and all during the harvest season, folks came to expect us on their particular day. Pa was made to feel most welcome by people who didn't have their own land to plant or had grown too old to work what they had. He often left off food at the homes of those who were not able to pay. He called them, "the least of these, thy brethren."

In helping Pa this way, I came to learn all the roads and territory around Gettysburg for many miles. What was more important to me was that I also took note of every brook and stream that looked big enough and cold enough to hold trout or minnows and hellgrammites to catch for bait. On occasion, I got the day off to check out my theories firsthand. The main reason I got to go fishing on this particular first of July was because, as I recall, we were in sort of a lull between beans and squash, and I had worked hard and had a little time coming.

I looked back one final time while old Sport plodded along and thought our farm was probably just about the prettiest place God had ever blessed. Whenever I topped the rise where I now sat on my way back home from school or with Pa or from somewhere else, this very scene was always as welcome to me as my mother's cool hand on my fevered brow.

I turned around and rode out the lane to the old trail that ran along Willoughby Run up towards Fairfield Road. The better fishing in Marsh Creek lay to the south, but if I was to get Bill to go with me, as I said, I first had to go a few miles north and then backtrack. In order to get to the Bayly place, I'd ordinarily cross the Chambersburg Pike just west of Gettysburg, and cut northeast another mile or two, which is exactly what I now set out to do.

As I rode along, I kept thinking I heard this funny sound, way off somewhere. And then again, I wasn't so sure I heard it at all. It reminded me of what it's like when the black locusts are in bloom and full of bees. You hear this kind of deep murmur that keeps getting louder and louder the closer you get. And then when you get right underneath, you realize it's the sound of thousands and thousands of honeybees high up in the trees collecting nectar. It was something like that, but I couldn't tell for certain what it was, and if I strained to listen, it seemed like it wasn't there after all. It did bother me enough to make me wonder, though.

I can tell you this much: I never got anywhere even close to Bill Bayly's house, and before the day was out, I would be sure as sin that I had not picked a very good day to go fishing after all. Not by a long shot.

Chapter Two - This Sure Messes Up a Good Fishing Day

If I could feign turn back the clock,
Who knows what might have been;
Perhaps some other path I'd walk,
Perhaps the same again

As I headed north on the Black Horse Road, a whole separate course of events was bearing down upon us. Rumors about the whereabouts of the rebel army had tied people's stomachs in knots for a week. Everyone's nerves remained on edge, and every conversation was abuzz with alarm.

Ten major roads radiate outward from Gettysburg like spokes on a wheel and lead to the neighboring towns of south central Pennsylvania and Maryland. This morning, as it turned out, most of these roads were occupied in their outward stretches by converging units of both armies, and no one knew just where everyone else was at the time. The short story is that they were all headed towards Gettysburg.

That's about where things stood that morning as I moved along half-dozing in the saddle on my way toward the Chambersburg Pike with a vague aim to find Billy.

The day was free and delicious and for the moment all mine. My faithful Jack trotted alongside and zigzagged back and forth sniffing out one mystery after another. Sport's rhythmic swaying in the warm morning air made it hard for me to keep my eyelids open, and I remained upright by only the slimmest of margins and in such a delicate state of balance, a sharp puff of air could have blown me off.

Farm dogs barked here and there from habit, mainly, and roosters still crowed for no good reason as all decent folks were long since up at this hour. I held onto the saddle horn and swayed dreamily from side to side to Sport's steady rhythm, beguiled by sounds and smells gentle and familiar – whiffs of barnyards and dank woodlands, of horse sweat and horsehair, the little squeaking sounds of saddle and leather, and the steady clop, clop of Sport's big feet, birdsongs high above – and buzzing insects that folks around here called "locusts." I told Gramma the teacher said they're not really locusts but are called "*sickadys*." Gramma says they are, too, locusts, like in the Bible plagues, because their haunting call says, "*Pharaooooh!*" I said it seemed pretty fine that bugs spoke Egyptian way over here. She threw her dishrag at me.

And I could still hear those strange sounds like bees way off somewhere.

DID YOU EVER DO SOMETHING that seemed like a good idea at the time, and later on you wished to high heaven you could take it all back?

The crack of a single shot not too far away brought open an eyelid. It seemed to be a mile or so to the northwest – or was it? Maybe someone had popped a woodchuck in his garden patch. Or maybe I imagined it. I strained to listen. Then there were more.

Now both eyes were open. I noticed a parade of light thumps coming from within my breast all on their own. Did this mean I should turn around *now* and head for home in strict interpretation of my promise to Pa? Surely my day was not meant to end so soon. Maybe I should find out for sure before I allowed it to be cut short. Maybe my curiosity was already too far along to permit any consideration other than to keep on going and see what happens.

The notion came to me that if the rebels really were about to "start the dance," I hoped they would respect the time-honored practice among farmers around here to keep to the roads and not tromp all over our carefully cultivated fields. As most of them were farmers themselves, I expected them to do their best to be mindful. But if there was to be a battle of any sort – if one couldn't be avoided – where on earth was there a piece of uncultivated land big enough to accommodate one? I thought on it a while, ran my mind over all the fields around and concluded that there just weren't any that would do. A pasture, maybe. Somebody's pasture was going to catch it, and whose it would be, I reckoned, would be up to fate and the Good Lord.

I pondered that grownups seem to understand what they're doing, mostly, and that this war was surely necessary or we wouldn't be so deep into it as we were. For certain, the rebels had invaded our homeland and had to be driven out.

And then there's this issue about Negroes. The first time I ever saw one I was about three years old and had gone with Pa to drop off some produce to a family of them. The little children all came running up to Pa shouting, "Mars' John! Mars' John!" Their little black faces scared me and I pulled around behind Pa and held on to his pants leg. He said to me, "Don't be afraid, Reisie. Their skin may be black, but their hearts are white." Well, I took Pa literally, and for a long time, I marveled at the image of their little snow-white hearts. Sometime later, I realized that Pa was trying to tell me we were all the same beneath the skin, and it was a lesson that has shaped my life in that regard ever since.

But either Negroes are people or they're not. If they *are* people, and I was raised to believe that they are, I just can't help but feel in my heart they should be as free as anyone else. If they are not people, then what are they? And who says so? Pa says it's no sin to make a profit from another man's labor but that he should profit also. It *is* a sin to take away a man's freedom and profit from his work and suffering. Pa says the North is not fighting to free the slaves, but that the South is fighting to *keep* the slaves, who they fear the North intends to set free as soon as they get the chance. I guess there's some grown up logic in there someplace, but it seems too much for my mind to deal with just yet.

Soon, we came out on the Fairfield Road a little bit northeast of Black Horse Tavern. I turned right and rode a mile or so until I came to the little hollow that runs between the Seminary and McPherson Ridge at which point I turned left and rode north a ways along the edge of somebody's wheat field. Before long, I could see uniformed riders racing back and forth and trampling down the planted fields up ahead — and they were *our* soldiers! I guess that answers my concerns about showing respect for the farmers' fields!

As I got closer, I saw all kind of goings on and people dashing off in every direction, civilians and military all a-flurry and all mixed up together. Whatever was going on, there was an air of urgency hanging over everything. I guess Bum was right. The rebels must be about to arrive in our bowels, as Pa would say (a reference that made Ma wince). What else could possibly have everyone so stirred up?

Here and there, small squadrons of cavalry galloped out toward the ridgelines, flags and pennants flapping proudly in the breeze. It was an uncommonly beautiful sight that lifted up some new feeling inside me and made it thrilling to be there. Other riders dashed up and down Seminary Ridge at full gallop, carrying dispatches and orders and such back and forth. I found it terribly exciting and felt envious.

Posted on the path a little further along, was an old cavalry sergeant with arms full of stripes and chevrons. Everything he wore was faded and worn from years in the sun and the rain. He and the horse and the saddle all looked to be cut from one piece. I guess he was posted there to shoo the civilians off, and, Lord knows, there seemed to be enough of them poking around, all of them in the way and none of them helping worth a hoot.

His eyes locked onto me and Sport and Old Jack coming up the way. I stiffened expecting him to bark at us, and he didn't disappoint me as we came near. "Boy, what the hell you doin' around here?" I shrugged and flapped my gums a bit, but nary a sound came out. It was the best I could come up with, beings I felt so outnumbered. His steel-blue eyes pierced me from under the visor of his forage cap. I sat and squirmed, then tried to be nice and appeal to his vanity.

"What's life in the cavalry like?" I asked pleasantly.

"A long stretch o' nothin' and a whole lotta horseshit!" He turned aside in the saddle and spit down from his chaw.

"My Gramma says she thinks cavalrymen are glamorous!"

"Yeah, well, you go tell Gramma after twenty-four hours in the saddle the glamour goes right out of it. What else you need to know, kid, before you git on out of here?" he snapped.

Dismissal. And then an order: "You git on home! This here's no place for you, now!"

Well, you don't have to tell me twice where I'm not wanted. Course he couldn't know which way home was in my case, so I just said *"Yes, sir!"* and kept on riding in the same direction.

A few hundred yards north of the Fairfield Road, I cut to the right and crossed the field towards the Seminary. I felt uneasy that Sport and

Old Jack and I might be about to ride into a mess we would regret, but there was also an inkling that something exciting was about to happen. And I just didn't have it in me to pass it up.

FROM SEMINARY RIDGE, I looked to the east and saw many wagons piled up with trunks and boxes and belongings, headed south and southeast through town, like people expecting to be away a long time or maybe forever. I saw a line of darkies – men, women, children, old folks – almost all on foot, some balancing bundles on their heads, everybody carrying something, hurrying along in the same direction, like Gettysburg was slowly oozing everybody and everything out the bottom. I guess a lot of folks really *were* leaving town. It crossed my mind that I would be wise to turn around and do likewise before the roads got clogged up or closed off completely. Well, right there is where I should have taken heed of my own better counsel. I was about to get drawn into events that would cause me to grow up fast and leave childhood behind.

But I continued along in the same northerly direction, and braced myself to get yelled at and ordered home again at any moment. There were other civilians milling around up ahead but the soldiers were too busy to chase them off. Everyone seemed to have his hands full and his blinders on and pointed towards Cashtown. No one was paying me any mind whatsoever, so I just kept old Sport moving along. Well, actually, it wasn't so much that I decided to keep on going as it was that I made no effort to stop Sport's progress, and before long, we were in the thick of it and all tangled up with horses, buggies, wagons and people surrounding us on all sides.

The tension was so uncomfortable it stopped your ears up. All the horses sensed it, and it put them on edge and made them restless. Sport had a hard time keeping his feet still, and Old Jack kept looking me over for clues and reassurance. The air felt thick and full of electricity the way it does just before a summer storm. It gave me a hollow feeling that gnawed at my insides, and I didn't like it. I felt as though I was in a fairy tale and knew that the dragon was just over that low hill yonder.

A scattering of shots rang out from one of the ridges a mile or so yonder. Up by the McPherson place, I saw a man throw up his hands and fall from a white horse. This was the first time I ever saw a man hit, and it was strangely not real. It was too far away to register properly, and the reality didn't quite make it all the way back to me. But it made clear that war was close and getting closer, and the time had come to heed Pa and head for home.

But I got distracted once again.

A party of fifteen or twenty mounted men came galloping up Chambersburg Street from the direction of town and rode into the midst of the confusion on Seminary Ridge. They came riding up powerful and strong in a cloud of dust, and you could feel the deep rumble of hooves stirring your insides. In the lead was a stern-faced officer with a generous mustache behind which was an otherwise clean-shaven face so square it would fit nice in a box. He sat in the saddle like he had been born there. I guessed the placement of buttons on his coat meant he was a general, a one-star, *bonney fidey* general, the first one I had ever laid eyes on.

The whole bunch was headed in my direction, and I didn't know if I should try to run or freeze. Mostly, I wanted to disappear, but that's hard to do on Sport. The whole pack thundered up and reined in half a barn length short of where I sat and paid me about as much mind as if I didn't exist, for which I was exceedingly grateful. Then a rider galloped up and saluted General Squareface, and shouted, "General, the enemy are advancing about two miles west with their artillery in the van!"

The general took out his field glasses. "Now why the deuce would they do that? They must not know we are here." Then he turned to a subordinate whose mustache grew itself clear into his muttonchops.

"Colonel Gamble, form your brigade and advance and hold that ridge yonder. We must hold here until First Corps comes up!" The colonel replied, "That we will, General," with the accent of an Irishman, which makes some folks smile, including me. I don't know why that's so, but it is. Gramma says they have a twinkle in their voice.

Then I almost jumped out of my skin and fell out of the saddle when a bugler nearby let loose with a blast of *"Boots and Saddles"* which is the noisiest and busiest bugle call in the whole U.S. Army. Then the cry, *"To horse!"* sprung up among the men and horses that had been standing ready up and down the ridge. Men scrambled and leaped to their mounts, while I struggled to back Sport up and retire out of the line of action.

The sounds and smells of cavalry assembling are exciting: the snort and snuffle of the horses, their pawing and kicking up dust and dirt; the muffled clinking of stirrups and trappings, the clanking of swords all mixed together in a mass and flurry of urgency and preparation. Everywhere was the heroic smell of horse and leather and fresh earth and trampled grass, of sweat and metal and axle grease and gunpowder.

Inside of a moment, a thousand men were ready to go forward. More bugle calls split the air. Commands rang out from strong voices, and the riders went forward and out the pike in columns of four, in concert and towards who knew what fate. I heard the general call after them again, "We must hold this place, boys, until First Corps comes up!" It was such a sight as to fill every loyal Union heart with pride.

A DOZEN OR MORE REBEL GUNS out on Herr Ridge opened up in earnest into the woods south of the pike and kept hammering away there for half an hour. Anyone who'd had the bad luck to start out in those woods surely would have been gone after the first few minutes, but the guns continued to pound away. Not long after that, a battery of six cannons of our own pulled by teams of six horses each came thundering across Seminary Ridge and out the pike at breakneck speed amid loud shouts and cracking whips. The guns spread out along McPherson Ridge north and south of the pike. Each team swung its gun around in a half-circle and stopped with the muzzles pointed west. They had no more than come to a stop, when a gun posted just north of the pike boomed out a puff of white smoke. Sport's ears twisted and turned, and he flinched a little and took a step sideways. I thought it was a wonderful sound. I learned later that what I heard then was the first Union artillery round fired in the Battle of Gettysburg.

The other cavalry brigade was under the command of a colonel whose mustache was so big it blocked all evidence of his having any mouth at all. "Colonel Devin, this is the key to the army's position. We must hold it if it costs every man in our command!" The general then ordered him out the Mummasburg Road towards Mr. Forney's place where his men dismounted and formed a line against a large enemy force that was now advancing towards Mr. Forney's hayfield.

Over by the McPherson place, troopers were tearing down fences and building a breastwork of rails and stone north to south. The corn and wheat and hay so carefully planted and tended by Mr. Slentz, who rented out the place from Mr. McPherson, were now well on their way to becoming casualties of war.

I started thinking about all the uproar I'd have to wade through, now, to go north to the Bayly place, and the idea was beginning to lose its charm. That uncomfortable feeling came over me again, and I felt about as helpless as a leaf in a creek. I had more than half a notion to turn back, but the other half plus my overriding curiosity once again clouded my judgment. I fooled myself into believing I would know before it became too late to turn back, and then I would go. But here I was, and right before me in full view was all the excitement of an army about to engage the enemy, and now everybody was too busy to run me off. This was the kind of show all boys dream about and seldom see from a front row seat. I began to rehearse what I would tell the boys from school, all of whom would listen enthralled and envious, and every one of whom had the misfortune to be safe at home this very minute – everyone except me!

At least that's what I thought at the time.

I TURNED OLD SPORT ABOUT and coaxed him into a shuffling trot over towards the Seminary. As I rode up, I saw that some men had taken up in the cupola. One had his field glasses trained toward Cashtown, and another was looking south in the direction of the Emmitsburg Road. The artillery duel had now warmed up considerably. Our guns on McPherson Ridge were greatly outnumbered and were taking heavy fire from the rebel guns on Herr Ridge. A mile or so west, rank after rank of graybacks poured over the rolling ridges and down the pike. These were rebel infantry, and they were coming on strong and full of purpose.

I could see that men had fallen up on the ridgeline, but it didn't seem at all real. I tried but couldn't fix my mind on the fact that men were wounded and dying out there. Things were so far away it was more like watching people on a stage than for real.

Word came back that the rebel column had split off north and south of the pike and had spread out into a battle line. On McPherson Ridge, a shell exploded beneath a team of horses, and four of the six horses were down. The gun crews struggled to cut the team loose and withdraw their gun to safer ground pulling it by hand.

There was now a stir in the cupola, and I looked up and saw fingers pointing south. In a few minutes, a small band of eight or ten riders came galloping over the ridge from the direction of the Emmitsburg Road and reined up not more than thirty feet from where I sat on Sport.

And then and there I saw as perfect a man, mounted on as perfect a horse, as I was ever to see again in my whole life. From his dress and bearing, I knew he must be an important general. Above his boots, his dark blue uniform was smooth and clean except for a faint coat of dust. It sported shoulder straps with two gold stars and a double row of gold buttons in groups of three. He wore soft yellow gauntlets, and a brushed and spotless officer's hat adorned with a single gold cord sat perfectly on his head. His face bore the look of quiet strength of a man experienced and greatly at ease in commanding other men. There was something else in that determined yet gentle face, something strong and good but fleeting and hard for me to grasp back then. In time, I came to recognize this look on the faces of men for whom long devotion to duty has become characteristic, a second nature.

He called up to the general in the tower in a voice easy and relaxed as one who had come for a nice visit. Both generals called one another "John."

"What do we have here, John?"

A voice from the cupola called down, "Things are about to come to a head here, John, and there'll be the devil to pay!" It was then that I realized the call came down from the general with the square face.

"First Corps is maybe an hour's march away. Can you hold here, John?" asked the perfect soldier. He tightened the reins on his magnificent, shiny coal black charger that pawed the ground restlessly to get on with the day's business.

"I reckon we will," said Squareface. "That's Heth in front of us. He outnumbers us more than two to one and there's more behind him, but his deployment is badly flawed. We'd be worse off if they'd had Pender lead. I can't figure why Hill would lead his advance with Heth."

"Hill is as tough as they come, but, as a corps commander, he is impetuous. His decision probably rested upon some whim," called up General Soldier.

"And Heth has his artillery in the *van*," called down the general in the cupola, "and his two weakest brigades next and his best brigade bringing up the rear. And Pender's behind Heth, yet. Danged if it's not all bass ackwards. You'd think Hill would lead with Pender, and Heth would lead with Pettigrew, but leading his attack with his artillery makes little sense. They clearly don't know we are here in force. But they're about to find out."

"Maybe it was Pender's turn to eat dust today," said General Soldier.

"I expect."

"So much for superior southern generalship. This might give us an edge. We'd be worse off facing Longstreet, but Longstreet doesn't like to be in front. He swings a big hammer but wants someone else to hold the spike."

"Yep," General Squareface smiled and nodded in agreement.

I learned later that General Heth had come all the way from Cashtown expecting to find shoes that were reputed to be in Gettysburg in sufficient abundance to justify such a foolish move. I would think that anyone who gave the subject half a thought would have concluded that General Early's division, which had swept through only a few days before, would have ferreted out and confiscated every shoe without a foot in it, and maybe some that had. Not only that, General Heth had been cautioned by General Pettigrew (whose brigade Bum had told us about) that Union forces were in Gettysburg in strength. Perhaps because he got whacked in the head early on, he threw caution to the wind and led the march with his artillery and his weakest brigade next in line.

The perfect general was now joined by some of his staff that came up to accompany him back through town. "Hold on, and hold this position, John!" He shot a parting salute up to the cupola, and I heard him say to his aides as they wheeled their mounts to ride off, "We can thank our stars we have John Buford holding here." He then turned to one of his staff.

"Captain, General Wadsworth is in the van and advancing on Emmitsburg Road. Find him and tell him the pioneers have opened a path south of town so he can cut across directly towards the Seminary. And urge him forward on the double-quick! Then ride with utmost speed to General Meade and tell him the enemy are advancing in force on the heights west of town. Tell him I will fight them inch by inch and barricade the town if necessary!" The captain saluted, wheeled his horse and headed south at a furious gallop.

Now one of the troopers stationed by the Seminary looked my way and saw me as if for the first time. I don't know what took him so long. I must have looked like a midget sitting on an elephant, an image that doesn't exactly blend in with the U.S. Cavalry. He fixed me with a look so intense, I felt like I was caught naked.

"What fer general was that?" I called over as pleasantly as I could.

"That was General Reynolds, boy, and none of your goddamn business. Now git on out of here!" he growled. "All hell is about to break loose, and when it does, you are going to be very much in the way until you get shot, which probably won't be long in coming. Gitchee on home now!"

Well, I embraced his wisdom, if not his manner and swung old Sport north away from the direction of home, because by now, the road south was all blocked up with artillery and wagons and an accumulation of dismounted troopers. If I rode into that, I was going to get yelled at and cussed at even more, and I probably wouldn't get through at all. I felt my options dwindling and got that sick little feeling once more. The thought crossed my mind that I might be able to make it to Amelia Harmon's aunt's house on the other side of Willoughby Run. It was three stories high, and I think it had an observation room on top. They said it had stone walls almost two feet thick, which should stop anything the rebs could throw at it, and me and Sport and Old Jack might be tolerably safe there.

But that was only wishful thinking. The idea would never work now. I had waited too long, because from what I could hear and make out, it appeared that the rebels would be massing along a mile-long stretch between me and the Harmon place before long, and I sure as fire didn't want to try to win *that* race.

I had been poking around here and there I guess for more than an hour by now. You could hear from the sounds of firing that this was now developing into a major fight and was drawing everything to it like flies to a dunghill. I thought I would be wise to remove myself somewhere to safer ground and was about to do so when I heard a cry from up in the cupola.

"General Buford, I see First Corps approaching on the Emmitsburg Road about two miles away," called down a young officer. With that, General Buford, who had come down a few minutes earlier, dismounted and went back up for a confirming look. He called down, "It's Reynold's corps, all right. Now we can hold this place!"

I crossed the Chambersburg Pike, and picked my way carefully through the low end of an unfinished railroad cut, and set old Sport on his way north towards Oak Hill, maybe a half-mile distant.

Before long, lo and behold, up ahead and off to the left a little, I spotted Billy Bayly and two other boys picking raspberries along a fence line halfway between the Chambersburg Pike and the Mummasburg Road as though they were on a Sunday picnic. What a sight for sore eyes they were!

"Hey! What are *you* doing here?" I yelled down from atop old Sport. "I see no one's run you off yet. I got run off at least twice getting this far."

"Well, what's it look like we're doing? We come to pick raspberries — and watch the show," Bill yelled back. "What's your excuse?"

"Well, I *was* on my way to your place to see if you wanted to go fishing, but I didn't expect all this! I think I just seen a man get shot way out there." I waved my arm in an arc to the south and around to the west to take in the whole battlefield that was forming up. "And the artillery are pounding one another hot and heavy. It's mighty exciting, but it's gettin' kinda scary, too. This sure messes up a good fishing day!" I was running my mouth out of breath. "Who's your friends, there?"

"This here's my cousin, Adam Snook, and you know his brother, Daniel."

"Well, I do now. Howdy boys, my name's Reis."

A round of nods and howdies went back and forth, and I slid down off Sport and commenced stuffing raspberries with them for a spell. Next to strawberries, black raspberries are the best. Well, maybe I'd put huckleberries in there somewhere, too. After we had eaten our profits, we all had a drink of water from my canteen, and I poured some into my hand for Old Jack to lap up. Then we sat on the fence like a row of blackbirds to see what would happen next. It was not long in coming.

WE HAD BEEN HEARING ABOUT IT, and we had been fearful of it, and now here we sat fascinated by it; and it was all about to unfold before our very eyes. Who would believe that in all of Pennsylvania, in all of America, they picked this very place right here in front of us where the four of us would live to tell about it. It was the most exciting place to be as I would ever expect to see again.

"I don't know if I'm ready yet to see anyone get killed," I said. "I mean, I think maybe I did already, but it was too far away. It looked like a man fell from his horse, but it was a long way off."

"The only killing I know about is the slewing and slaying in the Bible," said Billy. "I never could fix much horror to it. I guess I thought if the hand of God was in it, it must have been deserved."

"I heard once about a man who got killed in a farm accident, but they spared my tender ears the details," said Adam. "It must have been pretty bad because the umm-ing and aw-ing went on for quite a spell."

"Remember that big fight outside the saloon last year?" I asked. "It was in both newspapers for a week, and nobody even died over it. I expect people will get killed here today, and I guess the town will get all upset about it." We knew it made sense that men would get killed and wounded in battle, but somehow the glory a fellow was bound to take on as a result took the sting out of it and made it different from ordinary murder, or so it seemed – I guess that's so anyway. Otherwise how could both sides – which were both Christian for certain – be able to live with it alongside the commandment, 'Thou shalt not kill?' We thought on it and convinced ourselves we were not going to come up with anything that would persuade us to change our front row seats, so we planned to sit tight and see what happened.

THE FOUR OF US SAT ON THE FENCE and saw a man on a black horse ride out from Seminary Ridge to direct the placement of men and guns. As a battery struggled to get through the fence, the rider on the black horse wheeled around and galloped back to wave the approaching infantry forward. I noticed that he wore yellow gauntlets and realized then we had been watching General Reynolds, that perfect soldier whom I saw up close only an hour before.

"See that man on the black horse?" I said. "That's General Reynolds, the head of the First Corps. Less than an hour ago, I was as close to him as I am to you," I exaggerated a little. I'm not sure how much they believed me, but at least they knew I knew who he was.

Then, a thrilling sight appeared on the field below us. Just beyond the Seminary and from the east or to our left, a whole blue-clad brigade of the First Corps broke over the ridge in column on the double-quick. We cheered them wildly. The midnight blue of their tunics contrasted sharply against the pale green fields of timothy and the golden yellow of ripening wheat. The day was hot, and the men had been pushed hard and were arriving after great exertion from a long distance. Many stumbled along barely able to take the field. Some collapsed and fell. But more and more came, more than a thousand now, up the eastern slope of Seminary Ridge, pouring across the swale just to the west and fanning out in battle line as they neared the McPherson place.

General Reynolds rode about everywhere and directed men with commanding gestures as if he were a great wizard, creating swaths of soldiers with every wave of his magic wand. Five regiments were now on the field. Two rushed toward McPherson Ridge in support of a battery being posted there. Each gun was pulled by six frantic horses. Teamsters' whips cracked the air like rifle shots. The six big guns were wheeled into place and immediately began firing into the ranks of the rebel infantry rapidly closing on them. The other three regiments quick-timed along the low ridge that lay just to our right.

"Look, look!" cried Adam, pointing around to the right. "That cavalry up yonder is falling back!" We swung our eyes to the right and behind us. The dismounted cavalry that had been holding the line up near the Forney place were now falling back in our direction. They had held bravely, but they were being driven by rebel infantry.

Then we realized that two of the three Union regiments now heading north along East McPherson Ridge were also moving toward us so that both sides appeared to be converging on the very fence upon which we were sitting! Every hair on my body stood on end! One of the Union regiments suddenly formed a line facing the approaching Confederates and fired a volley. This was the first volley I ever heard and was perhaps the first one fired in the Battle of Gettysburg. The rebels were far off enough that our fire seemed to have little effect on them. The rebel regiment, which was much larger than ours, advanced and returned the fire, and some of our boys went down. We looked at each other with our mouths hanging open.

While we spun about looking for something or someplace to get behind, another brigade in tall black hats broke from behind the Seminary to the south and stormed across the ridge. They crossed the field on the run and with a resounding cheer disappeared into Herbst's Woods just south of McPherson's farm. We had heard of the famed black-hats they called The Iron Brigade, and it was exciting to see them take the field. A great, continuous roar of musketry came out of the woods where the Iron Brigade had gone in, and a huge pall of white smoke came lifting out through the trees. Just to the right of the woods, the other cavalry brigade that had been holding on at the McPherson farm was also breaking and being driven back through the infantry by swarms of oncoming rebels.

Then, coming up the pike from the direction of town, we saw a strange apparition: an old man in a tall silk hat and swallowtail coat, carrying a long musket by the end of the barrel, headed straight for the action. We marveled at the sight. I squinted and blinked to see if my eyes were playing tricks. "What kind of soldier is that?" I asked.

"Good gravy! That's old John Burns! He lives just down the road a piece," answered Billy. "He used to be a constable or some kind of lawman. I don't think he's ever got over it. I guess he means to go out there and arrest all the rebels — or shoot them all."

"Well, he's certainly dressed fit to kill," I said. We all chuckled and snorted, and I said Pa would say old Mr. Burns was a young man trapped in an old man's body.

They told me later Mr. Burns got wounded three times but none of them all that serious. During a lull in the fighting, he asked a man to go down the road to his house and tell his wife he'd been shot and to ask her to bring the wagon to fetch him home. The man found Mrs. Burns sitting on the porch. She was a tough old biddy and folded her arms and made no move to comply with his request, nor was she at all amused by the idea.

"I told him not to go up there! He shoulda *knowed* better!" she snapped.

From our higher vantage point, we had seen a large formation of rebels go into Bender's field a few hundred yards to the west and quickly disappear in among the wheat. We had no doubt they were still in there and ready to do mischief. For several minutes, we yelled and hollered and waved our hats and tried our derndest to warn the next regiment now coming up in our direction, but they either couldn't hear us or had more on their minds than to pay attention to four ragamuffins sitting on a fence. Our boys were still in column and all bunched up when suddenly, rebels thick as fleas, rose up from among the wheat and fired a heavy volley as they crossed in front of them. Many men went down, and the rest tried to form on the left of the first regiment in order to fire back, but they continued to take such a vicious pounding from rebel infantry and artillery that it was some minutes before they were able to recover and collect themselves.

An intense fight then opened up all along the line, and for the first time, we heard the *whrrrp!* and *whiiinnne!* of minié balls in the air, and I marveled at how many different sounds they could make. I now knew that my immaturity had poorly prepared me for what I had got myself tangled up in. The four of us tumbled to the ground and lay there terrified and trembling and quaking with the sudden wisdom that we had failed to take the situation seriously enough soon enough.

Fwwwp! Fhewwwww! Fwwwwow! Spitt! Zheeeww! Pott! Phitt!

Under the fence, we pressed every part of our bodies from head to toe as far and as hard into the earth as possible and tried to scratch a little deeper. Old Jack did the same, and I tucked him into my side and held him down. A low line of stones beneath the fence offered spare protection. Trouble was, our fence line was actually perpendicular to the enemy line of advance, and as soon as their left passed north of the end of the fence, we would be exposed on both sides without protection. I asked God for some miracle that would protect Sport and somehow get him through unscathed ... and us as well.

Balls ripped through the trees overhead, and bits of twigs, leaves and small limbs spiraled down on us and around us. As the battle built to its full fury, and the harsh, rude, heavy hand of war came down upon us, I knew I was now in a fix I never bargained for and began to think unpleasant thoughts about what would happen if I didn't live through it. I tried to dismiss the persistent thought of what it would feel like to have a minié ball tear through flesh and bone somewhere on my body, and I began to cry.

TO THE WEST, DUST WAS BEGINNING TO RISE from the drying roads as wave after wave of rebels continued rolling over the low-lying hills towards the Union positions and the awful racket continued to rise from the woods south of the pike. Just this side of Willoughby Run, it sounded as if both sides were going at one another with everything they brought with them. Both armies were now locked in mortal combat from a point beginning just north of our fence line and running south for the best part of a mile.

After a half hour's fight, the two regiments in front of us were slowly being driven back. As the line began to collapse, I grabbed Sport's halter and made a spirited dash with the boys and Old Jack to the shelter of Wills Woods a couple hundred feet to the east where the cavalry also was taking cover. A third regiment that had been sent to support the battery out on the ridgeline was still hotly engaged with the rebels bobbing up and down in the wheat field. Bugles called for this lone regiment to retire, but none of them could hear above the din. They continued to be whittled away until a lone officer galloped out from the woods under intense fire to deliver the order to withdraw.

The first infantry to reach our section of the woods immediately fell to the ground from wounds and exhaustion. The clothing of some was stiff with drying blood. They reminded me of men on butchering day, constantly waving off blowflies and yellow jackets drawn to the smell of blood on their hands and clothes. As bad as it was, far worse was left behind on the battlefield.

The dead and the seriously wounded – men torn open, men with arms and legs smashed by balls, some cut off by shrapnel – and too much in agony to be moved had to be left lying unsheltered in the hot sun. Others, too exposed to enemy fire to be rescued, were also stranded by the hasty withdrawal. Without some kind of truce, no one was safe to go between the lines. No truce was forthcoming that day, and many would die before help came.

"See that man on the black horse? That's General Reynolds."

Our battery on McPherson Ridge had been hard pressed by the enemy. They were forced to withdraw one gun at a time through a gap in a fence the pioneers had failed to bring down and were having a hard time of it. They got four of the guns out, but the last two were in danger of being captured. As the rebels overran the position, a gunner mounted one of the horses in a team and spurred it forward in an effort to force the gun through the gap in the fence. A rebel officer rode up, drew his pistol and fired. The gunner fell from the horse, but the racing team plunged through and the one gun was saved. Then the rebels fell upon the last gun and began bayoneting the horses to capture it. I will never forget the screaming and plunging of those innocent horses trapped and tangled in their traces.

Now, an alarming report swept the battlefield that General Reynolds had fallen and had likely been killed. We were stunned by the news of the loss of this courageous soldier to the undiscriminating hand of war. I heard in later years that the deed was not a random chance of the battlefield but a deliberate act by a Confederate soldier who lived in regret for the rest of his days when he learned of the noble character of the man he had slain. But, as in the case of any murderer who repents, when the terrible deed is done, it is final and too late to call back.

The men in Wills Woods arrived parched and ravenous for water, having emptied their canteens on the long march and because of the urgent rush to battle had had no opportunity to refill them. The wounded were the most in need, having bled and seeped away so much of their bodily fluids, and I felt obligated to help if I could. I volunteered to go with Sport to the McLean farm about a quarter mile north where I knew there was a good spring and fill a few canteens.

"Give me your canteens and I will fetch you some water," I said to a few men nearby.

If I had been giving gold away, I wouldn't have had a greater run on the bank. Men rushed forward like nails to a magnet, and I wondered if maybe I had started something I wouldn't be able to handle. Directly a general came up and asked what the commotion was all about. One of the officers told him I knew of a "big spring" nearby and would bring back as much water as I could hang on my saddle horn and over my shoulders. I explained I would have trouble getting back up in the saddle thus burdened and asked if someone could go with me to help. The general, General Lysander Cutler, directed one of his orderlies to go with me to hand up canteens after I mounted.

We set out with thirty-six empty canteens hanging on both sides of my saddle horn and another twenty slung around both shoulders. I was so weighted down on the way back, I couldn't move an inch. The orderly was able to hang onto his own saddle and mount up with maybe thirty more, enabling us to return with forty or fifty gallons of precious water, which disappeared in no time at all. The orderly, Jim Barrett, and I made three more trips to the spring and back that morning. I figured we brought in enough water for almost two thousand men of General Cutler's brigade and the troopers from Colonel Devin's cavalry.

I got a lot of attention over it, like as if I was some kind of hero or something, and I was roundly embarrassed. A soldier put a forage cap on my head for which I was mighty proud but didn't let on too much. I received the personal thanks and a pat on the head by General Cutler himself. He was a big man and looked worn and haggard, like he'd aged a little too much for battlefield soldiering.

ABOUT THE SAME TIME WE WERE FETCHING WATER, the rebels overran the field just south of us, hundreds of them pouring into another railroad cut just north of the pike. I guess they figured on using the cut as a breastwork to enfilade our lines, but it would prove to be too deep for them.

A black hat regiment in reserve south of the pike saw the rebels taking cover in the cut and rushed northward to confront them. Under a withering fire, they climbed the sturdy fence that bordered the pike and took many casualties. Bodies were left hanging in the fence and littered the field. The officer leading the charge pitched forward as his horse was hit and fell to the ground. He jumped to his feet, took up their fallen flag with one arm and waving his sword with the other arm, continued to lead the charge on foot.

The cut must have been a good fifteen feet at the deepest, and the greater mass of rebels that had formed there tried to climb the steep sides to fire on the attackers but kept slipping back as the shale gave way beneath them. A company of Union troops formed at the east end and fired on the trapped rebels, chasing them towards the deepest part and penning them in. The black-haired, black-bearded officer, who had fought his way to the cut with only a handful of men, looked down on them, brandished his sword and demanded the rebels' surrender. I guess those down in the cut couldn't see the size of the force that threatened them from above, because after a short fight, they laid down their arms and surrendered.

SOON AFTER THAT INCIDENT, the firing began to die down all along the line, and for about an hour, the carnage abated. It was during this lull that other First Corps units began to arrive and take up positions all along Seminary Ridge for about a mile north to south. The smell of gunpowder hung thick in the air, and the dense smoke of battle drifted east revealing the pitiful wreckage of the field.

As far as you could see, the battlefield looked like it was slowly creeping in opposite directions as the many wounded of both sides limped and dragged themselves towards the safety of their own lines. Men too badly wounded to remove themselves lay between the lines, waved their arms in supplication and begged for water, that piteous, ubiquitous and universal cry of the battlefield. We could faintly hear them wailing for help, for mother, for God. Their mournful appeals drifted up from the terrible debris spread out below us. Other forms lay still and silent amid the scattered muskets, dead horses, overturned wagons and torn up fences and fields. My eyes filled, and I cried once more.

I found nowhere in my instincts or in any guidance under which I had been raised what it was that justified war to men, or what I had just witnessed they would do to one another in the name of it. As we stared at the fruits of war spread out before us, one thing now seemed clear without the need to say so: we saw no glory in it. To the contrary, it sickened and saddened us.

Billy spoke. "Well, fellers I think it's high time to git on home. This has been a terrible day, and I would just as soon have missed it. I seen all of war today I ever want to see. Ma thinks I'm somewhere off with Pa or home minding my own business, and now that things have quieted some, I think I'll try to git home while the gittin's good. Reis, why don't you come on and go with me?"

"Thanks, Bill. I would, but I still hope the rebels will move on and leave a way open for me to get home. Ma and Pa must be worried sick by now."

THE SNOOK BROTHERS ALSO DECIDED this was their chance to head for home. They lived several miles out the Mummasburg Road, which leads northwest and away from where the rebels had entered the field. We had heard some officers say that the Confederates that left Carlisle and Harrisburg were close by and would probably be coming in from the north, possibly blocking the route the boys were planning to take. They said they'd just have to take their chances and that the further they got, the safer they'd be. As for me, the way home lay in the other direction and seemed hopelessly closed off for now. We said our goodbyes with prayers and good wishes, and the boys got set to leave.

Soon after the boys left, artillery opened up from Oak Ridge a half mile north, announcing the arrival of the Confederates expected from Carlisle and causing me to stay put for a while until I could get a better feel for what to do. I was plumb tuckered out and beset with an agonizing hunger. I slid down a tree I had been leaning against and sat on the ground pondering the terrible things I had seen. I was so tired, and in spite of the alarming new turn of events with the arrival of more rebels, I drifted into a reverie of thought and gave in to a half-sleep of exhaustion.

The knowledge now that men were lying torn and dying around me and the thought that I had once intended to make use of it to entertain my peers now played on my conscience. I felt guilty and stupid for ever wanting to see any part of war. I had focused on these thoughts so hard and so long, I had lost my attentiveness to everything else for what seemed a long time.

I was jolted alert by Jim Barrett's shrieking.

"Hey, Reis! *Reis!* Your horse's got away!" I swung around and looked where I had left him, and there he was, gone *indeed! Great Jumpin' Jehosephat!* I immediately thought of Pa and how I was to explain what on earth was so fascinating and distracting that I lost old Sport.

Then I spotted him clean on the other side of the field up by the Mummasburg Road, standing there with his head drooping and his bridle hanging down, cropping great swaths of grass like as if he had all day. I had tied him loosely to a small sapling, but he must have broken loose during all the racket and just decided to heck with all *this!*

I dashed out into the field towards him and froze in my tracks. A thousand rebels were coming down from Oak Ridge and heading for the open in front of Mr. Forney's place. Just into the field, the rebels swung left and formed into line. I hesitated. Oh, lordy, I thought, if I have to go home without Sport, I might just as well keep on a-going. That decided it. I figured I'd have barely enough time to get to Sport before they swept across. There was no time left and no other decision to make. I had to do what I had to do. As I started to move out, Jim Barrett called out to me once again.

"Hold on, boy! Don't you dare cross in front of that brigade. You won't get fifty yards!"

"Well I just have to," I yelled. "I'm sorry, but I just *have* to! If the rebels don't kill me, Pa will, if I was to come home without the horse!"

"All right, God Bless you then, boy! But take that dang Yankee hat off and hide it! And write me a letter some time and tell me you made it home! You hear?"

I tucked my new forage cap (which I still have) deep in a pocket and replaced it with my old battered straw fishing hat. Surely they wouldn't shoot a barefoot boy in an old straw hat! Then it came to me as I ran into the field that a lot of *them* were barefoot boys in straw hats themselves! So Old Jack and I went tearing across right in front of them just as fast as the legs God gave us would go.

"Oh, lordy, lordy, lordy, and Lord forgive me for sayin' it!" I puffed and leaped through the tall timothy.

I hoped Mr. Forney wasn't looking out the window to see me running through his hayfield. I also hoped I was far enough away that he wouldn't be able to recognize me and later tell Pa how he saw me and my dog running through his hayfield, because I had let the horse wander off. I took relief in the thought that Mr. Forney was likely to be distracted by a lot worse than me running through his field at that moment.

As the rebels closed, I could feel the long, hellish, bony finger of death upon my back – clawing, clutching, cold, fearsome – the inevitability of being brought down by a great blow, piercing, tearing away my flesh and bones and insides. I prayed with all my strength and faith that somehow the inevitable might pass me by. My leaden feet dragged me down, and it seemed that the fence line, so close ahead, would never come. I felt as though I was running along the edge of a great knife. Had it not been that I was so afraid of losing Sport, I would never have found myself running across a live battlefield. At the time, I was afraid of so many things, I wasn't sure what I was afraid of most.

When Old Jack and I got about halfway across, something else happened to scare us out of our wits. Suddenly, about a hundred yards to our right, a whole line of Union infantry that had been hidden behind a low stone wall at the top end of the field where the crest of the ridge joins the Mummasburg Road rose up as if by magic and took aim right at us! I knew without any doubt my end had come! But they all just froze with this surprised look on their faces and held their fire for a split second, and in that same split second, I saw for the first and I hoped only time for the rest of my life what it was like to stare into the business end of a thousand loaded muskets ready to fire. I dropped to the ground like a sack of potatoes and pulled Old Jack tight against me when they let loose with a deafening blast of musketry that few people ever hear this close or from this perspective and live to tell about it. The rebel soldiers sent up a great cry of surprise and fell together as if someone had cut them down with a giant scythe.

It was terrible. And me, I lay there gasping for breath, my heart pumping itself out of my breast! Our boys had stopped them dead in their tracks, but in that moment, I felt grief for all the rebel boys who would never be going home again.

With my head as close to the ground as I could make it, I could see through the stalks a young rebel's dirty butternut shirt turn bright red in a widening circle. His face slackened and paled as the lifeblood went out of him. He sank to his knees and pitched slowly forward face first into the dirt, and the thought passed briefly that a mother somewhere down south would learn her son was gone. Then she would sink to the ground also.

During all that went on, Sport hadn't budged an inch and continued his business of tearing up grass. As both sides paused to recover and got set to volley again, I rose up and made a beeline for the fence on the dead run. I was up in the saddle in a flash and don't remember how I got there. I reined Sport around and the three of us headed down the steep slope to the plain that spreads out north of town. By then the Yanks had reloaded before the rebels recovered, and I heard them fire again.

I hopped up and down in the saddle and kicked at old Sport to urge him along with every strong word and device at my disposal, but he had spent too many years not hurrying to turn over a new leaf this late in life. He just moved along in his ordinary fashion with no more acknowledgment than if I had been a horsefly on his arse.

SOMETIME IN THE MID-MORNING after the First Corps had become heavily engaged, the Eleventh Corps, under General O. O. Howard had come up through the town to support and reinforce the First Corps on its right. The timing was such that the Eleventh took the field just as two Confederate divisions arriving from Carlisle and Harrisburg hit them hard.

By the time I rode down from Seminary Ridge, the Eleventh Corps was engaged in a major fight but not faring well at all. The plains east and north of the town were strewn with the dead and dying. Wounded men pleaded for water where they had fallen and licked their lips and convulsed their mouths in a futile effort to produce a little moisture. I considered going back to the McLean farm for water but gave up on the idea, as the way was now under intense fire and the mission not likely of success. I heard from Bill later that his mother, Mrs. Harriett Bayly, came down to this same field from their place and bullied the Confederates into fetching water to aid the wounded of both sides. She later gave refuge to a young rebel and took him into the family, and he stayed with them for many years.

What with the whole rebel army now smack dab between me and home, things were going to have to change considerably before I got out of the fix I was in. I thought again about what Pa, Ma and Gramma must be going through with all the commotion around and wondering what in blazes might have happened to me, and I swallowed hard.

As I made my way into town, the noise of renewed battle from Seminary Ridge made clear that the First Corps and its tired, brave men had come under heavy fire once again as fresh Confederate brigades came up. I was tired and hungry and longed for some safe, quiet place to go rest and collect myself. Many soldiers were pouring back in retreat from all roads and fields west and north of town. On top of everything was the fearsome thought about what would happen to us if our army was defeated.

I thought of Christ Lutheran Church that was nearby on Chambersburg Street (some people called it the College Church). I guess a church would be as good a place as any to find sanctuary and comfort. Where better to shut out the terrible killing and wounding and mayhem? We attended church at Christ Lutheran occasionally as Pa was always seeking a preacher to his liking. I knew a pretty girl named Tillie Pierce who went there. She was about three years older than I was, but I harbored a sweetness for her that I had told nobody about. Some years later, Tillie would be married in that church but not to me.

Pa liked to try different churches and said he never tired of hearing the word of God from the lips of a truly humble man but that they could leave all the great orators at home. He allowed as how if he needed to hear any more "perorations" about "*Gaww*-deh!" to get into Heaven, they could just as leave keep the place. This kind of talk upset Ma. Pa said he'd even like to try a Negro church sometime, because they seemed to enjoy it so much and make such a wondrous time of it, but Ma and Gramma said they wouldn't hear to it. "Land sakes! What would the neighbors think?" Gramma said.

Pa said he believed that everyone had, for the most part, shortchanged God considerably with the notion that man was created in His image, which Pa said was all man's idea, not God's. Ma and Gramma feared that Pa was in danger of "losing his place" in line for Heaven with such talk.

Right now, the notion of going into a nice quiet, cool church to escape the awful things I had witnessed this day held great appeal. Since it was a Wednesday, maybe the church would be empty and I could sneak Old Jack along in with me and finally get a little rest, peace and reflection.

Chapter Three - Every House, Church and Barn a Hospital

And strewn upon the field of death,
This erstwhile cannon fodder,
Who supplicate with dying breath,
A little drink of water.

———————————————

I REMEMBERED AN UNUSED CARRIAGE HOUSE a little ways down the alley behind Christ Lutheran Church, where us boys used to get in a game of mumbly peg after services. If still unoccupied, it would make a good place to hide Sport while I went into the church to collect myself and pray and hide out some from the dreadful scenes of the morning.

I approached down the alley parallel to Chambersburg Street, hoping we might slip in unnoticed and avoid all the fuss and terrible racket going on out in the street. The whole town was filling up with retreating soldiers, horses, guns, wagons, ambulances and panic, all of which would soon overflow into this and every other passage and pathway in town.

By this hour, the meager lunch I had brought from home was long since gone, and the few raspberries I'd been able to work in just didn't do much for me, and I was empty as a drum inside. My stomach felt like it had dried up into a burning knot. Wafting on the breeze from somewhere was the most heavenly whiff of potatoes, onions and butter cooking. I knew the smell so well because of Gramma's potato soup. I thought about Ma and Gramma setting out supper in a few hours. It was torture to think about. I imagined Gramma going out onto the porch, banging on her triangle and calling for me in hopes that by some miracle she might conjure me up.

As I picked my way quietly down the alley, I could not get the thought of potato soup out of my head. I could see Gramma putting the old soup kettle on the hot stove. She'd cut off a big chunk of butter, and drawing the knife along the top of the kettle, swipe it off to slide down and sizzle in the pot below. Then she'd chop up a couple big round onions and scoop them up with both hands, pitch them in the pot and give them a quick stir with her wooden spoon. After a bit she'd pour in some water from the teakettle, then dump in a big bunch of diced potatoes and let the whole thing sit there and cook awhile. Then, she'd add a little warm milk and cook it some more until the smell escaped the kitchen and made everyone outside drop what he was doing and fetch himself in to wash up and come to the table. I got no real comfort thinking about it and only made matters worse for myself.

Lucky for me the carriage house was empty as I had hoped it would be. I took Sport in, took off his bridle, put on his halter and tied him to a hitching ring. As I was considering whether or not to remove the saddle, I heard, or thought I heard, a cry, or a scream – off somewhere. I stopped in my tracks and cocked my head to listen. I waited. There it was again. An awful thing, it was; it made me jump. I never quite heard the like of it before. There it was *again*! Something awful was going on somewhere, and I felt the chills fill up and over me as sudden as if the sun went out.

I latched the carriage house door quietly and walked gingerly towards the church, pausing every step or two to listen. Now I heard the murmur of many voices coming from inside. I wasn't close enough to make out what anyone was saying. There seemed to be shouts now and then, angry shouts, desperate shouts, almost, coming from the church. Could there be a fracas going on inside the *church*? I hoped not! The back wall of the church looked different. Something was missing. Like a man with no eyebrows. What in the dickens …?

I walked slowly and gingerly up towards the back door and froze in horror! A bloody leg flew out a back window and flopped in the dirt on the other side of a stand of hollyhocks. There was a *sock* still on it! Then out the next window beyond, a twisted and bloody arm went flying and rolled and slithered down a pile of arms and legs. *Merciful Heavens!* My stomach tried to run off, and I leaned over a hitching rail and threw up what little there was inside. I twisted up my face and braced myself for another look. Oh Lord! It was a sight I never could have imagined! A pale and bloody heap of blue-white arms and legs and hands and feet lay covered with blowflies and yellow jackets just beyond the hollyhocks. You could see where they had been cut off, like a cut of meat on butchering day. I could not imagine what it must be like inside the church. I was filled with dread now about going on in, but something compelled me forward. I made Old Jack sit outside and wait.

It was the church's shutters that were missing. They had been re-moved and spread across the backs of the pews and made to serve as oper-ating tables. They were laid out so that the sunlight fell on each one to give the surgeons light to do their dreadful work. Each shutter was occupied by a wounded man, some in blue, some not; some were crying, some were silent, and some lay still.

Two men were on their knees under the operating tables boring holes in the floor with large augers to let the blood run off. One of the surgeons called out to a man coming with a bucket of sand, "Spread some more of that sand over here. It's so slippery, we can't keep to our feet!" Awful smells combined to turn one's stomach — smells of blood and urine and feces, of vomit and burned flesh. I gagged again and again.

Around the walls of the church, dozens of men lay with all manner of terrible wounds, each awaiting his turn at the table and application of knife and saw to stave off death — to have some mangled and offending part sawed off, cut away and pitched onto the mound of other men's parts outside the windows. I stepped into a patch of blood in my bare feet and stood there for the moment unable to move, unable to turn aside and stared at the overwhelming sights arrayed before me, so very, very far from yesterday.

Old Mrs. Broderbundt, as round and white as a snowman, her eyes red from tears, passed among the wounded and assisted as she could, but it seemed to be too much for her. A surgeon near the door called to her to hold something, and she came waddling and whimpering and sniffling over to him. The doctor gritted his teeth and hissed quietly into her face, "These poor boys need a calming presence and a cool hand on their fore-heads. If you can't manage that, then please move on, madam!" Sniffling and suppressing her tears, Mrs. Broderbundt answered, "Yes … yes yes yes yes!" I felt sorry for her because I'm certain her day had started out with no expectation of what she must now endure. I knew I would never be able to do what was required of her.

The time had come for everyone to brace himself for what this thing called war was really like — a thing that everybody had so glibly bandied about when it was somewhere else and far away. It was easy then to make it out to be whatever you wanted it to be. But not here, not now. It was just outside and all around, and you could take nothing about it for granted. I was overcome with an urgency to get out of that terrible place and backed quickly toward the door. I slipped on out with little or no notice by anyone present.

BY NOW, EVERY HOUSE, CHURCH AND BARN available would be made a hospital to receive and repair shattered and mangled young men of both sides. Soon thousands from the Union First and Eleventh Corps would be driven through the narrow streets by yet thousands more Confederates. As the numbers accumulated, one young woman said the men passing by her window were so densely packed, she could have crossed the street by walking on their heads.

I decided to leave Sport where he was for the time being and look for something to eat. Although my appetite had left me for the present, I knew I would need something soon. I had watered Sport just before we stopped, and he had grazed all day long, so he could go a spell without food or water. I just hoped he didn't get impatient and cause a ruckus and tear the place down before I got back. Some old friends of Ma and Pa, the McGraths, lived a little further on and their back door looked out on the alley. They had always made me feel welcome in happier times, and I hoped they might take pity on me now.

I picked my way carefully down the alley with Old Jack. The rebels had begun to infest the town and were popping up here and there, and, all by yourself, you would stand out like a sore thumb. It might be better to be lost in the crowd. Trouble was, the crowd consisted mostly of Yankee soldiers in retreat from the mob of pursuing rebels. A feller could get trampled, and they'd never find anything left of him. For now, anyway, the alley was clear, and I didn't have far to go before I found myself knocking on the McGraths's back door.

"Reisie? Reisie Bramble! What in heaven's name are you doing in town on *this* day of all days? Come in come in come in, dear boy. Have you had your dinner yet?"

"N ..."

"What have you been up to? You look like something the cat drug in!"

"W ..."

"Come come. Have some fresh milk and a nice slice of butter bread I just baked. It's still nice and hot!"

"Th ..."

"What on earth are you doing in town with all these dirty looking scalawags all over the place? I'm afraid to go near the window, even!"

"I ..."

There was a pounding on the front door that made us both jump a foot! Mrs. McGrath froze in her steps, and then the pounding came again. This time, we knew someone should answer before the door came off its hinges. Mrs. McGrath gathered up her skirts and went to the door. She took a deep breath and bravely opened it to reveal a most distressing sight.

THREE RAGGEDY REBEL SOLDIERS with their muskets slung over their shoulders were carrying a wounded officer in a blanket. He appeared to be in great pain. One of them, skinny as a rail and dirty as a doormat, spoke up.

"Madam, we must have a doctor for this man at once! And a place to put him down."

"Well, there's no doctor here. I expect all of them are quite busy elsewhere or long gone by now," said Mrs. McGrath, hoping that'd be the end of it.

"Well, we have no choice. Your place is as good as any, and you can send that boy thar to skeer up a doctor," said the second one.

"No," said the first reb. "Don't bother sending the boy. He won't come back anyway. We'll have to make do with what we got."

They brought the man in and laid him on a couch in the parlor, much to his discomfort. Finally, after he had had a chance to settle and regain himself a little, he turned to Mrs. McGrath. He spoke in the soft, cultivated voice of a Virginian.

"May I ask your name, madam?"

"McGrath. Mrs. Taylor McGrath."

The man spoke hesitatingly, as if breathing caused him great pain. "Well, Mrs. McGrath, I need you ... to help me contain my innards ... as

I have been sliced open across the middle ... and am consequently inca-
pacitated ... to get up ... and help myself ... lest they tumble out."

"What a horrid thing to say, sir! I regret that you would feel free to
invade a person's home with such obscenities as that and would torment a
lady in such a manner!"

"I assure you it is true, madam .... You have only to look for yourself."

"Indeed I will not, sir! I won't have anything to do with it! Nothing
a'tall!"

"Then I shall soon die. There is no odor of penetration ... of the
bowel ... so my wound, while grievous, need not be fatal .... Will you have
it on your conscience that ... you refused to help? Is that what Christians
... in Pennsylvania are like?" In desperation to make his case, he opened
his torn tunic to reveal a gaping wound that further revealed his bloody
entrails on the brink of slithering over and out. I almost gagged at the
thought that it reminded me of a hog strung up on butchering day just
before you pulled his guts out.

Mrs. McGrath threw up her hands and screamed and then brought
them down to cover her face. "In the name of the Almighty, sir, what is it
you would have me *do?*" she shrieked.

"I would ask you to fetch the strongest thread you have ... and a
large, sharp, clean needle ... preferably curved ... like a carpet needle, and
sew me up. I trust these boys here with anything but a needle and thread."

"Oh, dear *Lord!* I could *never* do that!"

"Then you would prefer to watch me lie here and slowly die, madam?"

"Oh, dear God, give me strength!"

"Do you have any stimulants about, perhaps – for me, and for yourself as well?"

Mrs. McGrath left the room wailing and sniffling as she went about
rummaging and collecting paraphernalia and the 'anesthesia.' "I will never
be able to justify to Taylor the loss of his imported Irish whiskey!" she
whimpered.

After she left, I stood there in awkward silence and tried to look small
with the three rebel soldiers standing around the wounded man. No one
spoke, and no one's face showed anything. I made sure mine didn't. Un-

easiness hung in the room only a mite short of fear. The officer's breathing came hard and with hesitation, and I guessed he was in great pain but trying not to show it.

The other three were all young, lean, shabby, hairy, bearded and filthy. One had no shoes, and the other two weren't much better off. All had tattered hats of different description, which they had removed when they gathered around the officer. Their muskets were ominous and worn smooth and burnished from long use. They stacked them in a corner of the room along with their cloth haversacks, canteens, knapsacks, blanket rolls, ammunition pouches and bayonets. I tried hard to keep from staring at the muskets and bayonets. All three men wore simple tattered shirts and trousers of homespun. One man carried a long-barreled revolver tucked into a rope about his waist, and stood facing toward the window a bit where he could keep an eye on the approach to the front door. Other than that, there wasn't a whit of difference between them.

Mrs. McGrath returned with an agonized expression and a pan, some cloths, some lint, soap, a teakettle of hot water, a fearsome-looking curved upholstery needle and a few strands of catgut. Lying on top of the cloths was a handsome bottle nearly full of an amber liquid I took to be her husband's Irish whiskey.

We had never had spirits in the house, so this was my first look up close at the substance that seemed to strike such fear into the hearts of, and constitute the considerable preoccupation of, many a Christian congregation. I thought the pale green color of the bottle and the amber color of its contents made a right pretty combination, and I guess that thought alone would upset the righteous for fear that the Devil himself was already at work on tearing down my innocence.

Mrs. McGrath handed over the bottle, and the officer took a long pull. He then passed the bottle to one of the men who took a modest pull and passed it to the other two who did likewise. This act appeared to meet with great satisfaction all around, and the officer drank again. When offered a second drink, the first man put up his hand and said, "No, Major, the rest must be left for the ordeal through which you now must pass," and, nodding to Mrs. McGrath, said, "That is mighty fine substance, madam. Thankee." I found the accent of his voice soft and strangely appealing, almost kindly. The major took a few more drinks from the bottle and lay back to let the effects settle in.

Perhaps whiskey has become widely referred to as "spirits" because it tends to put a body in good spirits. I know this is not universally true, as I've heard there are some upon whom it has exactly the opposite effect, but in the major's case, there soon was indeed a noticeable improvement in spirit. A large heavy library table in the room was cleared and covered with a tick and several quilts and a sheet. A pillow was brought in for the major's head, and the three men very carefully lifted him from the couch and placed him on the table with great gentleness.

"All right, my good woman! Do your derndest! I await thy magic touch!"

WITH OBVIOUS TREPIDATION and extreme distaste, Mrs. McGrath laid back the major's clothing and exposed the terrible wound. She began by slowly and gently cleaning with soap and water the area around the long slice that ran clear across the major's midsection. The major lay as quietly and tolerantly as a petted cat. You could see his throbbing innards glisten and slosh around ever so little. Then, she poured a tiny amount of whiskey into a small dish and dabbed into it with a clean cloth. This she applied directly to the edges of the wound.

"*Whooo-eee! Lordy*, that stings!" The major lurched in reflex. The three men stiffened.

"I am so sorry, sir, but I am afraid there is worse to come, and we will all need all our strength to get through this as quickly as we can," said Mrs. McGrath. The major took another long drink.

"Right chyoo are, my good woman!" The major was beginning to slur his words a little. "And we should pause a moment and let the effects of this supreme nectar get down to where the trouble i ... *hick!* ... izh ...." He stared at Mrs. McGrath with a silly smile on his face.

"Please, sir, you are embarrassing me. And this is difficult enough." He turns his head to me.

"Aw, shoot. I'm not 'mbarrassing num, am I, boy? Am I 'mbarras – *hick!* – sing you? *Oh, Lordy!* Hic ... *hick!* ... cups for a man in my condition really smarts!"

It made me cringe for him. "No, sir," I told him. But he sure as heck was embarrassing Mrs. McGrath.

Mrs. McGrath had by now threaded her needle, winced mightily, gathered the two flaps covering the major's innards and plunged in.

He gritted his teeth. *"Ow! Ow! Ow! OW!* .... I think you're doin' that on purpuls just to shut me up, Miz M'Grabb!" The major twisted in extreme pain that seemed to hurt everyone else in the room as well.

Mrs. McGrath bent over the man in full concentration now. She furrowed her brow and squinted her eyes as if she herself was taking off some of his pain. With each careful stitch, she drew the gut up tight and as gently as she could while one of the men held a coal oil lamp in close.

"Careful you don't prick his bowels, ma'am, whatever you do, or he'll be as good as gut shot," said one of the rebels in a black hat. "And them hiccups ain't doing him any good either. Major, try and roll out a big belch just as you're at the edge of a hiccup."

"Oh, my!" The major gasped for breath and gulped air. No results. "Try again!"

"Rrrrpppp!" The major let out a prize belch.

"That oughta gentle them hiccups some now, Major," said Black Hat.

"Oh, dear Lord, dear Lord, dear Lord, dear Lord ...!" whined Mrs. McGrath.

The major began to sing:

"I knew a gal in May-hee-co,
She lived beshide the shee.
She wasn't quite a lay-dee-oh,
But good enough for me.

I knew she had some other beaus
And thish I didn't mind,
But when the need for love arose,
I had to stand in line."

Did you ever notice when grownups get flustered over something embarrassing, if there's a kid around, he gets yelled at like his very presence is what's embarrassing everybody? Well, this was no exception. Mrs. Mc-Grath looks over at me and says, "Reisie! Why are you standing there staring? It's time you made yourself scarce, and *forthwith!*"

I felt more than a little sorry for her. Here she was in this fix all by herself and no way out of it. If the officer died, no telling what the rebels might do if they held her to blame.

In the midst of all the gravity, I was occupied fighting off a mixture of emotions: the enemy was before me up close for the first time and I had no real confidence they would leave us unharmed and move on anytime soon. The major was grievously wounded and might not live through his ordeal, and I dreaded the thought of witnessing his death. Other than being the enemy, he seemed to be a good man.

And Mrs. McGrath was emotionally distraught and embarrassed at the improprieties of his song, which caused me to rift up the need to laugh from way down deep, and I hated myself for it.

I found myself struggling for all I was worth to keep from busting out laughing at this highly inappropriate time. Boys in church will sneak funny faces at you if they catch you fighting off a laugh during the sermon. And the harder you try, the worse it gets. It was like that, and I was in agony and desperate for relief. On top of all this, I'm ashamed to say, at this somber moment, I was trying as hard as I could to remember the words to the song for when I could use them to poke a little humor into grim times, or just to show off for the other boys. I was caught in the torture of a fight between desperately unwanted laughter and extreme pathos.

> "*I think I was her fa-vor-ite,*
> *And so she seemed inclined,*
> *'Cause sometimes on a Friday night,*
> *She'd let me jump the line . . . ."*

I looked at Mrs. McGrath's face and saw agony there. Then all the accumulated stresses of the day bubbled up and demanded release. I was choking to contain myself and could do so no longer. A laugh blurted itself out between my tightened lips like a string of smothered farts. I felt a humiliating blush creep over my face and broke into a trembling sweat. I prayed for help and thought of horrible things, disgusting things, but the laugh persisted to leak out in dribbles and drabs and my struggle continued without letup.

"One day, I up and made the choice,
And asked her for her hand,
But when I told the other boys,
They laughed to beat the band!"

"Please to God, sir! Will you not *desist?*" begged Mrs. McGrath.

I ran from the house like someone with a bad case of *dire-rear* and took refuge in the outhouse where I allowed myself the extreme pleasure of pounding the walls and letting it all come out, all of which puzzled Old Jack no end. Had anyone been passing by, I'm sure he would have reported a lunatic trapped in the McGrath's privy. It was likely the only case of wild laughter around Gettysburg that day. I stayed there a while, because just as everything seemed to settle down, Mrs. McGrath's face would appear and hiss the word "*desist!*" and the whole thing would start all over. You'd have thought the guilt I felt would have helped, but it didn't, not one bit. Finally, my spasms subsided and I returned to the house.

The operation had been completed, and the major appeared to have sobered up mostly but seemed to be losing ground otherwise. He seemed weaker, and his face was hot and flushed. He spoke to Mrs. McGrath with difficulty.

"Madam, I now believe I will not make it through. It has nothing to do with your good work ... as I was at the edge when ... the boys brought me here. I tell you now so you will know this ... and to ask you to accept my gratitude ... for performing what I know must have been ... a most difficult and demanding task. I hope I wasn't too offensive or too awfully much out of line. I guess ... I was simply trying to lighten the load a bit." Mrs. McGrath's eyes were brimming as she took his hand in hers.

The five of us sat there and watched his decline. Each of the soldiers made cool, damp cloths for his forehead, which seemed to comfort him some. In time, his breathing became difficult, and he lapsed into unconsciousness. Soon thereafter, the spirit left him.

"His life was a mean struggle," said one of his men. "He was away with the army for years in Mexico and agin the Mormons and Injuns out west. He leaves a wife and five little children." He must have got home to see the missus once in a while, I thought.

"What will they do without him?" asked Mrs. McGrath, tearfully.

"We will look after them as best we can — if indeed any of us survive to return home at all. But even those of us who are left will be returning to a barren land. We'll be hard-pressed to look after our own, but most of us will share what we have. It would be unchristian not to."

I PEERED OUT FROM BEHIND THE CURTAINS to discover that the multitudes in the street had made a transformation from blue to gray. Chambersburg Street was now full of rebel soldiers. My, but they were in high spirits. So much so that some took to opening doors of houses whenever they felt like it. I thought it was only a matter of time before one of them yanked open the carriage house door and discovered Sport, and what a prize he would make! As no one in the house now showed any care about me, I slipped out the back door and into the alley. I saw my mistake too late.

Before I could dash back inside, a small pack of rebels coming down the alley from the direction of the seminary spied me and came running up to me and Old Jack.

"Hold on there, boy! Where you headed so all-fired fast? And what fer dog is *that* anyways?"

"I don't know *what* he is; we just call him Old Jack."

"That ain't meant in disrespeck of our dearly departed General Stonewall Jackson, who *we* called 'Old Jack' — behind his back, of course — is it boy?"

"Oh, no sir! My Gramma named him that because 'Old Jack' is one of her favorite names for the Devil."

"Well, dagged if she didn't tag *him* right! Just look at them eyes, woodja! That dog's too ugly to let live!"

Old Jack dropped his ears and curled himself around and got as low down as he could without falling over while the tip of his tail beat quick little taps against the ground. He peered up at the rebel out of that one yellow eye of his. I had frozen in my tracks, and all sorts of things were running through my mind. Were they going to take me prisoner? And take me back south like Ma had worried about? Were they going to shoot Old Jack? And maybe *eat* him, hungry as they were? They looked capable of eating dogs or nails or anything. I hoped they wouldn't be able to hear my heart pounding and know how terrified I was.

"Well, if you was to die fer bein' ugly, we'd all be in Hell," said the one.

Then the other one spoke up, "Well, just to look at *him*! He's scared shitless. What have they been sayin' about us terrible rebels, boy? That we eat youngins?"

"Wha ... ba ... amah ..."

"Go on, boy, *git*! Before you git in somebody's way and git hurt! *Heah, now?*"

That would suit me just fine. My whole purpose in life right now would be to "git."

"Yes sir! I do. Thank you sir!" After they cleared away, I walked slowly towards the place where I had left Sport. I had to be particularly careful, as the rebels were now pouring into the streets. I sidled up to the carriage door, looked left and right and slipped inside.

WELL, OLD SPORT WAS RIGHT WHERE I LEFT HIM and cool as a cucumber. I climbed up the carriage wall and swung over and mounted. I eased him out into the daylight and halted him there a minute while I gritted my teeth. Not a rebel in sight.

I prayed that the Good Lord would somehow get me and Sport and Old Jack to safety of some kind. I don't know how I expected to get an animal big as a house past the eyes of them that coveted healthy horses and were confiscating them left and right. But faith and foolhardiness will sometimes take you a long way.

Rebels coming in from the north now occupied a large part of the town, including the town square or 'diamond' as it was known. I stayed clear of the diamond, but I was able to peer over a fence at the end of the alley and witness a most pathetic and repulsive spectacle. On the railroad siding just north of the diamond were several railroad cars of supplies the rebels had captured. They had torn the lids off tubs and barrels, and in their hunger, were stuffing their mouths with raw salt fish and flour. The sticky juice from the fish had run down on their clothes, and their faces and clothes were all coated in white. They looked as awful as if someone had just dug them up, but not a one of them showed the first sign of shame or remorse. To the contrary, they were all whooping and hollering for all they were worth and flinging fish and flour at one another in all directions.

I thought it high time for me to move on whilst some of them were so occupied and others had something else to draw their attention. I wheeled Sport around and made my way south through back alleys in the direction our retreating soldiers had taken. More advancing Confederates would soon fill almost every street and alley and nowhere in town could now be considered a safe path to the Union lines. People running down the streets were yelling that rebels now occupied the row houses on Baltimore Street and had knocked holes in the common walls upstairs between them so their sharpshooters could run through from house to house and take pot shots through the windows at our troops heading towards Cemetery Hill.

Several bodies lay in the street. The body of one soldier was missing its head. Poor, poor man. I prayed his mother would never find out that he was made to lie like that on a public street with his head missing. Here were more terrible images for my brain to contend with, and I wondered how other people would ever tolerate such things suddenly thrust upon them. Soldiers say they get used to it to the point where they hardly even notice anymore. I have looked upon a severed hog's head or a deer's head with dispassion, but never a man's. I hope never a man's. Also there were dead horses along the way, which made me all the more apprehensive about Sport.

As I proceeded to Washington Street a step ahead of the tide, I saw old Mrs. Carlisle in her sunbonnet and apron sweeping the sidewalk in front of her house. A lot of dust had been raised by men, horses and cannonballs bounding down the street. She was being pestered by three rebels who were teasing her about waiting a day or so until they got done making dirt. She was threatening them with her broom. I backed Sport into another alley and carefully laid back to watch.

"Careful, missus, that thar broom might be loaded! Har, har, har!"

"If you Pennsylvania Dutch could fight a war like you fight dirt, we'd o' been whupped long ago! Hee, hee, hee!"

"Maybe you should join the army. You Yankees seem a little short on people what kin wield a broom proper! Har, har, har!"

Mrs. Carlisle was flushed with anger and looked about ready to burst. Her tormenters hadn't noticed a rebel officer who came up quietly on his horse behind them. He drew his sword, and in a flash, laid the flat of it hard on the backside of the nearest one to him.

"*Whee! Damn* that smarts!" he yelped in surprise and rubbed his wound.

"You scalawags! Your place is up on the line! And not bothering the womenfolk!" The three scraggly rebels hurried on ahead.

The officer lifted his hat. "My apologies to you, madam. This war has hardened us all, some more than others. Those rapscallions are not typical of the army commanded by General Robert E. Lee."

"I've heard more than enough about Mister *Robert E. Lee* and what a good man he is," Mrs. Carlisle shouted up to him, her face red as a beet and smoking out the ears. "If this is what a southern gentleman does to people, I sure as blue blazes never want to meet one who's not!"

The officer nodded graciously. "Yes, madam, and have you been reading about Vicksburg and how the practices of General Grant are resulting in the death of women and children there? Such conduct would be unthinkable to General Lee."

"As far as I'm concerned, you could put 'em both in a poke and shake 'em up and it's hard to tell which one would come out first. Anybody responsible for this war ought to be taken out and dropped in the ocean. Just look at what you've done to us!" Mrs. Carlisle waved her arm around about.

"There's no such thing as a tidy war, madam. It was you Yankees who first invaded *our* land."

"Well, no one in this town invaded anything, but it was *you* people who started this war, sir, by your treasonous acts! It was *you* people who fired the first shot! And I think all of you will soon understand that you've more than met your match here in Pennsylvania and will soon see the handwriting on the wall. Remember, sir: '*They have sown the wind, and they shall reap the wild wind! Hosea 8:7*'" By now, Mrs. Carlisle was worked up and huffing and puffing.

The officer responded and quoted courteously. "*'But I scattered them with a whirlwind. Thus the land was desolate . . . for they laid the pleasant land desolate . . . and the Lord God shall blow the trumpet, and shall go with the whirlwinds of the <u>South</u>! . . . Zechariah*'"

She looked up at him in dismay and burst into tears.

"Well, then, damn you to Hell, and what do you say to that? This is *my* land and the land of *my* fathers. You've no right to be here, destroying our town and our good work of generations!" she cried.

By this time, some townspeople – a few ladies and an old man or two – had come cautiously out of their houses to find out what was going on. The rebel officer now spoke to the gathering.

"Y'all should see what the Yankees did at Fredericksburg," said the officer, again in a clear and courteous voice. "Our aim is not to kill Yankees but to be free of them." And then, as best as I can remember, he looked around said the following:

"Our cause is just, people! Many of us were against secession. But you Yankees invaded *our* land. And that obliged us to sacrifice everything except honor in defense of our homes. Would you not do the same ... if the seat of government was in the South, and we had invaded *your* land and crammed our government down *your* throats?

"We treasure our land as much as you treasure yours," the officer went on. "Remember! It was mostly Virginians that settled this country more than two hundred years ago and gave early voice to its ideals. We worshipped the same God as you and sang the same hymns. We lived in certainty that our lives were upright and correct, filled with rectitude and probity and dedicated unfailingly to the values set forth in this Good Book." He held a small testament aloft.

"Most people in the South do not own slaves and some despise the institution. General Lee himself does not favor it. Slavery is embraced mostly because, after two hundred and forty years, we've come to depend on it. Many people in the South see it as the natural order of things, and it has become something ensconced into our way of life. Most people never stop and think that there is anything wrong with it, because they've seen it all their lives. It is simply the way things are.

"Then came an iron heel under which we have been ground, not for a *day*, but for *two long years!* The unintended destruction you see around you is the accidental product of a few hours of war. Now imagine the condition of your land after two years of directed savagery, and you may come to some understanding of the condition ours is in and why we are here. We are here if for no other reason than to give our land and our people some *relief!*"

"Why didn't you think of that before you started this war?" shouted a lady from her doorway.

"I make no brief for those on either side whose actions led to this terrible conflict; their souls are assured a special place in Hell. But you will have some understanding of my bitterness, for I live in constant awareness that our people and their rights in 'the pursuit of happiness' have been shattered. No one will be untouched by this war," said the officer.

"Why don't you go on home, and leave us alone?" someone else shouted.

"We did not engage in this war in order to change anything about you, or to take over any of your institutions or territory. We did it to prevent you from doing those very things to us. Can you not understand this?" He said these words with much feeling and almost a pleading for the understanding of those who stood before him. "Do you not have the right— indeed the *obligation* – to fight someone who breaks into your house and threatens your family? Does not your honor require it?

"I have seen far too much of this war and would like nothing better than to end it right here today and return to the land I love. But would this damnyankee government be willing to leave it there?" With that, the officer tipped his hat once more and rode on, leaving the small collection of townspeople staring after him.

NOTWITHSTANDING THAT I HAD NOW WITNESSED the gentlemanly quality of at least two Confederate officers and the reasonable decency of a handful of ordinary soldiers, there were plenty of the other kind to go around. It was easy to be lulled into the notion that these men were not so bad after all, because that's what we all wanted so badly for them to be. In truth, they were hardened killers bent on killing our soldiers. War has a way of taking the edge off conscience. For some, it appears to remove it altogether. But they were the enemy. We hated and feared them and hoped and prayed for their defeat.

Notwithstanding also that General Lee had remonstrated against excesses towards civilians and ordered his army to respect all non-military citizens, what he did as well was to turn thousands of half-starved, desperate armed men loose in the streets of Gettysburg. It would be no wonder that some of them, swelled with the passion of their success against their hated enemies, would cut loose and do whatever they pleased.

Any time a house was unoccupied, it was not very long before some wild rebels would go in and tear up the place and take anything edible or whatever else struck their fancy. Often enough, they would smash up what was left. The rumor went around that they would not rob or smash up a house that was still occupied, probably out of deference to General Lee's admonitions. But many people were terrified at the thought of having rebel hordes pour into their parlors and had fled, leaving everything up to Providence. Whether to leave and risk the loss of one's home or to remain and risk one's life presented a universal quandary. Many did stay with their homes and, in the aftermath, all were surprised to realize that everyone except George Sandoe and Jenny Wade, who got shot by accident while baking bread at her sister's house, had survived.

Some citizens had left town ahead of the tide; some cowered in their cellars; others simply rose early and turned their attentions to the long string of chores attendant to survival as they did on every other day

WELL, I DECIDED THERE WAS NO GOOD REASON for me to do anything besides sneak off, which I did and left Mrs. Carlisle and her broom to fate. I had not gone far when I came across an acquaintance, Albertus Mc-Creary, who hailed me in the street.

"Reis Bramble? What on earth are you doing roaming the streets on your horse? It's not safe around. Come on in the house. Pa is chasing us all back down in the cellar until this thing blows over. You don't want to be out here. Half the rebel army is about to come charging through town after our boys who are making a stand on Cemetery Hill."

"Thanks, Bert," I said. "I can't think of anyplace I'd rather be right now except home."

"What are you doing here anyway?" asked Albertus.

"Well, mainly, I was on my way to Bill Bayly's house, and by the time I knew what was going on, the way back was closed off," which stretched the truth just a little, but I'm sure the lack of the details didn't do him any harm. "I was out by the railroad cut and got swept back here along with everything else, and now I'm trying to catch up with the army again. I figure I'll be as safe with them as anywhere until I can find a way home."

"Well, who knows when that could be? Come on in and be safe with us a spell. Let's hide your horse out back, or you won't have him long."

"I've been trying to hide him all day. I appreciate it, Bert."

"We have a barn out back, and part of it is closed off secret like, where we also set a few hens away from egg thieves. You'd miss it sure if you didn't know it was there. Will he tolerate being cooped up in a place like that?"

"I don't know for sure. He'll just have to, I guess. If we can give him some oats and water, maybe."

We saw to Sport's needs, and I brushed him down a few strokes with a currycomb I found hanging on a nail. Then, we went directly to the cellar through double doors that lie over the stone steps that led below. As my eyes adjusted to the darkness, I could make out Mr. McCreary and a few others I didn't recognize. Mrs. McCreary and their girls were huddled back in a corner scared out of their wits. Mr. McCreary closed the double doors and slid a flat iron bar through the handles.

After a bit, Mr. McCreary struck up a spirited rendition of *The Battle Hymn of the Republic* and encouraged all of us to join in. Everybody started out a little weak, but before long, we put some life into it. Then we sang *Battle Cry of Freedom* followed by *Onward Christian Soldiers*. I didn't know a lot of the words, but I faked my way through the gaps and opened and closed my mouth like a sucker thrown up on the bank. Every now and then, we heard the sounds of footsteps clomping around upstairs, but who they were, we knew not. Each time we heard them, everyone would pause with their mouths hanging open until the footsteps stopped. Then we'd pick back up where we left off and sing some more. We must have stopped and started a dozen times.

We were well into *Aura Lee* and getting all teary over it when Old Jack's ears went straight up, dropped and then went back up halfway. He commenced a low growl. Somebody rattled the cellar doors and tried to yank them open, and all of us froze. Jack set in to barking up a storm when there came a banging on the doors that jolted us like a thunderbolt.

"Open up in thar afore we brek it down!" came a voice with the twang of the deep south.

Mr. McCreary went to the doors and lifted off the iron bar. "No need for that!" he said. "No need for that!"

Five skinny, dirty rebels armed with muskets poured into the cellar. The womenfolk pressed themselves into a corner and began to whimper with fear. One of the rebels spoke.

"Thar, thar, ladies, we didn't come to do you no harm. We're only in-terested in Yankee soldiers, and clearly you ain't them." The speaker was young and red-haired and covered with freckles. His hair was matted with dirt and sweat, and he commanded things with a manner well beyond his years.

"Would there be any Yankees in hiding hereabouts?"

"As you can see, there are none here," answered Mr. McCreary. "I cannot answer about elsewhere."

"I'm afraid we will have to search the house," said Red. "And you folks will have to come along. You ladies have nothing to fear from us."

We all trouped up the cellar steps and were led to the parlor and told to please be seated while three rebs went off to look for Union soldiers.

BEFORE LONG, THEY BEGAN TO RETURN with prisoners, which they turned over to Red and the fifth man. One came back with a young feller with his hands over his head. "I found thissun tryin' to squeeze hisself into the py-anner!" he laughed.

In all they found thirteen. I never could imagine there were that many hiding places in the house, and I guess none were good enough.

Everyone was all tensed up and filled with alarm about what might happen next. These were the people who were trained to kill our boys and had been trying very hard all day to do just that. Now that they had them at bay, would they show them no mercy? Lord knows what we should be required to witness. The McCreary daughters had already hidden their eyes in anticipation that something awful was about to happen.

First, they checked the prisoners for weapons and possessions, all of which they confiscated. Then they took down their names and told them they were prisoners of war. The redhead stood by and waited for the others to quiet down.

"I want to know if any of you damnyankees is hidin' a pack o' cards in yer sock!"

"Huh?" said several prisoners at once.

"*Cards!* Cards, cards, cards, cards, *cards!* Don't y'all know what cards is?"

One fellow very gingerly put up his hand and pulled a deck from his sock. "Fork 'em over Yank, and consider them contraband. All our cards is worn out jist like everything else. Now, does anybody here know how to play whist? I jist love to play whist!"

Another Union soldier said, "I know how to play whist, Johnny!"

"Well, pick ye a partner, come over here and sit down, and make y'self ready to get your ass whipped! Johnson, you be my partner. Sorry, ladies. When you've been in the field for months, it's easy to forget yourself when you get back among decent folk. Mister," he said to Mr. McCreary, "could you possibly spare anything for my poor boys to eat?"

Mr. McCreary was so relieved by the way things were turning out, he took on an extra layer of Christian hospitality. "Why, certainly, sir. We were about to sit down to supper before I thought it best to seek shelter. You are all welcome to join us."

With that, the notion of a card game took a hind seat, and the whole pack and passel went to the dining room, took up plates and went around dishing up food as if they were at a church covered-dish supper, while the ladies rushed to keep food on the table. Twenty-five in all, mixed together: rebels, Yankees, the McCreary's and me, all behaving like ladies and gentlemen as far as the eye could see.

"Down where I come from, it's too warm to have cold milk in the summertime."

"Is that so? We are quite fortunate to have a spring that runs cold all year 'round."

"Where'd you say y'all was from, Yank? VER-mont? I heard o' VER-mont. Just where in tarnation *is* VER-mont?"

"It's over from Maine a piece. Mighty pretty place."

"I 'low it's not prettier than Virginia — that is, before you Yanks got a-hold of it. At least you'll go back to a place that's still there. Most of Virginia has been stomped down, burned up or carted off!"

"I'm sorry for that. It wasn't any of my doing, of course."

"I guess none of us here picked this war for career or pastime. It's hard to find anyone who did or is willing to admit to it. I myself never had anything against you people. The war just came along, and we were required to go."

I can guarantee you I kept my mouth shut, got my share of Mrs. Mc-Creary's home-cooked food, hoped Sport would stay quiet and thanked the Good Lord and my lucky stars for food and for the high quality of the dirty rebels I had met so far. And so, for a little while, a few people, at least, stopped trying to kill each other and behaved like human beans once again.

It was like one of those games of war we played at school. We'd all be waving our stick swords and going at it *what for* until someone's shoe got untied, and he'd yell "Kings!" and everything would stop whilst he tied his shoe. I about half expected somebody to yell "Kings!" here today. Anyway, I was sure the war would soon return to normal again, and everyone could go back to pounding one another's lights out.

After a game of whist and a right smart jawing session, the rebels packed up their prisoners and went off with them. It was time for me and Sport and Old Jack to move on as well, if we were going to go through with our notion to find safety with the army and perhaps a way home. I had hoped to be safe within our lines while the way was clear, and it was getting late. The three of us made sure the coast was clear, then headed out in the direction of Ziegler's Grove.

In the early evening there appeared in the sky east of Gettysburg a most beautiful rainbow, which gave me great pangs of homesickness. I remembered seeing my first rainbow sitting on the porch with Ma when I was just a little fellow. She told me the rainbow was a symbol of God's promise that He would never destroy the earth by flood ever again. I told God that that was not exactly the sign that fit the circumstances of the day, but, if, in that same spirit, He was to show us something that might be taken as a promise to get the rebels out of Pennsylvania, I would be ever so grateful and would try to do good for the rest of my life. Or, if a rainbow was all He had to spare in the way of signs this evening, it would do fine, and I would be grateful for that too.

Cemetery Hill and safety now lay just ahead. A wonderful feeling came over me that Sport and I had beaten the odds and gotten through town clean when an ugly, snaggle-toothed rebel came dashing out of nowhere with his musket at the ready and blocked my path. Several others just as ugly and cut from the same cloth backed him up.

"You kin jist git your scrawny ass down offin that horse right now, boy!"

Chapter Four - Mad Scramble for Cemetery Hill

The battlefield is quiet now,
But enemy are nigh;
What are they up to anyhow?
Perhaps they'll pass us by.

WELL, I THOUGHT WE GOT AWAY clean, but we got hauled up short.

"Oh, you don't want this *here* horse, sir!" I said in the inspiration of the moment without having a thing in mind for what to say next.

His squinty eyes nailed me, and he hissed through clenched teeth. "And why is that, you li'l scudder? You best just do as I say, and move down offin that horse, *right smart!*" This one was so dirty and mean looking, I knew he could bring down his musket and put my lights out and not blink twice.

"I will, sir, but ... but ... well, Pa told me to warn anyone I came across that he has the dreaded Pennsylvania Dutch foot-and-mouth disease, and if he gets around other animals, it spreads like wildfire. One sick horse can infect a whole herd in a day, they say." I tumbled out the words, and felt certain my trembling would let the outrageousness of my lies show through.

"Oh, is that so, now?" He narrowed his eyes and left a little space between each word. "Just what the hell you take me for, boy?"

"It's true! And because it's so catching, they passed a law here just last week that all infected animals has to be taken out and shot and burned immediately." I looked over my shoulder and lowered my voice. "What they don't want to get around is that human beans can catch it too. It's so bad, there's only one man around here willing to dispose of 'em for you, because if you catch it yourself, it's like hydrophobia. You die a horrible death, wailing and frothing and clawing at everything! I only seen it once before, and that was once too often, I can tell you!" I shook my head at the very notion.

"Oh, is that so, now?" he repeated. "How is it your Pa sent *you* to do the dirty work, then?" The rebel paused but had enough suspicion in his voice that I knew I was far from being out of the woods. I gave him a quick shot of the famous Long Face.

"Well, this is very sad for me personally. First is because I'm the only one in the family that's come in contact with old Sport here, so why risk anyone else? And second is, and it hurts me to say this, but my stepmother would rather see *me* catch it than one of *her* boys." I was moved to tears by my own performance and choked out the last few words. "And you can understand a mother's favoring her own. I won't hold it against her. I figure my days are up soon anyway." I was surprised at the quality of my act and promised myself I would do some thinking on career possibilities at some better time.

"You must think I'm stupid er somethin', don'tcha, boy!" And I thanked my lucky stars that he was. "I don't believe you one whit! Now git ... down ... offin ... that ... *horse* before I *shoot* you off it!" He looked mean enough to do just that, and I thought of George Sandoe and knew they didn't waste time on anyone who gave them trouble. I also remembered Pa's expectations, so I was in hot water either way.

"But it's true, honest!" That was one solid lie I felt no remorse in telling. "That's why he looks so swelled up. Don't you get it down south, too? Go look at his mouth, how his teeth are all covered with green stuff. Careful you don't get any on you! And just part the hair aside down on his fetlocks. See those little bags of pus? Some of 'em's broke open already. Or go around and look up his rear end. If you look close, you can see awful stuff oozing out. You don't have to believe me. See for yourself!" I reined Sport's back end around towards him.

The rebel shrunk back and wrinkled up his face in revulsion and distaste. He stared me deep in the eye. I looked back at him with the best face of youthful innocence and simplemindedness I could muster. His eyes narrowed again into an ominous threat for a second or two, and then he conferred aside with the others who went to mumbling amongst themselves and looking askance.

"Well, I ain't lookin' up *no* horse's ass! Much less *that* one. And don't get it near *me*, that's all *I* got to say!"

"It's too much of a goddamn monster to get any use out of anyways. Shit, I don't think I could even mount the goddamn thing!"

They decided on the side of prudence.

"I still don't believe your lyin' ass, boy, but all the same, you get the hell on out of here, and take that walking pus bag with you!"

WITH THE LATEST RUN-IN WITH REBELS behind me, I made my way on south and hadn't gone very far when I heard the most wonderful sound of band music and men's voices raised in song. It seemed every regiment had a band of sorts in those days that often played at grim and discouraging times to boost morale. If it was a good band, it oftentimes did just that; if it wasn't a good band, they made do with what they had.

Near where Washington Street, Baltimore Street and the Emmitsburg Road all sort of come together, along about the Dobbin House, I converged with another small regiment that sported those black hats of the Iron Brigade. I halted Sport and waited as they passed. On horseback and bringing up the rear was the same young officer who had led the brilliant charge against the rebs in the unfinished railroad cut. His hair was black and thick out from under his kepi, and his beard had a distinctive shape that took in a generous mustache and goatee all in one piece. Otherwise, he was pretty much clean-shaven. As he came alongside, he paused and eyed me carefully.

"You there! Aren't you the water boy that brought all the water to General Cutler's brigade?" he asked. I guess he recognized me by my horse. I pulled alongside and rode with him.

"Yes, sir, but I had help. It wasn't just me."

"That's not the way I heard it. What are you doing here on that gigantic beast with the rebels hot behind us? They'll swoop you up and take your horse for certain."

"They just tried, sir, and I talked my way out of it."

"I'd sure like to have heard *that* exchange. I can't imagine what you could have said to talk them out of it."

"I told them he had a terrible disease and that human beans could catch it, too."

"And they believed that?"

"Well, we're still here."

"You are a man of many talents." I could feel a blush creep up my face. "What's your name, son?"

"Reis Bramble, sir."

"My name is Rufus Dawes, and I'm glad to meet you."

"Me, too, sir. Colonel, sir, do you think I could stay with you and your men 'til I can get Sport here to a safer place?" I asked, figuring I had a little credit built up with the U.S. Army.

"Well, I don't like the idea, but I'll think about it." Which is what older people usually say when they feel a 'yes' coming on but aren't ready to let go of it yet. "If we start to take fire, you'll have to break off immediately." Well there it was, an unspoken yes but a yes if ever I heard one. He spoke up again as we rode along.

"The First Corps acquitted itself with high honor this day, lad. It simply fought itself out after many hours of brutal fighting. I'm not so sure about the Eleventh Corps. They took the field much later and yet withdrew about the same time we did. But it's not for me to judge without knowing what they faced; time will bear it out. However, this regiment is beat to shit, boy, and your town has saved all our backsides."

"How was that, sir?" I asked.

"Had we been in open country and in full retreat like we are, we would have been swallowed up by such an aggressive enemy coming at us from two directions. As it was, the streets and buildings of the town diffused and dispersed their lines like a windbreak while they stopped to grab whatever they could eat, drink or carry off. They are now momentarily scattered and reduced in effectiveness, which should give us enough time to withdraw and re-form on the high ground ahead. I pray this will not have caused too much damage to your town."

"I live out in the country, but I'm sure folks here would be glad to know you said the town did its part."

"Do you live near where you got the water?"

"No, sir, I live a few miles southwest of there and had come up to see a friend. All the roads home got shut off before I could go back."

"It was fortunate you knew about that spring."

"Well, I pretty much know where all the springs are around Gettysburg. And all the roads and things, too. I help my Pa take produce around, and I like to fish, so I know all the streams for miles around."

The colonel thought for a moment. "You could be of considerable service to this army while it's here. What would your folks think if you didn't show up for a few days?"

"It looks like there ain't no way I could get word to them, anyway."

We rode on a bit in silence, and then the colonel turns to me and says, "All right, lad, here's what I want you to do. When we get up on that hill, find where all the brass are. Ask someone how to find Second Corps headquarters and go there and ask for General Gibbon's quarters. The man you're looking for is Lieutenant Frank Haskell. Can you remember that?"

"Oh, to be certain! Yes, sir!"

"Good. Now you'll need a pass through our lines and a purpose for being there."

Colonel Dawes took out a dispatch book and wrote the following:

1 Jul 63

Grant passage to the bearer, Rice Bramble, scout to Lt. Franklin A. Haskell, 2 Div, 2 C.
Rufus Dawes, LCol
6th Wisc, 1-1-1, Cmdg

"*Scout!*" The word ran through my innards and out my goose hairs and thrilled me no end. I was determined to wear that title proudly all my days. But surely, Colonel Dawes knew what my reaction would be and had meant it to appeal to a young boy's adventurous side. I had no idea back then how much fame the two names contained on that scrap of paper would engender in the years ahead.

"The First Corps gave a good account of itself, but took terrible punishment. Some regiments are reduced to a mere handful of survivors. The loss in field officers will leave many units without leadership. Some are down to captains and lieutenants. It will be up to the Second and the other uncommitted corps to bear the brunt of what comes tomorrow," he went on.

"Lieutenant Haskell and I both started our terms of service with this regiment. Then it became part of the Iron Brigade under General Gibbon. He's the one that got our boys the black hats. When Gibbon was promoted to division command, he took Haskell with him. There's no particular glory in his job and little chance for advancement in rank, but Haskell took it out of loyalty to Gibbon, and he'll know exactly how to use you. Frank Haskell and I had our differences once, but that's all behind us. I know of no wiser or abler man."

We continued on. After a while, Colonel Dawes spoke again. "Our brigade commander, General Meredith, received a head wound today. I'm not sure how severely. We all pray for his recovery."

"I think I was down near there when they carted him off. Is he a great big man?" I asked.

"Oh, yes," answered Colonel Dawes. "'Long Sol' they call him. He's six foot seven. He succeeded General Gibbon in the command of the Iron Brigade."

"Biggest, strongest looking man I ever saw," I said. "They could have made him a general just on looks alone."

The colonel gave a small laugh. "Some say they did. Find Lieutenant Haskell. He's as fine a man as they come. Tell him I told you to make yourself known to him for the purpose of serving as a local scout." His use of the word sent a thrill up my spine once again, and I had a flicker of thought about what degree of modesty to employ when telling the other boys about it. "The army looks for local people who know the lay of the land, and where good water and the roads are. Such arrangements are often of great service and save time in locating suitable water and favorable sites for the field hospitals. They'll be most grateful for your services, my boy."

BEFORE LONG, WE ENCOUNTERED UNION PICKETS, and the colonel inquired as to the whereabouts of the First Corps command tent. As we approached the cemetery, he spied General Doubleday, who I think was commanding the First Corps at the time, and asked him where the regiment should be posted. The general indicated a position further along the line.

"Too bad about Meredith," said General Doubleday. "I understand his wound is severe enough to end his career, perhaps."

"That may be," answered Colonel Dawes. "Of course, we all hope that is not the case."

"I am proud of First Corps today, but our losses are appalling, the loss of Reynolds most of all," said General Doubleday.

"It is truly a loss. There is not nor could there ever be a replacement for Reynolds," answered Colonel Dawes. "I regret Eleventh Corps did not seem to be more effective out there today."

"Well, Howard is like Burnside: he means well, but he somehow seems to fall short," responded General Doubleday. "Some people think that about me, I hear." He changed the subject.

"Who's the young feller on the big horse?" he said with a nod in my direction.

"This is Reis Bramble, the young man who fetched water for General Cutler's wounded," said Colonel Dawes. "He knows the streams and roads and terrain hereabouts, and I thought he might come in handy for placing our medical units and the reserves. I've told him to report to Frank Haskell of Gibbon's staff, because I know Haskell well and know he will use this boy to good advantage."

"All right, lad. General Gibbon and Second Corps are not up yet and probably won't be until early morning. You'll do to stick around here until then," said General Doubleday. "That indeed is some horse you're driving there."

I thanked General Doubleday but didn't have the gall to ask him where I might find something to eat in the morning.

✞   ✞   ✞

FOR THE NEXT FEW DAYS, and much to my surprise, I was to find myself in a role that cast me among the high brass of the Union army. I was about to enter the rarified atmosphere of what I called *The Land of the Generals*. I would learn later that over a thousand generals served both sides during the Civil War. Not all had field command, but most of history is drawn from those who did, and they are the ones we remember. Over a hundred were present at Gettysburg, the Union having about sixty and the Confederates about fifty.

There is a particular air about generals that sets them apart. In their presence, lesser officers tend to be fidgety and nervous, whereas the generals never are. They have achieved a lofty place, a club, an exclusivity. I read somewhere about a king who had this fellow whose job it was to follow him around with a chair. Whenever the king felt ready to sit down, he simply did so without looking back, confident that the chair would be there. Generals are something like that, particularly the ones with two stars. They stand central and look yonder, while those of lesser rank hover at the edges and are quick to cater to their orders and demands. Generals have a look, a posture, a commanding presence about them, and you'd know they were generals even without their stars and buttons.

By the time of Gettysburg, there were largely, I think, good men in command on both sides. The weak, the incompetent, the ineffective, the vainglorious and the stupid had been mostly culled out, relieved of command or relegated to non-combat roles where they could do little harm. The rest had been tempered and hardened by the realities of combat into first-rate general officers — for the most part.

The three or four days I was with them was sufficient to observe and reflect that they were intelligent and able and were, to the man, highly dedicated to the preservation of this union of states, the United States of America. It was they who made the decisions and took the actions by which victory or defeat would be determined.

Some were graduates of the U.S. Military Academy at West Point; many others were volunteers up from the ranks and came from non-military backgrounds. Some enjoyed the status of general with no other credential than appointment by the President in an attempt to strengthen his coalition for prosecuting the war. And every one was different.

IT IS THE FASHION OF THE ARMY to post artillery on the downward slope of a hill just below the crest. They do this so when the piece is fired, the recoil sends the gun uphill. If it fired in the other direction, it would haul off downhill and be a chore to get back, plus it's much easier to fire down into an attacking enemy. Also, guns posted upon the crest would be silhouetted against the sky, making them and their crews easier targets for enemy fire. Cemetery Hill just happened to occupy a position of high ground most favorable for the defense of the northern curve of the Union line. This high ground stared down on the town and looked off in the

"You could be of considerable service to this army."

direction from which an enemy attack was expected. As such, the cemetery was suffering widespread and extensive upheaval in preparation.

My mother had always taught me to honor and respect graves and cemeteries. I was admonished never to step on a grave or even step over one, and I have carried the habit throughout my life. Now, here in front of me, the old Evergreen Cemetery was being torn to shreds and it went against everything I had ever been taught.

All manner of tombstones, monuments and iron fences had been turned up, knocked down or broken. Trees were being chopped down, and men were digging frantically in the soft earth and piling dirt against the front of the breastworks as fast as they were put up. Everywhere, batteries of artillery were arriving and being posted in a mad flurry to secure the position against attack, which everyone was saying could come at any moment. Men piled up mounds of dirt into crescent shapes they call *lunettes*, or 'little moons,' which curve around in front of a gun to protect it from enemy fire. Coffins were exposed by the shovel brigades and smashed apart under the wheels of the guns and hooves of the racing teams. Here and there, corpses had tumbled forth, grinning at being released from their ancient confines. A few shovels of dirt had been thrown on some, but hands and feet and the grinning skulls still stuck out ghostlike and fearsome in the fading light.

Everything was in shambles. Regiments from First and Eleventh Corps were in such tatters and so exhausted that many men dropped to the ground where they were halted and immediately fell asleep among the dead. Many of the surviving regiments coming in were pitiably small, having been cut down to less than company size. One regiment that just arrived, which I was told was the 24th Michigan, mustered only twenty-seven survivors! Some paused to pray and sing hymns. *Abide With Me* was one of Gramma's favorites, so, full of homesickness, I joined in from the saddle. We also sang *Nearer My God to Thee*, which was a new one everybody was singing, and *Bringing in the Sheaves*. When I was little, I thought they were singing "Bringing in the Sheep," which made perfect sense at the time.

This gruesome desecration and disorder were appalling in the extreme. And, as if the Devil himself sought to make light of this terrible scene, a sign over at the gatehouse proclaimed:

ALL PERSONS FOUND USING FIREARMS IN THESE GROUNDS
WILL BE PROSECUTED WITH THE UTMOST RIGOR OF THE LAW.

Then, into the midst of all this violation and chaos, rode an odd-looking brigadier general screaming a string of incoherent orders and cussing a blue streak. He was hatless, his tunic was open and his round and florid face was framed in an unruly tousle of hair matted with sweat and dirt. His wide, wet mouth reminded me of a frog's. He gasped for air between shouts and croaked loudly.

"You goddamn sunsa bitches are a buncha no-good ... *hick* ... cowardly goddamn ... *hick* ... *sunsabitches!*"

"Great Lucifer, it's Rowley! Drunk again!" said General Doubleday.

The newly arrived general suddenly whirled and looked directly at me and shouted, "Get that goddamn mastodon off the line before I put a ball in both of you, you brazen, dis ... *hick* ... respekkful brat, *you!*" Well I clean knew where the 'hicks' were coming from. Before I could do what he said, he was off berating some sleeping soldiers.

"Get off your asses, you cowardly wastrels, and come to attention when your corps commander co ... *hick* ... mands it!"

"Now there's a good way to get yourself killed," observed Colonel Dawes. "Someone who has dealt with the Devil today is going to come out of a deep sleep and act before he thinks." Dawes looked around. "Orderly, get the provost here on the double-quick!" A soldier saluted and dashed off. By that time, General Howard, who had lost his right arm the year before, rode up full of agitation, demanding to know who was making all the ruckus and why.

"We are expecting the enemy to attack us here at any moment, and things are in disarray enough without this! Someone get him off the field at once!"

With that, the provost, a young first lieutenant, came up and explained that General Rowley had apparently lost track of his division and was under the delusion that he had acceded to corps command. He had just come from cursing and berating Wadsworth's division where he had branded them all cowards.

"Do what you have to do, but get him out of here *at once!*" said General Howard and rode off.

"He fell from his horse, and I went to look for General Wadsworth but couldn't find him," the lieutenant explained to Colonel Dawes. "I am about to place him under arrest. Will you support me, sir?" General Rowley was flailing his arms and swearing loud enough to wake some soldiers – loud enough to wake the dead, said Colonel Dawes – and, swinging wildly, fell from his horse once again. The provost helped him to his feet, and General Rowley stumbled, rudely pushing him aside.

"Hell, yes! *Do* it! It suits me," answered Colonel Dawes and turned to General Doubleday.

"Yes, for Chris' sake! Do it now!" hissed Doubleday.

The provost came to attention before the errant general and saluted. "General Rowley, for the good of the army and for your own protection, I am placing you under arrest, sir," he said in a level voice.

"Oh *yeah*? You and just who the goddamn bloody hell else?"

"Rufus R. Dawes, Lieutenant Colonel, Sixth Wisconsin, Commanding, *sir!*" announced Colonel Dawes.

"Well, I'd just like to see you try it! And on what author ... *hick* ... ity?" The general staggered and tried to appear as menacing as possible but simply looked pathetic. Here now exposed was the bad side of spirits.

"At the request of the provost, General," said Colonel Dawes. "This hill is about to come under attack. We cannot afford to be distracted by your loss of lucidity and self-control. We will need to focus our every means to repel the enemy." A rattle of gunfire was heard from the direction of Culp's Hill.

From the ranks came a voice, "And to save your goddamn drunken ass, you stupid fool!"

"You have two choices, General Rowley," said Colonel Dawes. "You can go quietly or at the point of the bayonet."

"And *you* have two choices, you brazen son of a bitch! You can kiss my ass, and you can go to hell!"

"*Sixth Wisconsin! Bayonet!*" The unforgettable sound of a hundred and fifty shissing, clanking bayonets pierced the air in a single instant. There was a pause, as all the players froze in a moment of expectation.

"All right, damn you! But, mark my words, I am bringing charges against you … and you … and you …!" His arms cut the air wildly once again as he threatened everyone at all points of the compass generally and was marched away. I never would have believed such a thing if I had not seen it myself. I heard later that they restored General Rowley to the Third Division, First Corps, after he sobered up. Sometime later, they sent him off to duty in Maine or somewhere where he could little damage.

I was accumulating some mighty fine stories, but the tragedy was that I would never be able to give many of them full flavor without substituting a lot of 'blankety-blanks' for tender ears and the ladies.

"Well, that takes care of that … I hope," exclaimed General Doubleday. "Quite a way to welcome you back into the ranks. Slocum is in charge here until Meade comes up. Meade had sent Hancock to take command while the Twelfth Corps and Old Slow Come was plodding his way forward, dragging his seniority behind him. When Hancock came on the field, loud cheering went up and down the line from the men in the ranks. When Slocum took over, you could have heard a pin drop.

"Hancock and Howard had had a little set-to over command seniority, but Hancock simply said, 'Fine, I'll go tell Meade I'm not needed here now.' Howard harrumphed a little, stood aside and deferred to Hancock and allowed as how the situation justified that both their talents would be needed." He went on. "After Slocum finally came up sometime before six o'clock, Hancock departed and rode back to his command at Second Corps." (I guess the general and the colonel must have been pretty thick friends to speak as openly about other officers as they did.) They said Second Corps would be up in the morning, whereupon I would seek out Lieutenant Haskell and make myself known to him.

About then, as I recall, the Sixth Wisconsin had no more than sat down to rest when it was ordered to join the rest of the Iron Brigade over towards Culp's Hill. That was the last time I ever saw Colonel Dawes who I held in high esteem for all my days. I do know that he survived the war and came out a general, enjoyed fame and honor for his wartime exploits and was elected to several terms in Congress from Ohio. Late in life, I would be proud to vote for his son, Charles, as Vice President on Calvin Coolidge's ticket. After the war, I read somewhere that, of the 1,058 men who served in the ranks of the Sixth Wisconsin during the course of the war, the only one who came through alive and without a scratch was Rufus R. Dawes.

OUR MEN TOOK FIRE FROM THE REBEL SHARPSHOOTERS holed up in people's homes along Baltimore Street, and heavy firing was heard from time to time from Culp's Hill until long after midnight. But the enemy did not launch a general attack on our positions that evening, much to everyone's surprise and relief. Our exhausted men would spend the night improving defenses, and by morning we would be ready for them.

I laid low and listened and was able to glean from the all comings and goings of the aides and couriers that the Army of the Potomac would come together during the night to form on and around Cemetery Ridge. The Second Corps, under the temporary command of General Gibbon in the absence of General Hancock, was posted a mile or two to the south. The Third Corps, under General Dan Sickles, was advancing from the direction of Emmitsburg, and the Fifth Corps, under General George Sykes, was coming up on the Baltimore Pike as the reserve. The big Sixth Corps, under General John Sedgwick, would be posted half a day's march to the southeast to cover a retreat of the army should one become necessary. All this I heard that evening or pieced together afterwards. The vulnerability of the remnants of First and Eleventh Corps now in position on Cemetery Hill was improving by the hour. In any case, everything was coming to a head at Gettysburg, but I didn't have much confidence that there would be an easy way out for any of us.

Just before twilight, the last slanting shafts of the red-orange setting sun peered from between dark clouds and pierced the deep woods with patches of light so brilliant it was as if the woods were on fire. The striking beauty of it somehow made my homesickness all the more acute. Soldiers milled about in all directions, tearing down fences and seeking anything burnable with which to feed a thousand campfires. Stately old trees, heretofore sacrosanct and untouchable, were felled in and around the cemetery to build defensive works and to clear fields of fire for the artillery. Our quiet glens and flowered fields lay open and vulnerable, and cool virgin streams would soon run red with blood. Among my many fears that day was a deeper one that said that nothing here — not flowered field, or sheltered wood, or pristine stream, perhaps even a way of life — would ever be the same again.

About dusk, General Sickles showed up with a few aides. General Howard seemed glad to see him, and showered him with compliments and led him and a major over to the gatehouse where they sat down to a supper of pancakes. I sure could have used a stack of those myself, and I wasn't the only one. The commissary wagons with all the rations had been left behind to clear the roads of everything but ammunition and artillery — and were ordered to stay clear for now in case of retreat, so the men were left at the end of a long march with nothing much to eat since yesterday.

NOT LONG BEFORE MIDNIGHT, in a late note of drama to end the day, General Meade arrived leading a small contingent of riders who rode up near where I was standing next to General Doubleday's tent. He looked tired and haggard after his late night gallop all the way from Taneytown in the dark of night on crowded roads or fields or woods. Remarkably, it took him less than an hour, some said. He had taken to the fields to avoid the congestion of the roads and had been knocked from his horse by a limb that came up in the darkness. He had lost a pair of glasses and, all in all, was in no mood for pleasantries. I was told to keep myself and Sport and Jack out of the way as General Meade had a short fuse. Behind his back, they called him Old Snapping Turtle. Maybe it was because of the flickering lantern light, but I thought he looked more like an old tom turkey. He began an immediate review of the dispositions of his army.

Generals Howard, Slocum, Sickles and Shirts gathered around General Meade, and sought to reassure him that the position occupied by the accumulating army was a good one and highly favorable for defense. General Warren, chief of engineers was also present and agreed. General Warren seemed aloof and more refined than the rest. I thought General Shirts to be an odd-looking man with an unlikely name. His face had a fearsome appearance in the shadows, but I learned that he was a man of great courtesy and intelligence and was held in high regard by his peers and by President Lincoln as well. (I also learned sometime later that his name was spelled, "Schurz.")

Then General Meade looked all of them over and responded by saying, "I'm glad to hear you are in agreement on this position, gentlemen,
because I'm afraid it's too late to leave it. General Warren, I would like you
to assign me a good man who can draw maps in the dark to conduct me on
an immediate reconnaissance of the lines."

General Howard said with obvious relief, "We are fortunate the enemy did not strike us while we were most vulnerable. By morning, we will
be ready for him, should he care to try us. They hurt us today, but we hurt
them also, and they need time to recover and re-form as well."

Shortly thereafter, General Meade went forth in the wee hours of the
morning to scout his lines accompanied by a Captain Paine, who had the
amazing aptitude to draw maps in the dark of night resting his sketchbook
on the pommel of his saddle. Heroes do come in all shapes, sizes and
talents.

THE NEWS WOULD COME FILTERING BACK over the days ahead that the
rebels had been having unaccustomed troubles. So, to that extent, thank
the Almighty, we were lucky. Fortunately for us, the Confederate high
command seemed to be out of sorts with itself and off its mark following
their success in the earlier part of the day.

The Confederate advance which had chased our units through town
and had menaced us here on Cemetery Hill seemed to peter out late in the
day and missed its chance to hit our lines when they were weakest. Both
their Second and Third Corps had seen intense action most of the day and
were dazed and battered by late afternoon, as was our side as well.

General Ewell, rebel Second Corps commander, had had a terrible and exhausting week and some say he was so tired, he couldn't think
straight. Because he lost a leg at Second Manassas the previous August, he
had to be strapped to his horse, where he had spent most of the last few
days. His corps had fought magnificently and routed the Union Eleventh
Corps but at the price that many of its officers and men were lost and the
rest were pretty much asleep on their feet.

General A. P. Hill, commanding the Confederate Third Corps, had
been sick for days and was becoming sicker and appeared to be absent
from active command altogether. General Jeb Stuart's cavalry had been

missing for days, leaving General Lee in the dark about our strengths and movements. General Lee, himself, was said to be not well. Only General James Longstreet, "Old Pete," commanding the Confederate First Corps, seemed to be more up to snuff, but even at that, as it would turn out, he found himself in disagreement and at opposition with General Lee on just about everything.

THE DAY ENDED WITH ME in as safe a situation as any. Without my having to ask, General Doubleday had kindly seen to it that Sport and I were fed rations, such as they were, and I gave a piece of salt pork to Old Jack. Otherwise, I failed to draw anyone's attention, which suited me fine. I don't know whether it was because everything and everybody was so occupied or because God was looking after me, or both, but no one told me to "git on home" this evening. I was just powerful glad for whatever reason and was too plumb tuckered out to make adjustments.

A great thunderstorm crashed and raged over the city after midnight. Afterwards, a full moon peered down through fleeting clouds to reveal the vast desecrations that appeared and disappeared ghostlike in the coming and going of the moonlight. I shuddered at the awful sights and marveled that not even a full day had passed since I left home.

Somebody gave me an old army blanket, and I tried to get some sleep but couldn't quite get down to it. What would tomorrow bring? Will the enemy, having done such damage far and wide already, by some miracle be satisfied with that and depart and leave us in peace? I know my folks must be worried sick about me, but the way home is perilous now, if not impossible.

Strange dreams of chaos and death came and went during the night. I felt fearfully adrift and marooned in another world, and that Ma and Pa and Gramma and home were far off and drifting, drifting away from me. Or maybe it was I that was drifting. I guess it seemed even worse than that: it was almost as if here in this terrible cemetery was the real world and the only world there ever had been, and all the rest of my life had only been a dream.

I missed my home and my bed … and somehow most of all right now, my gentle and familiar chickens. I tried to hold down a big lump deep in my throat that was trying hard to work its way out. I awoke and stared up into the night and felt as far from home as if I was one of those distant stars, all alone away up there in some far off corner of the sky.

I reached over and hugged Old Jack just to bring me back down to earth. He answered with a reassuring flap, flap of his tail.

Chapter Five - Forging a Fishhook

If they predicted yesterday
The kind of day tomorrow
Not in their wildest dreams could they
Imagine such a horror.

I FINALLY DRIFTED OFF and awoke at first light to the sounds of heavy firing over towards the Culp farm. I was too tired to stay with it very long, and it just wasn't enough to keep me awake. I remember the beginnings of a beautiful red sunrise when I must have drifted off again and slept until I smelled coffee. In that last little fog of dreams just before waking, there were two that I remember. One was Bum Piles sitting on a tombstone hee-hawing away, and the other was of Gramma making coffee.

I stretched and yawned awake to the sounds and smells of a wak-ing army. The air was thick and damp and already hot just as it had been yesterday morning. Off somewhere, bugles were calling men to task like a bunch of brass roosters. Up and down the Cemetery Ridge line, drum-mer boys sounded the long roll and men poured from their shelters as if someone had kicked over a giant anthill. As far as I could see, smoke rose above campfires fueled by fence rails and Lord knows what. No one had much to cook, as the commissary wagons were still not up, but somehow there were enough coffee pots going to put the smell of coffee in the air. I guess that explained the dream about Gramma.

I rubbed my knuckles into my eyes and sucked in air for another yawn and was just fixing to go beg some of that coffee and a bite to eat from somebody, when, lo and behold, I couldn't believe my eyes and just sat there with my mouth hanging open. Not fifty feet yonder stood Bum Piles jawing away at General Meade seated on a tombstone! So the Bum part was real, too. That does beat all! Why on earth would the general of all this army be having a confab with someone Pa might charitably refer to as one of the "least among us?"

Bum must have felt my eyes on him, because he turned toward me and caught my eye. He kept right on talking away to General Meade like as if he was awful much at home. Finally, he paused and shouted over to me, "Well, do tell, Reisie! Fancy meeting *you* here. Git over here a minnit.

98 Sing Before Breakfast

There's somebody I want you to meet!" Aw, no. Not me. That's the Old Snapping Turtle, and he has his hands full, and you're not going to catch me getting in *his* way. No, sir!

But daggone it, Bum keeps on a-pumping his arm, making little Cs in the air that mean *Come on! Come on!* With that, the general faces me with an exasperated look, and I think, uh-oh, guess I better get on over there before he starts in to snapping.

"Git on over here and make y'self known to Gen'l Meade here, the boss of all these people."

I stumbled up. "Th ... thank you sir for coming to save us from the rebels," I stammered foolishly.

"Well, if you're not the first person that's come to me and said thanks and didn't want something or have something to complain about!" said the Old Snapper not unkindly.

"Gen'l Meade, this here's Reis Bramble. He ain't growed all the way up yet, but he knows every road and hill and dale for miles around, and he fishes all these streams," Bum swept his arm around in a wide arc. "He goes everywhere hereabouts with his Pa and heps deliver vejabuls and such. He'd make ye a good guide to have around."

Well, you could have knocked me over with a feather, and I wasn't sure I was out of dreamland yet. Colonel Dawes had said it was a common practice for a military commander to engage one of the locals to guide him around in unfamiliar territory. It came out later that Stonewall Jackson used a local boy to guide him through the woods and back roads on his flank march on the Union army at Chancellorsville two months ago.

Then General Meade, he says, "Hello, son. I'd like you to make yourself available when I need you." Oh, my. Now I didn't know whether to feel proud or get sick. Here was an offer way beyond *my* abilities. I was certain I would be exposed as a complete humbug. I tried to think of ways I might duck out first chance and find a way home. Maybe if I went far enough south and circled back around ....

"What would you say to that?" asked the general.

"Um ... I'd be proud to, sir, but I ... I ... already was promised to another." I felt my face reddening once again at the foolishness of my remark.

"What in thunder does he mean by that?" the general asked, turning to Bum.

"Beats me," said Bum. "Reisie, what in tarnation are you talkin' about? You sound like you went out and got y'sef betrothed."

"W ... well, I ... promised Colonel Dawes of the Sixth Wisconsin I would look up Lieutenant Haskell ... on General Gibbon's staff and make myself known to him for use in the capacity of scout." I waited for the laughter, but none came. I produced my chit signed by Colonel Dawes and showed it to them.

"I know Haskell, and he is a superb staff officer," said General Meade turning to Bum. "Perhaps it would indeed be well for this lad to be under his wing." Then he turns to me and says, "Find Lieutenant Haskell and tell him to quarter you and make you ready to come when I send for you. The Second Corps is coming up and will be posted to our left." The general interrupted himself. "Better yet, I'll tell him myself. *George!*" General Meade called aside, and a young captain came quickly. "Send someone to fetch Lieutenant Haskell, at Second Corps – with Gibbon ... and tell Gibbon I'll send him back forthwith."

George went off on his errand, Bum mounted old Rip, gently reined him around, tipped his hat and quietly departed, and I was sent on my first official scouting mission to fetch a pail of fresh drinking water.

I returned and sat down on an empty cracker box in General Meade's headquarters and awaited Lieutenant Haskell's arrival. The general's headquarters was in a tiny house belonging to the Widow Leister that sat along the Taneytown Road just south of Cemetery Hill. They said the general took over the house by putting out the widow, but it happened to be right where he needed it. It was far too small to recommend it much as a farmhouse. It was so small that when the general held a council of war, the place got so crowded only a few had room to sit down, and everyone had to depart in reverse order, that is, the last ones in had to be the first ones out. I could hear Gramma say, "And they who would be first shall be last."

So now I had a job, and all three of us would have something to eat.

BESIDES EVERYTHING ELSE he had to worry about, General Meade was confronted with a steady stream of citizenry, each of whom wanted him to do something or wanted something from him. This morning, the flow had been continuous since daylight, and the general was in a state of high agitation.

Typical was an old German farmer who demanded payment for some animals that had been killed or carted off. The general's temper had been rising as the old farmer enumerated his demands for "compenzation" and "zatisfaction" from a list he had been reading from. He said hungry soldiers had pulled whole limbs from his "churrie" trees and ate the fruit as they marched along. His well had been knocked over, his water ruined, his chickens stole, his pigs stole, his sheep killed and his porch all tracked up with muddy footprints. Worst of all, his wife was furious and insisted he do something about it. General Meade waved him off a time or two, but the farmer persisted. Finally, the general had had enough and blew up. General Meade brought his fist down with such a bang everything on the table jumped six inches.

"I am absorbed here with trying to make sure you will have a farm or *a nation* left at all, sir, and you're worried about your blasted *sheep*," he shouted, "and I haven't a minute more to spare you, sir! If you do not depart at once, I will put a musket in your hand and send you to the front of the line where you can visit your dissatisfaction upon those properly responsible for your complaints!" With that, the old man turned red, spun around and scurried out.

I was in sympathy with General Meade's position, but I also understood, being half German myself, the pride that German farmers had in the meticulous care they took of their homes and farms, their fences, their grounds, houses, gardens and animals. I knew it broke their hearts to see the things they had worked so hard to make right torn up and abused. They had come from across the ocean to escape poverty and the oppressions of aristocratic Europe and had borne too many hardships for too long simply to stand back and allow themselves to be violated by scalawags. It was not uncommon to see an old Dutch farmer come running from his house shaking his cane and taking on a whole regiment if it offended him. The men would jeer and mimic his accent, but those old Germans had the courage to stand their ground.

I meekly tried to soften matters by saying, "These old Germans are proud of the fruits of their labors (I had heard Pa use that term)."

"Saving your place from an army is about like trying to save your garden patch from a plague of locusts," countered the general. "There's just too many of them."

If you asked ten thousand people to come for supper, and even if they all behaved themselves, their sheer numbers would simply trample your place to pieces. Combat veterans, even the best among them, faced with the brutal particulars of life on the line, often lose their attachment to ordinary niceties and behave in a way that would astonish the folks back home. Add to that hunger, anger, fear, homesickness, military necessity and the expectation that life will be short, and you get some idea about the frame of mind of whomever might be setting up camp in your yard. There were a lot of mean things said about local farmers afterwards and some were true, but mostly, they were just afraid to open up their beautiful properties while being surrounded by so many soldiers in need, as they were. There just wouldn't be any way to keep them from overrunning the place and stomping it to smithereens.

Both armies arrived at Gettysburg famished and short on food. Most soldiers respected the lovely farms of Adams County, but misfortune falls to any farm that becomes a battlefield or lies in the path of an army. Of course, there were rapscallions on both sides who held nothing sacred and who, through mischief or thievery or just plain carelessness, or to comfort their own miserable situations, were capable of anything. But, with 170,000 men converging to do battle, no one had time or inclination to seek justice for a few Dutch farmers, and they were simply left to God and fate.

Next, a preacher came to the door with a family of Negroes with small children and all the possessions they could carry. The preacher spoke for them. "These are not runaway slaves, General Meade. These are citizens in good standing in our fair land and should be treated as such. Our white citizens have places to go, people to take them in — even strangers will do so in this crisis."

"I can give them no comfort here. We are fully occupied preparing for this fight and must not be distracted from it for any reason," snapped the general.

"But these people have no one else to turn to in this dark hour. They live in dread of being captured and sent south because of no other reason than the color of their skin. All I ask you to do is to show them some fundamental Christian kindness and a little food, sir, and, if you could find it in your heart, perhaps a single mule and wagon to ease their burden, that they might then be on their way to safety." The preacher was not going to give up easily.

"I'm sorry, but they will have to fend for themselves." Turning aside to his son, George, the captain who served as his aide, he snapped again. "No more civilians until this thing has passed!"

"With due respect, Father, it seems to me one of the very reasons we are in this fight is to see to it that these people will *not* be forced from their homes in fear ever again."

General Meade fixed his eyes on The Reverend a moment, lowered his glasses and cast his gaze to those about and, looking back to his table, said in an almost kindly manner, "George, see to it these people are fed and get them a mule and wagon and a day's rations. And then you people best move on quick. This place is about to become a hornet's nest. Keep in mind that the mule and wagon are the property of the U.S. government and are to be turned back over to the army as soon as you are able to return home. George, draw up a pass for the mule and wagon."

Pa says Negroes have mastered a bland expression that shows nothing behind it. He says they do so because some people get offended if they think they see character and self-confidence – or what they might take to be determination – in the face of a Negro. I was always taught that character and self-confidence were to be prized. This is another example of what I don't understand about grownups. What did they fear for a Negro to know? Were they afraid he might show up better than they would? It seemed to me that people couldn't bring themselves to tolerate in the Negro the things they admired in themselves.

THE REBEL ATTACK over in the vicinity of Culp's Hill seemed to intensify about mid-morning. Captain Meade reported that Second Corps was in position, and Fifth Corps had come up in the rear. General Meade expressed anxieties about the army's left flank, and instructed the captain to see if Third Corps was in position on the far left, and if not to tell

General Sickles to take up positions without delay. Captain Meade rode off to do so.

Before long, Lieutenant Haskell arrived and reined up in the small barnyard and dismounted. General Meade beckoned him over. They saluted.

"Haskell, this lad will serve as a guide for me. I am told on high authority (surely he didn't mean Bum Piles!) that he possesses extensive knowledge of the geography hereabouts that could be of value to the army. Quarter this lad at Second Corps and keep him handy for me so I can have him here on a moment's notice, and otherwise look to his needs. And get him a proper mount to replace that behemoth he rides (Sport sure was getting a lot of new names). That beast will draw fire like a four-legged barn. Heaven knows how he's made it this far."

It took an effort to keep a straight face.

"Yes, General Meade," said Lieutenant Haskell, saluting. "I'll get him a new mount forthwith."

General Meade touched his fingers to his forehead. "I have convened a council of war for after dinner and would like to hold the boy here until it's over. I would like you to stay as well. Has Hancock returned to command?"

"Yes, General. General Hancock met up with us early today and is back in command."

"Very well, Haskell. I will apprise Gibbon at council that I held you here."

Again, salutes and flourishes.

Lieutenant Haskell looked different than I expected. He seemed too old to be only a lieutenant and was losing his hair. There was a gravity, a solemnity, yet a fearlessness and a truthfulness in his face. Somehow, I felt assurance that I would be in good hands. Soon, I would discover that Lieutenant Franklin A. Haskell was more by far than any words I could ever find to say about him. He shook my hand and said, "What is your name, son?"

"Reis Bramble, sir. That's spelled 'Ar — ee — eye — ess'." I figured he might as well get it right from the start.

"All right, 'Ar ee eye ess Bramble,' I have a few other things to attend to right now, but let's you and I come back here after dinner and go listen to what the brass have to say."

No report had come in from Third Corps confirming compliance with General Meade's orders, even though Third Corps was nearby, so the general sent Captain Meade back again to make sure that they were in position on the far left. Captain Meade shortly returned with the disappointing information that not only was General Sickles not in position but also was in doubt as to where that position should be. Clearly exasperated, General Meade instructed the captain to go tell General Sickles in no uncertain terms that he was to go into line on the left of Second Corps and deploy south to "that little sugar loaf mountain."

Presently, General Sickles's aide, Major Tremain, arrived (I understood that he had made other trips to headquarters that morning, and it was clear that General Meade's patience was now near its limit) asking General Meade for permission for General Sickles to move the Third Corps from its presently assigned position. General Meade returned his salute like he was shooing flies. "General Sickles has his orders!" Even I knew it was high time for General Sickles to let the matter drop. After Major Tremain departed, I heard General Meade mutter into his beard, "I'm tired of Sickles's bellyaching!"

After a while, General Sickles himself strutted in to make the case. I had seen him from a distance last evening, and now I better understood some of the things I'd been hearing about him. General Sickles seemed shorter than I remembered with a long droopy mustache, a patch of a goatee and a chip on his shoulder. He cocked his head to one side and looked up with one angry eye and the other slightly closed whenever he talked to someone. He made me think of a banty rooster looking to fight anything that moved and someone whose path I would be obliged to clear in a wink. He wore his cap at a careless angle and his blouse was unbuttoned down to the tops of his huge, muddy boots. His eyes were tired, puffy and suspicious. He spoke.

"My compliments, General Meade. I have come to clarify personally exactly what leeway I may exercise in the posting of my corps. It appears I have been assigned the lowest, most indefensible position on the line, and, out of concern for my men and in loyalty to my commanders, I would like to improve on this condition to an extent consistent with your orders and your intentions."

That sounded like a reasonable statement to me.

"General Sickles, as I have relayed to you by way of Captain Meade, and as I have said a number of times to Major Tremain, your corps is ordered to occupy ground on the left of Second Corps, thereafter following the ridge line south to General Geary's position."

"General Geary has no position, sir. General Geary is gone."

"Well, then ... to where General Geary was or *ought* to be if he'd stayed!" General Meade was gritting his teeth and struggling to maintain the military decorum of high command.

"I am certain the enemy will attack where we are weakest, which is the position you have assigned to me." General Sickles appealed once more.

"Generals always expect an attack will open upon their position."

"General Meade, with all due respect, sir, might I not post my corps as I see fit, sir!" General Sickles seemed to be having a little trouble keeping his lid on, too, and I expected both men were about to crank things up an embarrassing notch, and as I looked aside, I knew what men who run from battle must feel like. But General Meade let the steam out with the following answer, as best as I can remember:

"All right, General Sickles. As long as you operate within the limits of the general instructions I have given you, I will leave the details up to you." His answer was very close to that, and I say that carefully because the controversy over this particular issue that followed the Battle of Gettysburg will never go away. In any case, I am afraid that General Sickles took General Meade's attempt to settle the thing and move on to be a license to do whatever he pleased. General Sickles rode back to his corps amidst the sounds of intensified firing over towards the Bliss barn.

The Bliss farm found itself in an intolerable position between the two lines, and firing from that direction was intensifying. Presently, the first wounded began coming in over the ridge and were taken in the direction of Second Corps hospital, which had been set up along Rock Creek in a series of large tents.

"What do you know of the people who occupy that farm, lad?" General Meade asked me.

"Not a whole lot, sir," I answered. "They don't buy from us. The place belongs to William Bliss. As far as I know, they are good people."

"They had the hard luck to build it in the middle of a battlefield. The rebels are firing on us from there, and if it persists, we'll have to send someone over there to burn it down," said the general.

GENERAL BUTTERFIELD SENT ME OFF to see Lieutenant Haskell about finding me a better mount. Because Lieutenant Haskell was an aide to Brigadier General John Gibbon, who commanded the Second Division of the Second Corps, I would be spending a lot of time on the other side of Cemetery Ridge where Second Division was posted.

Lieutenant Haskell had recommended that Sport be retired to where he would be safer in the care of a farmer I knew named Schwartz who had a place four or five miles down the Baltimore Pike. "He makes too big a target and will draw fire. And he is bound to be wounded or killed in the big battle that will come soon," said the lieutenant. "The general expects you to be ready whenever he snaps his fingers, so you'll need to be able to move quickly and keep up." I agreed with everything he said and made ready to take Sport down to the Schwartz place.

Lieutenant Haskell's orderly showed up with a pretty little bay mare named Sally for me to use. She had a sweet disposition and was as pretty as a young girl and came with an army blanket and a McClellan saddle. She wore a 'U.S.' brand on her rump. I could barely contain myself at the prospect of mounting up, and when I did, I knew at once that I was in love. I caressed and patted her neck, and she gently tossed her head and looked around in response. My, how I had come up in the world!

I guess the single thing that made me proudest was that Lieutenant Haskell had fixed me up one of General Meade's pennants on a small switch for me to carry when I was by myself so no one would run me off for being where I wasn't supposed to be. It was midnight blue with two gold stars, and it was all I could do to keep a straight face as I rode with it fluttering shamelessly beside me. (It has been one of my most cherished possessions that I have kept with me now for almost seventy years, and I've asked to be buried with it.)

I had to explain things to Sport, of course. He bent his head down while I rubbed his forehead and gave him an old turnip I had found and let him know I was going to lead him a few miles out the road to the Schwartz place for safekeeping a few days, which I did. For his own good, of course.

On my way back, I let Sally have her head. She rode smooth and sweet, and we covered the ground back to Cemetery Ridge in a matter of minutes. And not too soon did we do so, because I began to see all around us the preparations in anticipation of the coming battle. Men were moving faster now and more often. I heard all around me the rattle and rustle of thousands of men doing little things to make ready for war. Some were quietly writing what might be their last words to loved ones. They put these letters in their knapsacks to be mailed should they not survive. Others were hiding their playing cards under rocks or in crevasses. Cards were held to be sinful by many, and most boys, in case they were killed, did not want cards sent home with their other belongings, so they hid them where they might pick them up after the battle. People walking the battlefield found some of these sad little mementos many years later.

Some men wrote their names on scraps of paper to put in their pockets so their bodies could be identified. Some checked weapons and cartridge boxes, and yet others were seeing to lesser things. Some sat and smoked their pipes. Still others appeared to be praying or deep in thought.

As I moved north and returned to Cemetery Ridge, I could see down both sides of the low rise. Generals and their staffs rode among the troops and checked the preparedness of their commands. Couriers galloped off in all directions.

Between Cemetery Ridge and Rock Creek were hundreds and hundreds of wagons of all kinds: ambulances, ammunition wagons, caissons, limbers, artillery, officers' wagons, surgical and hospital wagons, wagons carrying forges, horseshoes and farrier's tools, water, tents, spades, carpenter's tools, feed and forage, and pitifully few commissary and mess wagons, all with thousands and thousands of horses and mules in attendance and trampling the place to pieces.

Until yesterday, I had probably never seen as many as a hundred horses all together at one time. Now, every battery was assigned a hundred horses – or more: six guns pulled by six horses with as many in reserve. Add to that those necessary to pull caissons and supply wagons. Every battery had a blacksmith with all his accoutrements to move around. There were about a hundred men associated with each battery as well, and when they and everything else got together, it covered quite a patch of ground, kicked up a lot of dust and made quite a crowd – all that for just a single battery. And there were many batteries posted on the line to my left as I rode the crest of the ridge and many more to my right in reserve down behind in the meadows around Rock Creek.

Elsewhere, medical teams were laying out medicines, bandages, lint, brandy, whiskey, beef broth, surgical implements, stretchers and supplies. Others were attending to ambulances, boiling water and laying out straw to receive the wounded. Further to the rear, hospitals were putting up huge tents and marking their locations with red or yellow pennants. The troops on Cemetery Ridge casually viewed these preparations and wondered who among them would soon find themselves in need of the grisly services these medical workers would be giving out and tried not to think on it too long.

Skulkers and skedaddlers that had been caught running to the rear or pried from their hiding places were being brought forward and put into the line by the provosts (they would later come to be called military police). Some were being whacked forward by officers using the flat of their swords. They were a miserable and embarrassing lot. Better to be a live coward than a dead hero, they said. More to be pitied than censured, as Gramma would say, and pity them I did.

Lieutenant Haskell had given me a short lecture on the importance of an officer's sword. Infantry officers rarely sharpened their swords. They used them more on the backs of shirkers than they did as weapons. The sword was more a symbol of command. Regardless of rank, when the sword came out, men were trained to respond, so no officer, if he could help it, would lead a charge without his sword, the symbol of his stature and authority. That's why, when an officer surrendered, the first thing he surrendered was his sword; he was turning over his authority and his symbol of power to his captor. When it had been given to him as a gift of honor or by a loved one, the parting was bitter indeed.

There were drummer boys my own age and even younger, but I never fell in with them much. They endured a hardened life and probably bore some resentment to my favored status: riding my own horse with my dog alongside. I imagined them to be particularly envious of Sally, a luxury beyond their imagination.

After a while, things fell quiet all along the line as if the time needed to make ready had been about the same for every man.

THE TERRITORY OVER WHICH the battle would be fought, including staging areas for reserves, animals, artillery, ordinance, wagon trains, ambulances, quartermaster supplies, field hospitals, cooks, musicians, blacksmiths, and all other non-combatants, covered an area about four miles east to west and at least six miles north to south or about twenty-five square miles. I was intimately acquainted with this land and most of the families who occupied it.

All my short life, I had heard the names of the families who lived nearby and knew many of them personally – Weikert, Codori, Klingle, Trostle, Sherfy, Rose, Hummelbaugh, Bliss, Ziegler, Spangler, Pitzer, Rodgers, Bryan. Some of these names would be immortalized through the years in the thousands of books that would be written about Gettysburg. I had been back and forth over this ground many times before yesterday and never thought it particularly distinguished from anyplace else hereabouts. Yet I never could have imagined all that was now laid out before me in this little space.

As it turned out, today and tomorrow the battle would concentrate on that portion of the field that lay between Cemetery Ridge on the east, Seminary Ridge on the west, Cemetery Hill to the north and two small hills to the south, an area of three or four square miles (the smaller one would become known to history as Little Round Top). The land between the two ridges was comprised of a gently rolling terrain of planted fields, pasture and patches of woods. At the south end of the field was a complex and difficult terrain of woods, small streams, hills and humongous boulders. The small hill was mostly devoid of timber on its western slope and was studded with granite outcroppings that would make it virtually impregnable.

As soon as he had cleared a few more civilians out, General Meade called for his council of war, and the little Leister House soon filled with more brass behinds than there were places to put them. Just before the meeting started, General Warren came up with the surprising news that Third Corps was still not in position, which pretty much astonished General Meade. His ears had just begun to smoke when General Sickles himself and his staff thundered up. General Meade was furious.

"Do not bother to dismount, General Sickles! Go and tend your front! You are much needed there. Go and tend to your front, and I will join you there presently." General Sickles and the rest wheeled their horses obediently and went back as quickly as they had come.

Inside, Captain Paine's map had been enhanced and lay smoothed out on a small table. I peered at it as I walked by and could see enough to know that he had done a pretty good job with the details. I marveled again that he had been able to do a draft of it in the dark with his little desk resting on his pommel. At that point, it was anyone's guess as to the exact location of the enemy other than "over there" somewhere behind Seminary Ridge.

Attendees and arrangements for the council of war are noted following:

Maj. Gen. George Gordon Meade, Army of the Potomac, Commanding – standing;

Maj. Gen. Daniel Butterfield, Chief of Staff – seated at the table and prepared to take notes;

Maj. Gen. Winfield Scott Hancock, Second Corps – seated;

Maj. Gen. Oliver Otis Howard, Eleventh Corps – seated;

Maj. Gen. Henry W. Slocum, Twelfth Corps – seated;

Maj. Gen. George Sykes, Fifth Corps – seated;

Maj. Gen. John Newton, First Corps – seated;

Brig. Gen. John Gibbon, Second Division – lying on the bed;

Brig. Gen. Gouverneur Kemble Warren, Chief of Engineers – sitting on a cracker box;

Brig. Gen. Henry J. Hunt, Chief of Artillery – sitting on the edge of the bed;

Lt. Franklin A. Haskell, Aide to General Gibbon – standing;
Chester R. Bramble, Scout – stuffed in a corner and making himself scarce.

The little house had only two rooms. It appeared the widow had
carted off anything she could carry, as the house was plain and spare inside
with precious few amenities. Besides the table and candles, there was a bed
with a tick in one corner and a few chairs and cracker boxes to sit on.

Outside in Mrs. Leister's yard, which had suffered greatly, the staffs
and orderlies attendant to each officer that had gone inside awaited their
return and tended their horses. It was quite a crowd, and it filled the little
yard and spilled over into the adjoining field.

I was permitted to write a few words in a blank dispatch book to
bring to mind the gist of things when I would have time to write it all out.
I'm sure some things got by me, because a body can only do so much. A lot
of what they said was over my head and beyond me. I can write down what
a person says, or I can remember most of it, but it's hard to write and remember what's being said at the same time. Anyway, I did the best I could.

General Meade spoke.

"Gentlemen, we face a grave situation. The fate of the nation is at
stake, time is short and the responsibility to act is ours. I doubt if the sum
of all we do for the rest of our lives will be as important as how well we
perform until this present issue is decided." As he spoke, General Meade
cast his eyes to the face of each man.

"Most of you know as much about what to do here as I do, but for
reasons I cannot fully comprehend, I have been charged with the command
of this army. I hold neither wisdom nor device that is not held in equal or
greater measure by most of you." He paused. "It seems to me the situation is straightforward and clear. We are confronted with perhaps the largest Army of Northern Virginia yet to take the field. We may outnumber
them by a corps or better and are able to refit and re-supply our forces to
a degree that cannot be matched by the enemy.

"I have consummate faith in each you and your commands to see us
through. The enemy we face has a reputation for whipping us. I see him
as no less ominous because he has been mostly quiet in our front thus far

today. I take little comfort in that. I expect him to come roaring at us at any minute. But let him come.

"I would remind you to remind everyone under your command that the enemy, any enemy, fearful as they may be, are, after all, only men, and it is imperative that we contain them here. They are deep into our country and their lines of communication and supply are long and thin. Their need to be reinforced and re-supplied will soon become critical. Therefore time is on our side – up to a point. Their resources will dwindle with each passing hour. We should be able to bring far greater resources to bear upon them than they upon us ... if ... we are able to keep our lines open." General Meade paused and looked around for response. There was none, which seemed to confirm all he had been saying. He continued.

"I have examined our ground and am impressed that we occupy a very favorable position to receive them. Lee would prefer to be on the defensive here, but we have stolen it from him. I know also that he will not hesitate to strike us. Defensive or not, our work is cut out for us. We could also withdraw to another position, or we can, of course, attack. I seek your advice and counsel with respect to these three alternatives. We bear the hope and trust of the President and the nation, and we must not let them down. Our troops are seasoned and have just demonstrated the march to a remarkable degree. They are healthy. And they are chafing to drive the enemy from our homeland. The men will do their part; now let us do ours.

"If anyone has anything to add or sees otherwise, let's hear it now."

All agreed with the general's summation. At least no one disagreed. There was a sense in the room, I remember, that seemed to be felt by all that the army was finally in the hands of a competent (I heard General Hunt use the word, "pragmatic") leader.

There was agreement that the army should defend from this strong position and let the enemy attack. The Union line was taking on the shape of a fishhook, someone observed (it seems to me it was General Butterfield), being formed with Culp's Hill anchoring the point of the hook to the right, curving around to Cemetery Hill to the west, then directly south several miles to the eye that ended at the little rocky hill. The distance from point to eye on the inside curve of the Union line was at most three miles, whereas the outer curve of the rebel line required a ride of nine miles from one end to the other, making the task of travel and communications three times longer for the Confederates. The Union positions made it relatively easy to move troops and units on short notice to meet changing battlefield conditions. The same was virtually impossible for the Confederates.

Without much further ado, the council ended, and various aides and staff officers were given orders and galloped off to see to their several commands. I think it was about here that General Meade told General Sykes to be prepared to use the whole Fifth Corps if necessary and to hold the left at all costs.

PA SAYS MOST PEOPLE WILL SEE what they want to see and hear what they want to hear out of all you show them and tell them no matter how much you put into the effort. I guess that's what we had here, because before too long, Captain Meade burst in the door to announce that the Third Corps was heading for the high ground out along the Emmitsburg Road. This put them a good half-mile west of the assigned Cemetery Ridge line and appeared to be aiming to locate their center right in the middle of Sherfy's peach orchard and *smack dab* between the lines.

"What in the Lord's name is he doing out there?" asked General Meade, astonished and incredulous at the same time.

"General Sickles said he did it to improve his position. I guess you didn't make it clear what he could do," answered the captain.

"Well, thunderation! I guess he improved his position, all right, but it sure as Hades plays crunch with the rest of the army! He may as well go on over to Seminary Ridge right now. It's a better *position!*" By now, General Meade was stomping around in the tiny room, and his agitation was reaching a high point. "Someone needs to go over there and pound some sense into Sickles," he said, smacking his fist into his palm, "and I guess that someone will have to be me! Sometimes I think Sickles is not worth the powder to blow him up!"

General Newton made no bones about his feelings for General Sickles's predicament. "Sickles is so full of himself, you couldn't fit him into a twelve-foot room without knocking out a wall."

"Well, I don't cotton to him, either, Newton," said General Meade in a rare criticism of what he called "a fellow officer." "I often lack confidence in what he might do next.   And I never expect him to say anything that's going to change my mind.   But I have to listen to him, because sooner or later he likely *will* say something I need to hear."

"I avoid him as much as I can," said General Hancock, who was just fixing to leave, "It's a shame, really.   He's intelligent and brave enough, and if he would take well to direction, he could be a great soldier, except that he's got a screw loose somewhere."

"I'm always a little afraid of any man with a screw loose," General Newton said.

"I'm not afraid *of* him, the little fart," said General Hancock, "but I do fear his unpredictability.   You have to have confidence in the man beside you.   I don't question his courage, but you can never be sure what the son of a bitch is going to do.   And not just on the battlefield.   If you get drawn into a scrap with him, he'll blow it up and see it to its bitter end whether it's worth a fight or not.   And I don't care to put that much fight, or *any* fight, into anything connected with Sickles.   I think they decided right when he beat that murder charge and they called it 'temporary insanity.'   The only part I disagree with is the 'temporary' part.   And if you let yourself get drawn into a fight with a crazy man, you're a fool yourself."   With that, General Hancock departed to see to his command.

"Come boy," General Meade said to me.   "I want you to ride with me while we head over to see General Sickles in case I have any more questions about the lay of the land.   Ride with the staff, and lay low until I call you forward.   And forget what you heard here."

"Yes, *sir*, General Meade!" I said – a little strongly, perhaps – but my blood was up and I was so proud to be where I was it was almost enough to make me pass out.

Everyone dashed from the little house and mounted up and hauled back over the ridgeline to see what was going on.   General Meade and his party reined up alongside Generals Hancock, Gibbon and Caldwell who were scanning to the southwest with their field glasses.

"My, don't Sickles's boys make a grand sight?" said General Gibbon admiringly, staring after the vast formation of the Third Corps on the march.

I had to admit to myself that the sight of thousands of soldiers with their gleaming muskets and banners flapping in the breeze, and their artillery and mounted officers advancing in fine order did indeed make the heart swell.

"Yes, that's Humphreys hell bent for somewhere. And Birney's out there, too, but hold on a while, and you'll see them all come tumbling back," answered General Hancock. "And then it will fall upon us to save Sickles's ass."

"Did you say save his *ass*?" asked General Caldwell, smiling and turning to General Hancock and lowering his field glasses.

"Indeed. Get ready to go save his ass." General Hancock paused, still peering into his glasses. "And when you do, Caldwell, you can leave the rest of him out there!"

Chapter Six - At All Hazards

They saw a cloud of birds so vast,
They took it as a warning
Foreboding that their lives would pass
Before another morning.

LIEUTENANT HASKELL SAYS THAT Thursday started out as Thor's Day, the day of the Viking God of Thunder. It would turn out to be a day Old Thor could be proud of all right and then some. In the morning, things had been so quiet on our front, I had hoped the rebels might be giving up and going home. But that turned out to be more wishful thinking. In the four hours from late afternoon until sunset, in some of the most savage fighting of the war, the two sides incurred and inflicted horrendous casualties all along the line. When the day ended little had changed except for the loss of men, horses, ammunition and equipment with the issue still undecided.

BALDY, GENERAL MEADE'S REGULAR HORSE, was getting shod or something, so the general borrowed General Pleasanton's horse. General Pleasanton commanded the Union cavalry, so I guess you could figure that he of all people would ride a fine horse and offer one to General Meade he could be proud of. You would think so. But this one was cranky and trouble from the start.

Sometime in the afternoon, a little before the shooting started in earnest, we mounted up and rode south for a piece looking for General Sickles and the Third Corps.

"See how far we've come?" I asked Old Jack. "You stick with me, old buddy, and you'll go a fur piece! Now, let's go see to General Sickles."

As expected, Third Corps was nowhere near where General Meade had intended it to be. The entourage swung around and rode west in the direction of the Trostle farm at a gallop. As I rode along with General Meade, General Warren and a dozen or more others, amidst pounding hoofs and pennants all a-flutter in the breeze, I have to admit that the thrill of it was reaching new territory deep inside me. Here was adventure beyond every boy's dream. I was caught between wanting to focus on every detail to strut about later, and being under such a spell that I simply wanted to let the adventure carry me along without thinking about it. Who besides Bum would I ever get to believe that General George Gordon Meade would want *my* services and specifically ask for me, old C. Reis Bramble, to accompany him on a mission to pound sense into General Sickles? Now, if that just don't take the cake! I wished Ma and Pa and Gramma could look in now and see how far their boy had come since only yesterday!

We were crossing the field above George Weikert's house when here came none other than Bum Piles riding up in a hurry. He came in on our left riding an army horse for all it was worth. I had never seen Bum in a hurry about anything before. He hailed General Meade and we reined up.

"What do you have for me, Bum?" asked General Meade.

"Howdy do, Gen'l Meade and all y'uthers. Well, now, Gen'l Geary was up on that hill yonder, but he left just after sunrise to pick back up with Twelfth Corps, so they ain't *nobody* there right now. A brigade could hold off a whole army from up there, but, by cracky, you can't hold off nobody without *somebody!*" Bum paused to catch his breath.

"And they was thousands o' rebels a-pourin' across the Emmitsburg Road and into the woods just south of here a little while ago, I expect headin' for that same hill," said Bum, waving around to his right. "If you hurry and git some men up there, the rebs'll never be able to knock 'em off once they git there. The woods below is full o' boulders that run from a bushel basket to big as a house, so when the rebs come out, they'll come out all scattered and slowed down because it'll be dang hard to get through. Your people can pick 'em off as they come out," Bum explained. "But you dang well better git 'em up there *right smart!*"

Bum said all that as calm as if he said it every day, and I marveled at it. He's either brave as all get out, I thought, or crazy, or knows he's old and his time's about up anyway. But none of that seemed to fit any of my ideas about Bum somehow.

General Meade called to General Warren. "Warren, go over to that little hill yonder and see if there is a problem, and if there is, tend to it. That position is the left of our entire line. Get some men up there and order it held at all hazards!"

General Warren saluted, reined his horse left and waved up two of his aides, an orderly and a couple of couriers that had been following a few rods behind. The six of them broke away and galloped south in the direction of the hill.

WE FOUND GENERAL SICKLES in a field between the Trostle farm and Sherfy's peach orchard and reined up to where he sat mounted to receive us. Salutes went around, and the two principles went immediately into serious discussion, while the others and I sat a respectful distance. The Old Snapping Turtle wasn't exactly snapping, but he didn't appear to be full of warmth either.

"Are you not too extended, here, General Sickles?" said General Meade stiffly. "Are you able to hold this ground?"

"I am certain Third Corps can hold this ground, General Meade."

"I don't think so," said General Meade. "But we will have to make the best of it now. It is too late to undo it. You have stretched your line so thin there are holes in it, a half-*mile* hole between you and Hancock. What are we to do about that, sir?"

As General Meade spoke, artillery rounds began coming in from south and west of the peach orchard. One burst nearby and gave me a start. I hoped no one noticed. My little Sally stood her ground, and I took some courage from her. In our present position, all of us were exposed to enemy fire. Everyone else, having had plenty of practice at this, sat his horse calmly except me. I tried to hide what I really felt and hoped no one had reason to look my way and see that I was petrified. I knew right then that no war was ever going to include me long enough to get used to it.

"This is neutral ground," said General Meade forcefully above the sound of exploding shells. "The guns of both sides command it, thus it cannot be held by either side, sir!"

"Are you advising me to withdraw, General Meade?" asked General Sickles.

"Well, I wish you could, sir, but it is too late. I'm afraid the enemy will not let you off without a fight, now."

IF YOU MEAN TO BE A SUCCESS at being a scout to a general, you have to know how to handle your face. Sometimes it's best to laugh at a general's

joke, funny or not. There are other times when you'd best pay strict attention and look him straight in the eye. Then there are still other times you'd
better pretend you don't have any face at all, or stare at the ground, or look
the other way – like if a general has had too much to drink, or throws up,
or farts even. Woe unto he who laughs at the wrong time. And you must
never, *ever*, catch the eye of either party when one general is out of sorts
with another, like General Meade was with General Sickles in the present
instance. You need to send your face away someplace or disappear right
where you stand, so they can feel as though you don't even exist until they're
ready to let you come back among the living.

I was thinking about whether I should ease farther away from the
two generals, when a strange and unexpected thing happened that alarmed
everyone. General Pleasanton's horse, with General Meade in the saddle,
was spooked by an exploding shell and reared up and made a beeline at
full gallop toward Seminary Ridge, General Meade and all! Such a sight
that was! Here was the commanding general on a runaway horse hell-bent
for enemy lines! After what seemed like forever, the general got the beast
under control just as one of his staff officers pulled up beside him. The
two of them galloped back to where the rest of us sat frozen. "Someone
tell Pleasanton I gave him credit for knowing more about horses than this,"
said the general calmly as he came up.

At this point, we left General Sickles to his fate and turned back in
the direction of Cemetery Ridge. After he returned to headquarters, General Meade replaced General Pleasanton's horse with Baldy again. "It's a
relief to be free of that confounded animal," said the general as he mounted
up. Unfortunately for them both, Baldy was severely wounded before long,
and the general had to mount his third horse of the day. (Old Baldy would
survive his many wounds, fourteen in all, and outlive General Meade by ten
years.)

As we passed back over Plum Run, several regiments that had
formed to our right crossed over the Millerstown Road to Rose's wheat
field and formed behind a stone wall on the south edge of the field. At
that point, they opened fire on rebels advancing through the woods. We
were close enough that the rebels' return fire was snipping at leaves over
our heads.

Sometime after four o'clock (everybody's watch ran a little different in those days), heavy firing broke loose along the left of General Sickles's line from the Rose farm all the way to where Plum Run enters the woods at the place called Devil's Den. The attacking rebels now posed an alarming threat to the left flank of the whole Union army, just as everyone except General Sickles, it seemed, had predicted.

Then intense firing began to pour down from the little hill. General Meade and his staff took this to mean that General Warren had been successful in getting troops up there in time to defend it from falling into rebel hands, or so everyone hoped. For the next couple hours, the battle there raged on without letup.

GENERAL MEADE'S PARTY RETURNED to their vantage point atop Cemetery Ridge to watch the fight proceed and to direct the placement of reinforcements. Couriers bearing reports began flying in from all directions, and General Meade was constantly referring to his map, giving orders and dictating dispatches. He even had me dashing off when they ran short on couriers a few times, which I was proud as punch to do.

I was busier carrying messages for General Meade then than at any other point during my time of service. Couriers were coming and going in flocks. Lieutenant Haskell had said that it is usually the practice of the commanding general to step aside once the shooting starts and leave the details up to his individual corps commanders. General Meade would normally position the corps broadly or direct any reinforcements as needed but would otherwise allow his generals to have full "discretion." With so much at stake, General Meade did not hesitate to step in and command directly where he felt his experienced hand was needed.

Sometime that day, I can't exactly place the hour, a strange phenomenon occurred. A massive swarm of pigeons swept the battlefield and continued mile after mile, millions upon countless millions filling the skies. In their aimless urgency, they brought a sense of apprehension and restlessness to the men. Some called it a bad omen, a portent of death.

The rebels had spent most of the morning getting themselves in position to launch their attack. They marched first one way and then the other, backtracking some miles until they came out directly east of our farm. Mind you, some of them had already marched the twenty-five miles from Chambersburg and, having arrived all lathered up and tired and thirsty, were ordered to march around some more after they got here. One of our neighbors told us that he asked them what in Sam Hill they were doing with all that marching back and forth. One of them told him they were trying to position their units out of sight of the Yankees. Well shoot, he told them, if the Yankees just bothered to look around, they'd know what was going on by all the dust being raised now that the roads had dried out. But now, it appeared they were finally set to do business.

In the next half hour, more rebel firing broke out continuously from Little Round Top all the way out to the Emmitsburg Road and thence north all the way up to the vicinity of the Bliss farm, a distance of maybe two miles. From within Rose's Woods came a terrible intensifying fire of massed musketry that produced a deep guttural sound like someone ripping a huge piece of canvas, only a thousand times louder.

The time had now come for Second Corps to go save General Sickles's backside and carry it off to safer ground. Turning to General Caldwell, General Hancock boomed the order, "Form your men, General!" The long roll sounded, and two of General Caldwell's three brigades under Colonel Cross and General Zook made ready to go forward.

General Hancock saluted Colonel Cross and said, "You've been looking for a star, Cross. There's one out there waiting for you today!" Colonel Cross was a strong looking man, hard and unsmiling, with a long red-brown beard. He sat a horse with ease, like an Indian, some said. His men were proud that he always had a red bandanna tied around his head when he went into battle. Not one man in his brigade failed to notice that today he wore one of black.

"No, General, not this time. My last fight is out there," he answered calmly and solemnly.

General Hancock stared after the two brigades as they moved out to support the crumbling line in the wheat field. "Zook and Cross are different as hell, but both are tough as nails and the best damn brigade commanders in the whole corps, maybe the whole army, Caldwell," said General Hancock as he stared after them through his glasses. "Cross is mean as shit but even-handed and looks after his men. Zook is a stickler, but he looks out for his men, too. The men know it and love them both and will fight like hell for them today." Both brigades disappeared and formed in Trostle's Woods and got set to cross Millerstown Road into Rose's wheat field.

GENERAL MEADE HAD ORDERED that any man who fails in his duty in this hour was to be shot, and this seems to have had no effect at all on skulkers cringing in the ditch or skedaddlers waiting to fake injury and limp off to the rear. The order seemed harsh, but it was given to compel weaker men to hold fast in time of great peril. I don't know that anyone actually shot cowards very often, but they were free to do so.

Any army has its share of cowards, I guess. Yet, there is a kind of calling that sends men forward into great mortal danger and uncertainty. Amidst thoughts of life yet to be lived, each man is drawn by his own measure of courage, his heart heavy with fears and hopes and resignations. Some are patriots and devoted to an ideal as yet unfulfilled. Others are drawn by a peculiar wanting-to, a faithful association to the whole, a loyalty that grows with training and conditioning and is inspired by good leadership. Still others go, brimming with fear, quaking, cringing, praying and trembling – afraid to go forward and afraid not to – alert to any opportunity to hole up or break and run.

Fear touches upon every sensible man, some more than others, and weighs down upon each like a lead mantle. But regardless of all the measures of men, regardless of fears great and small, for any and for all reasons, forward they go.

GENERAL CALDWELL'S THIRD BRIGADE, popularly known as The Irish Brigade, was then called up and went into formation with its flag with the golden harp flapping brilliant bright green in the breeze alongside our nation's flag. Their commander, Colonel Patrick Kelly, addressed the men.

"Boys, you are about to carry into battle once again the honor of the Irish Brigade." He raised his sword above his head. "Remember *Antietam!*"

The cry, "*Antietam!*" rose in unison over the brigade from a thousand voices.

"Remember *Fredericksburg!*"

"*Fredericksburg . . .!*" they cried.

"Remember that the honor of the comrades left behind on those distant fields is in your hands this fine day. Remember the honor of the old country! And now, you are again called upon to bring honor to your new country, *the United States of America!*" Again, the men raised a resounding cheer.

"*The United States of America!!*"

"Now if any of ye have been a-waitin' for that eleventh hour to offer up repentance for your sinful lives, I would bring to your attention that life has crept up on ye, and that hour has now arrived. Hell is half a mile yonder, boys, and ye'll be wantin' to go clean, now. So gather 'round Father Corby here as he is about to offer absolution for our sins."

Father Corby stood on a large rock and performed the Sacrament of Absolution over the sounds of the battle roaring ever louder now just across the way. He called out a bunch of words, none of which I understood, and then made the sign of the cross. The men, who had removed their caps and bowed their heads, did likewise. General Hancock was present on his horse, and also removed his hat and bowed his head, as did others of his staff. So I did, too.

The good Father held his right hand aloft and shouted out from a Bible he held in his left, "*. . . for the living know that they shall die, but the dead know not any thing . . . for the memory of them is forgotten . . . also their work, and their hatred, and their envy, is now perished . . . God now accepteth thy works . . . And whatsoever thy hand findeth to do, do it with thy might!*" He now shouted the words louder to be heard above the raging noise of battle. "'*For there is no work, nor device, nor knowledge, nor wisdom, into the grave, whither thou goest!*'"

Father Corby made the sign of the cross once more, and the men responded, and tears poured out from somewhere and down my cheeks.

And I was not the only one.

"Now go forward . . . for the honor of the Irish Brigade! And *remember . . .!*" The priest slowly spoke his words of warning. "The Good Lord and the Catholic Church will refuse a Christian burial to *any* man who turns his back upon the enemy in this hour!"

The brave Irishmen and their waving banners marched off towards the sound of the guns, and I put in my two cents in my own way and asked God to protect them all and bring them back. Soon the sound of battle was heard even louder yet from one end of the field to the other. The smoke blocked out the sun like the swarm of pigeons, and I wondered who among those that passed by so proudly just minutes before were now among the dead and dying out there on the field.

It had been common to hear Gramma rail against the Pope and the Catholics, whom she claimed meant to take over the country and rule it from Rome. I had been raised Protestant, mostly. Pa and Gramma were Methodist and Ma was Lutheran, and although I was not Catholic and knew little of their ways, I was inspired by what I had just witnessed and thought this was as good a time as any to make my peace with the Lord. I prayed I would have time to think on each of my family and say goodbye and tell them how much I loved them as the life passed from me. I thought about how I had never really kissed a girl yet or got to know much about the different spirit that always seemed to be a part of them. But if it was my lot in life to bow out early, I guess I would have to accept that. I tried hard to be noble, but I really didn't feel very noble. I still felt the need to cry and be comforted.

I knew I would leave a pile of things undone, a hundred chores to finish, the letter to Aunt Banner for the socks she gave me last Christmas, the things Ma had asked me more than once to fix for her, an apology to Gramma for hurting her feelings, all kinds of loose ends; but most of all I would feel remorse to leave behind a grieving mother and father and grandmother.

There's a part of me that wants to go along with what everybody else seems to take in stride: to be manly, to be brave, to laugh at fear and to pretend not to notice the poor devil that lies pleading by the wayside, broken and torn, then dead, then blackened and bloated, no longer a person, just an awful *thing*. A soldier must abide. He must learn to live outside the dreadful things before him, or he would go mad in his first mile.

There is another part of me still the child, a part not yet hardened, still tied to a sheltered world that somehow believes a happy childhood goes on forever and expects goodness and charity and rightfulness to be the distinctions of a proper life. I have not yet given myself up to hardness and will struggle to hold on to that which is good, hoping someday these awful things shall pass. Yet how can I reconcile the terrible deeds of this battlefield with what is in the Good Book and all I have been taught about what is proper and decent and fair?

I must have got some of it across to Old Jack, because he leaned over and licked my face.

ABOUT NOW, GENERAL MEADE began riding off everywhere and anywhere. I ran to mount Sally and had to ride her hard to catch up with him, not that he appeared to have much use for me, but I had a job, and I was determined to whatever extent possible to be a success at it. The general had couriers coming and going in abundance. Much of his attention was now focused on a wide gap in the Cemetery Ridge line between Second Corps and parts of Fifth Corps which had been ordered up to support Third Corps that was on the verge of collapse. At one time or another, General Meade was occupied with directing the movements of parts of the Second, Fifth, Sixth and Twelfth Corps to those places on the line where need was greatest. In all, I'd guess these four corps carried as many as fifty thousand men.

The battle up on Little Round Top was still going full blast when more troops from Fifth Corps crossed Plum Run into heavy firing from the small rise immediately to the west. There was one continuous racket from Devil's Den around and up past the Codori barn. At many points along this line, hundreds of stragglers and wounded and suffering men came streaming back through the lines. At the same time, new regiments and brigades formed up and moved forward into the fight.

The smoke became so intense it was next to impossible to distinguish friend from foe in the late afternoon light. Up at the peach orchard, after a savage fight, our troops had given way to an attacking rebel force that brought up artillery to pound our lines. Many of our batteries had been pulled back to various places nearer to Cemetery Ridge and faced danger of being overrun.

SOON, A REPORT CAME IN THAT GENERAL SICKLES had been hit by a cannonball and had lost a leg. As they carried him from the field, hundreds more of his men from Third Corps fell back in retreat and in great disorder through the Second Corps lines ("tumbling back" as General Hancock had predicted). Ordinarily, the call to honor or the fear of disapproval – or the predisposition towards cohesion and reliance – will cause men to hold their post in times of great danger. But sometimes a peculiar thing occurs when a few men who break and run in the face of the enemy pull others with them. Next thing you know, they have a panic on their hands that turns into a rout. Lieutenant Haskell came up and tried to help turn the retreating Third Corps troops back to the line but without much success. He told me, "It is only when a man stands his ground under fire that he becomes a soldier."

On another front, the noise coming back all across the wheat field from Plum Run to a little stony hill out towards the Rose place was so loud it hurt. Our boys drove the enemy back into the woods and off the little hill but not for long. The rebels were soon joined by other units and formed up for a counterattack. They attacked, and our troops were forced back across the wheat field. Each successive drive from one side or the other moved the line back and forth for two and a half hours and left a new array of dead and wounded that began to cover the field with blue and gray.

Couriers began coming to General Hancock from General Sykes asking for help. His Fifth Corps had sent the brigade to Little Round Top and then sent two others to prevent a rebel breakthrough as Sickles's lines began to crumble; and now Sykes' diminished corps was hard-pressed itself with his two forward brigades being driven back into Trostle's Woods.

Sickles's men continued stumbling back, and General Hancock shouted at them and cursed them, and waved his sword at them and ordered them to return to the fight. They ignored him completely. Hancock shouted above the growing pandemonium, "Well, I'll be goddamned if there doesn't go Sickles's house of cards!" He turned to General Gibbon.

"They carted that bastard off with his leg hanging by a thread! What he did was a damned disgrace, Gibbon. If he was regular army, he'd be up for court-martial. Instead, he'll go back to Washington, and everyone, including his good friend, Uncle Abe, will flock around him and hear how he saved the army at Gettysburg in spite of old Granny Meade. The bastard will be back there and made into such a hero, and by the time the truth be told, no one will be able to touch him! General Meade has too much character to denigrate a wounded fellow officer. *That's* why I hate political generals, Gibbon! The son of a bitch should be court-martialed!"

"And he was one of the better ones," said General Gibbon.

General Hancock went on like he didn't hear him. "That irrepressible bastard!" he shouted. "He left here with a big black cigar stuck in his face claiming he'll have his leg preserved in a jar in his office. He'll call it 'Sickles's Pickle.' My, what flair! There's the hero for you: he makes merry over his own misfortune."

General Hancock took a breath, "Mark my words, Gibbon, maybe they won't bring him home in one piece, but you watch, they'll make the big piece out to be so much that one of these days, you'll find it back sitting in Congress again!"

General Meade had ridden up and had heard the last of General Hancock's harangue. "It is unseemly to speak so of a fellow officer, Hancock."

"But he's not a fellow officer, General; he's a politician. The closest he ever got to West Point was Tammany Hall. And now we are left to correct a folly that has endangered this entire army."

"I am asking you to take command of Third Corps and return Gibbon to temporary command of Second Corps," said General Meade firmly.

"So now I am asked to give up command of a corps that is functioning properly and take up one that is falling apart," responded General Hancock.

"That is correct, sir," answered General Meade.

"Would that you could have made that decision early this morning, General." said General Hancock, to which General Meade gave a small nod in response.

Now, one of General Hancock's aides rode up with another report. "General Barksdale of Mississippi has been captured and lies mortally wounded at Second Corps Hospital. He led his men all the way across Humphrey's front unscathed, screaming like a wild man to kill Yankees.

We got him when a captain ordered his entire company to 'fire on that officer with the white hair.'"

"Cheers for them. I for one am not sorry to see the end of that maniacal bastard," said General Hancock.

"Yet, one cannot deny that he was a very brave and dedicated soldier," offered the aide.

"He was dedicated to an evil cause. And I agree with Jackson about brave enemies: 'Kill them! Kill the brave ones!'"

AT THAT MOMENT, I FELT SOMETHING whack me on the head that in the instant of its occurrence caused me think of my Aunt Fidey. Aunt Fidey would dote on me shamefully, ordinarily, when I was a little fellow. She had a thick gold band wedding ring, and now and then when I did something to set her off, she would reach out and crack me on the head with it. It always surprised me and hurt something awful and would set me to whining. The difference this time was, when I reached up to rub it, my hand got all wet; and when I looked, it was covered with blood. Well, it scared me so much, the pain went right out of it. I tried to wipe away the blood with my shirt, but I couldn't keep up with it at first. Directly, someone wrapped a strip of cloth around my head and tied it tight. It turned out that the wound was slight and stopped bleeding as suddenly as it began. But it left a small red patch where the blood came through the cloth and made me so proud I never wanted to take it off.

"Wear this 'til it heals over to keep the dirt out. You'll feel better," someone said.

"Heck, I just might wear it forever," I cried.

I didn't feel a thing until later, and then I caught a whopper of a headache. My wound was the best kind, though: good enough for appearances and not bad enough to do any permanent harm.

From time to time, I went back and forth between thinking I would die and thinking I would survive. Now, a strange new confidence, almost an assurance that I would indeed survive, began to creep over me, and with this, I could again feel childhood slipping away. But I wasn't quite through with it yet and didn't want to let go of it, even as I knew I would soon be leaving it for good whether I wanted to or not.

I departed with General Meade back to his field command on Cemetery Ridge. I got the feeling now that some of the officers thought we might be getting the best of the rebels, but I guess you could never be sure about that until you saw how things finally came out. I was then given a dispatch for General Sedgwick and sent off to find him somewhere down the Baltimore Pike. He was not hard to find, and within a few minutes, I was on my way back.

In the eastern shadow of Round Top, some batteries posted along Jacob Weikert's stone wall had been in danger of being overrun but were now supported by new advance infantry units of Sixth Corps. The beautiful sight of more men from the big Sixth Corps appeared like magic as they moved toward the shallow end of Cemetery Ridge.

Up by the house, I caught a glimpse of a young woman hurrying out into the yard and recognized Tillie Pierce! I blinked by eyes in disbelief. She lived up on Baltimore Street, and here she was a long way off and in the middle of the battlefield. I called out to her. "Tillie! *Tillie Pierce!*"

She whirled around, and I could see her hair was plastered to the side of her face with sweat. Then I noticed with alarm the blood on her apron. They had been bringing in wounded to the house and barn, and I was relieved at least a little bit by the likelihood that the blood was not hers. But what the Sam Hill was she doing way down here?

"Tillie Pierce! What are *you* doing here?" I asked, amazed and not at all unthrilled to see her.

"Oh, Reisie," she cried in some despair, "my mother and father sent me down here to Jacob's, because they thought I would be safer here!"

"They guessed wrong, I'd have to say."

As I rode up to her, I saw the yard was full of wounded men that had overflowed from the house and barn and were laid out waiting for attention. About then, a shell came hissing overhead and exploded beyond the barn. Tillie shrieked and ducked behind a tree.

"Hey, Tillie! No need to fear," yelled one of the wounded. "*If you can hear it, no need to fear it!*' You never hear the one that gets you." The men in the barnyard all laughed, and I felt embarrassment for her.

"Oh, don't pay them no mind, Tillie," I said protectively.

"I want to be brave for the soldiers, Reisie, but it'll take me some getting used to." I never liked being called Reisie, except I didn't mind so much when Tillie Pierce did it. Actually, I didn't mind at *all* when Tillie Pierce did it. Come to think of it, I guess I *liked* it when Tillie did it. "I've been helping tend the wounded all afternoon. The house is full and the barn is full, and now the yard is full. Their suffering is almost unbearable to me, but I know it must be far worse for them. For all that, I'm holding up pretty well, but I'm still terrified by cannonballs!" Then she noticed the bandage on my head, I'm happy to say.

"Oh, my lands, Reisie! You're hurt! What *happened?*"

"I almost took a minié ball, but it's just a scratch. I guess I'll be all right." I hoped that would keep her concern going a little bit longer.

"But you should have that looked at, Reisie!"

"Well, maybe. But only after the ones that's worse off are taken care of," I said, as I slid down off Sally, hoping she would recognize the selfless courage of such a statement.

"Well, aren't you my brave fellow," she said and kissed me on the cheek. I blushed something fierce. "Right now, I need to go see to a fellow named Stephen who is very seriously wounded who they just put down in the cellar. You can come with me if you want." I was happy to go along just to be with her.

I left Old Jack outside while we went in the house and picked our way among men lying everywhere. I followed Tillie down the narrow steps to the cellar. I could hear the moaning and gasping of the wounded throughout the house, and as my eyes became used to the light, I saw a dozen or more men laid out on straw on the small floor. The place was a bit cooler than above but it stunk to high heaven. Over in a corner, a man was laid out still wearing his bloody clothes. He had been shot somewhere in the body, and, while I knew very little about wounded men up close except for that one experience back at Mrs. McGrath's house, it was instinctive to me that this man would not survive.

"Hello Stephen. You see, I did remember to come back. I have a drink of cool water for you and a nice damp cloth for your forehead. And also a little beef broth for you, Stephen. I brought my friend, Reisie, with me. Reisie, this is General Weed."

"Howdy, sir," I said. "I been scouting for General Meade, and I know he would want to know how you're feeling, sir."

"Tell Old Snapper I never felt better," said General Weed with difficulty. "I should be up dancing this time tomorrow."

General Weed was to say other things in his state that in a way made sense and in a way did not. Some of it bothered me a little, because it seemed a mite out of harmony with what I was raised to believe but made sense all the same.

"I guess I'm one of the few people who believe and will admit it that man is still in the process of becoming more than he is and that he's a long way from what he could be. I think God is far, far greater than we give Him credit for being or can even imagine Him being. Man lacks the imagination *and* the intelligence *and* the comprehension to come anywhere near knowing what God really is. But being mortal and in mortal danger as I am, I must cover all the bases and ask the only God I ever did know to help me through this."

With that, Tillie took one of his hands in hers.

"I believe we are headed for something far greater than what we are now, Tillie, something finer, more intelligent, more knowing, more comprehending. Hasn't this always been so? Each generation adding its small bits to that 'Something' we will become?"

Tillie now held his hand against her cheek. General Weed stared at the ceiling and went on in earnest.

"You would have to look back far deeper into the past than we can to see how far we've come. And you'd have to look far deeper into the future than we are possibly able to do to see what we will become." General Weed lay perfectly still as he spoke. "This is where faith comes in, *real* faith, personal faith, not what we are expected to believe because of what was written many centuries ago. I'm talking about my convictions about a better world that none of us will live to see. To me, that's faith." Tillie was crying openly now.

General Weed's words would come back to me many times over the years, but their hopeful philosophy was for the time overwhelmed by the brutality of this battlefield.

"Please promise me you'll come back in the morning, Tillie. In the absence of others with whom I would like to share my final hours, I take great comfort in your being here."

"I do indeed promise, Stephen. You must promise me you will be here as well."

"Where on earth would I be going, child?" asked the general. And in the silence that followed, all three of us held quietly to the same fateful answer.

In the yard, I mounted up and bade Tillie goodbye.

"Are you really a scout for General Meade?" asked Tillie with astonishment.

"It ain't nothing, Tillie. I've been with him regular all day long, and I have to get back now. I tell him things about the land and streams and such that he doesn't know. And I just carried a dispatch to General Sedgwick. Bum Piles, who I guess you never heard of, got me the job. It was a big surprise to me that he even knew the general. He lives out near us and is friendly with Pa and all." I was gracelessly sputtering and hating myself for it.

"Well, it certainly *is* something," she said. "And you're my hero!" She reached up for me and I bent down and about fell off the horse so she could hug me and kiss me again on the side of the head, and I loved the smell of her, sweat and all, and would try hard to remember it. All the wounded in the yard did a round of "*Wooo-wooos!*" and I know I blushed something fierce right in front of everybody.

Sometime after the war, Tillie got married and moved on to Selinsgrove where she would write a book called *At Gettysburg* about her experiences including administering to General Weed and other wounded.

As I was returning to headquarters, just north of the George Weikert place, General Hancock and his aide, Captain Mitchell, came riding through the smoke in my direction. Captain Mitchell had been wounded and was having difficulty staying on his horse. A small regiment occupied the position where the two officers and I came together.

General Hancock reined up beside the colonel commanding the regiment. He was quite agitated and pointed towards the late afternoon sun and a brigade of rebels approaching in our direction from the other side of Plum Run. This rebel brigade was taking fire from Second Corps on the right and a few of the retreating Third Corps remnants on the left. General Hancock rose up in his saddle and spun around to see what other men were close at hand to oppose the advancing enemy.

"Are you really a scout for General Meade?"

He looked down at the colonel and shouted out above the din, "What regiment is this, sir?"

"First Minnesota, General! William Colvill commanding, sir!" Colonel Colvill was a large man with a strong, clean-shaven face with a pair of muttonchops that poked around from the sides.

"How many men do you have, Colonel?" bellowed the general.

"Two hundred sixty-two, last count, General!"

"God *Almighty!* Is that *all* the men we have here?" General Hancock pointed towards the rebel brigade and shouted, "Then, by God, advance, Colonel, and *take those colors!* I need you to give me five minutes, sir!"

"Then we will give you ten, General!"

"Then do it! And do it damn well quick, sir!"

The regiment formed up with fixed bayonets, and the colonel waved them forward at the double-quick. These men faced a force five or six times the size of their own. I watched their steady line advance on the rebels who had crossed Plum Run. The First Minnesota came under fire, and I wondered if any would survive. As they closed upon the enemy brigade, the colonel gave the order to charge, and a cheer rose from the men in this small regiment as they lowered their bayonets and drove the rebels back across Plum Run.

Their spirited charge took the wind out the rebels' sails, and their brigade advanced no farther that day. In fifteen minutes, the survivors came back, but now, the regiment was so small, it could only be described as pitiful. Two hundred fifteen men were left behind on the battlefield, including Colonel Colvill, who was wounded. The First Minnesota suffered 82 percent casualties in that charge, the highest percent loss in a single engagement of any regiment during the war, they say. But they gave General Hancock the precious minutes he needed to find and order up additional units to secure the line.

I thought about General Hancock's command to "take those colors!" I had never understood all the fuss about carrying the colors or the frenzy to capture the enemy's colors until I witnessed something of its significance. I found that there was a very practical reason as well as an emotional one. The battle flag, the regimental unit flag, some lovingly stitched together by admiring ladies back home, served as a beacon, a rallying point, around which men could reassemble when they became disorganized in the terrible confusion of battle. That's why it was so important for someone else to take up the colors when the color bearer fell. At times, even an officer would take up and carry a fallen banner. The job of color bearer was most dangerous and few survived throughout the war.

I RETURNED TO THE LEISTER HOUSE and found General Meade there but not for long. A captain came in and complained that men were streaming back over Cemetery Ridge in retreat while First Corps sat idle on the back side of the ridge. General Meade instructed the captain to find General Newton and tell him to send his corps to the business side of Cemetery Ridge to help fill another gap on Second Corps left. With that, General Meade and staff mounted up and I followed after. As far as I knew, General Meade had ordered divisions from First and Sixth Corps to plug the gap in our line and was going to see that it was done.

The day had been long and hard for everyone, and here we were again headed for heaven knows what else. When the general's party arrived at the gap it was still unattended by any of the units ordered up. We could see vaguely outlined against the setting sun what we took to be a brigade moving in and out of the obscuring smoke and coming in our direction.

"Is it ours or theirs?" asked one of the general's aides looking through his field glasses.

"Well, if it's ours, they are for certain headed in the wrong direction," said General Meade. "I don't need glasses to tell me that."

Elsewhere, the thunder of nearby artillery shook the earth, and flashes of musketry winked at us through the smoke like red fireflies. From various parts of the field, Union cheers arose to compete with screaming horses and rebels' fearsome yells. Some Second Corps infantry were holding on and pouring fire into the approaching enemy's left flank until it had advanced so far that our troops had to hold their fire to keep from shooting across the gap and hitting some of our artillerymen. It was all total confusion to me.

Things seemed to be getting pretty hot in front of us, and it looked to be high time to head for the rear. I tried to find something in either the general's face or any of the rest of them to start us off. Nothing showing up yet. More seconds passed. Still nothing. Only that the general and the others rose up in their stirrups and fiddled with their equipment. Then the light came on that General Meade and his staff were preparing to *defend this gap by themselves!* This small band of men led by the commanding general had suddenly found itself required to stop a whole enemy brigade! Every hair on my body now stood at attention!

I marveled that these men made ready without alarm and without melodrama, without reservation or complaint ... without hesitation. And for whatever they might have felt inside, I was certain that none of them misunderstood the portent of events that were fast rolling toward them. The shifting fortunes of the battlefield now delivered up a time for each man to be stalwart and to expect those at his side to be likewise.

The general spun the cylinder of his revolver, felt around for his sword, adjusted his hat and straightened upright. Then came the call from within each man to be what a soldier is and do what a soldier does. Everyone brought his horse into line and faced the enemy, no doubt with final thoughts of home and some other life so far away. As an afterthought, the general turned toward me and with a small motion directed me to position myself further back.

Old Jack and I took our place with this small band who were preparing themselves to go down fighting. What I felt then was not so much fear but rather sublime pride, honored to be with General Meade, this old soldier who somehow got left off history's list of heroes.

Suddenly, someone shouted, "Here they come, General Meade. *Here come Newton's boys!*" Everyone spun around to the welcome sight of First Corps veterans pouring over the low ridge to our rear and as they came rushing forward, we cheered them on loudly.

General Newton galloped ahead of his men and reined up beside General Meade. "Well, you *are* a sight for sore eyes, Newton!" General Newton pulled out a flask and offered it to General Meade who took a good pull. At that moment, a shell struck the earth nearby and showered both men with dirt. Neither man so much as batted an eye, except for General Meade who gave a short nod in gratitude for the drink.

Newton's two shrunken divisions bore down on the gap at the double-quick and were more than enough for the rebel brigade. They swung into line of battle amidst wild cheering and a charge that carried them into the face of the oncoming rebels. The general's blood was up, and he galloped forward shouting, "Come on gentlemen! Come on boys!" and waved them on with great sweeping strokes of his hat. Overwhelmed, the rebels fell back, and the gap was secured. General Meade reined up and called Newton's men to a halt, reluctant to send them any further into the smoke and uncertainty of a darkening landscape.

SOMETIME AFTER DARK, GENERAL MEADE SUMMONED the corps commanders back to the Leister house. Most were exhausted by the events of the day and took to the chairs and bed without hesitation. General Warren had sustained a painful neck wound. "You'd better have that looked after, Warren," advised General Meade. Without comment, General Warren sunk to a corner of the floor and fell asleep from sheer exhaustion. Couriers came and went during the meeting, and we could hear the heavy firing east of Cemetery Hill that had been going on most of the day and into the night as the rebels tried unsuccessfully to wrest Culp's Hill from the defenders on our right flank.

The question of the evening posed by General Meade was to the effect: should the army remain in its present position or retire to another one? General Gibbon, being the junior member of the assembly, was required by tradition to speak first. He advised that the army should make such corrections to its position as practicable, but on no account should it be changed in any substantial manner.

Except for General Howard, who favored attacking the enemy, all the other generals in one way or another agreed with General Gibbon about holding our present position and waiting for the enemy to make his move. General Hancock said if we did decide to take the initiative, we couldn't wait too long and must move while the enemy was weakest. General Howard then proposed that if the enemy had not resumed the offensive by four o'clock tomorrow, Friday afternoon, that our army attack the Confederate positions.

Around midnight, as the generals were departing, General Newton turned to General Meade and said, "General Meade, I think you should be much gratified with the results of the day."

General Meade turned to face him squarely. "In the name of common sense, Newton, why would you say such a thing as that?"

"Because, sir," smiled General Newton, "they have hammered us into a position so strong they can't whip us out of it!"

As they all trooped out, General Meade asked General Gibbon to stay behind a minute. He scanned the map on the small table by candlelight. "He's tried our right, and he's tried our left, and it is fortunate for us that he couldn't do both very well at the same time. Tomorrow, I expect him to try us right here, and that's your position, Gibbon." He stabbed the map at the center of the long north-south ridgeline thrice with his forefinger. "We have the advantage of a strong position, and Lee is not fighting his best fight. So let's stay right here and let him keep up the good work. I would not want to interfere with an enemy while he is making bad decisions." He paused. "But you can never be sure what Bobby Lee is up to 'til he's up to it."

I managed to get in a word about General Weed and told General Meade it didn't appear he would survive. General Meade touched me on the shoulder and shook his head softly. "I know, son. I knew him well in Fifth Corps. This will be hard for Warren."

✣   ✣   ✣

LATER THAT NIGHT, I AGREED TO GO with a small band of men who planned to go out on the battlefield under cover of darkness to see if they could find and bring back some of their friends they had had to leave behind.

I swore to myself early on that I would try not to dwell excessively on the horrors of the field after the battle, as I found it difficult to do justice in the telling. But the scene is always just as depressing to one side as it is to the other. It is the saddest, most somber, most dismal sight on earth. The first day, yesterday, I had left the field before the fighting was concluded, and the worst part of that field was then in enemy hands. Much of the action happened afterwards, and what I did see, I mostly saw from a distance.

On this, the second night, we went out to search in an area that bore the most ferocious actions of the day. The moon had poured through broken clouds about midnight and gave enough light to the smoky mists to expose an appalling field of death. As we stumbled along in the inconstant moonlight (there was one lantern among us, and it was carried to the front, while I brought up the rear), the first thing I encountered was a mounting, unbearable stench. The aftermath of battle is nauseating and revolting. The smells are overpowering: stinging, burning, choking smells of smoke, fire and gunpowder, of metal, oil, grease; of fresh torn earth, of savaged oak and pine; of urine and bowel, of the sickening sweet smell of blood; of evisceration of man and beast.

We met streams of ragged and powder-stained wounded, limping or crawling to whatever places of shelter and succor were not already overrun by sheer numbers. Pairs of men joining arms at the shoulder came hobbling back across the field in search of help. Every building in all directions was filled to overflowing, and medical personnel were overwhelmed beyond all expectations. Acres of wounded would soon gather around the designated hospital areas along Rock Creek.

Out on the field, men with candles and lanterns were turning over corpses in search of friends. Their ghostly lights cast moving shadows on upturned wagons, cannons, muskets, mutilated men and horses left in the moment of their deaths in every conceivable position. They stumbled through the darkness, turning up one cold dead face after another, searching for anything – hats, rings, pictures – by which to identify faces mangled beyond recognition

Some tore their shirts and drawers into bandages to bind up the wounds of comrades. Some were too severely injured to move. In this long night of agony, most went without food or water. Great rains would come late tomorrow and continue for days. Many of those left behind would lie undiscovered and helpless in the mud, while others would pass from this earth quietly and alone. Haunting cries for water arose from all parts of the field near and far like strange and doleful birds of night. Poor horses whinnied most pitifully and struggled to rise on legs no longer there.

One poor group of men had taken refuge in a small building and was not found for several days. Their blood and body fluids had dried and hardened on the floor and held them fast as if they had been glued there. They were found dehydrated, starving and crawling with maggots. Some had died.

At another place, an officer lay severely wounded among corpses that were being eaten by a herd of huge white hogs, which he held off by jabbing them with the point of his sword until help finally came many hours later.

Stretcher bearers — musicians, cooks, clerks, and other non-combatants — were conscripted to go out and retrieve anyone they could find. Ambulances braved sporadic enemy musket fire and hurried to the rear bounding and bumping to the shrieks and screams of those inside. Rebels were picked up as well, although the crews usually left them until last after all of our boys had been accounted for. The ambulance crews worked until dawn to bring off all they could find.

In the bloody wheat field a measure of truce had been achieved so that each side could collect its dead and wounded. In the darkness, a Confederate soldier sang hymns for a long time. His voice was clear and sublime, and men on both sides stopped to listen to this reminder of a civilized world. When he was done, cheers and applause went up from all along the Union positions.

I GUESS I WAS BECOMING USED TO the battlefield some. I was shocked at first by things that were becoming easier to abide. I had a relative who lived in a town with a tannery. We visited there once and the smell was so awful, you didn't want to draw a breath. I asked my cousin how he could stand to live in such a place, and he said you get so after while that you don't even notice it anymore. I hadn't gotten that hardened yet, but some things that had first offended me I could now take somewhat in stride even after less than two days.

One more horror that evening is burned into memory.

As I said, I had gone out with some of the men to look for friends that hadn't returned and might still be lying out there unable to move. Our lantern was turned down as low as it could so as not to draw fire when, suddenly and without warning, I came face to face, literally, with another of those horrible sights I was to see on that battlefield. Draped across a fallen log not two feet in front of my eyes and ghastly brilliant in the moonlight was a *face!*

It had been sliced or torn from its owner by some stroke of battlefield violence, as cleanly as a savage takes a scalp, and flung through the air to come to rest as neatly on this log as if someone had carefully laid it there. Of course the eyes were gone but the rest of it lay drying out like a mask – cheeks, lips, nose, chin, moustache, a little patch of beard at the bottom and a little patch of hair clinging to the forehead – all in one piece. At first, I had the senseless impulse to pick it up in case I came across its owner, but on second thought, I figured he would be long past the need for it by now.

I was taken by the notion that out of the whole body a face weighs at most maybe a pound but draws all the attention away from the rest of the creature. I had listened to soldiers talk about what parts of their body they would want to lose least and heard what you might expect: eyes, legs, arms and other things, but I never heard of anyone afraid of losing his face – probably because no one ever expected you could be separated from it. If a man was to lose his face, I guess the rest of him wouldn't bring much. There are some men who seem drawn to war, that is, until they come right down to it directly. I'm sure the poor fellow who owned this face went proudly off to war and felt, in his concluding moments, that he would have just as soon passed the whole thing by.

BACK AT THE RELATIVE COMFORT of Second Corps headquarters, into the late, late night, the haunting calling of the rolls went on for a long time in the dark – the answering to the names for some, the testimonial silence that followed for others.

I sought out Lieutenant Haskell. He patted my head and asked after my wound, and compared to the experience of the last few hours, being with him was as welcome as being with an old and treasured friend. I told him I was afraid I would be a failure in his profession as I could never get used to anything so terrible.

Lieutenant Haskell sat on his haunches and poked at the fire with a stick. "Good for you, Reisie. It's when you get so used to it and don't hate it anymore that you have cause to worry. After a while, war can become part of you. It becomes commonplace as surely as if you had been born on a battlefield. There's no use in saying, 'I don't want anything to do with it.' You can no more turn from combat or resist it than you can keep from being swept away by a raging flood; you fight your way out or drown in it.

Most men know they can't do much about it; they just grit their teeth and try to ride it out. You have a long way to go before that, Reisie."

Lieutenant Haskell rose up and stood before me. He tapped his forefinger lightly on my chest. "There's a fine man growing in there, and I hope he will still be around after this thing is over. This country is going to need him."

Far into the night, the bands on both sides played hymns to soothe the anguished men to sleep. They all picked up on that new one, *Nearer My God to Thee*, and played it and played it and played it. At first, everybody thought it was the most beautiful hymn he had ever heard. But they played it so much, they wore it out, and no one could stand to hear it anymore.

"Enough! *Enough!* Tell them to play something else!" shouted General Hancock. "They'll still be playing that goddamn thing on the road to Hades!"

THE EXHAUSTED ARTILLERYMEN busied themselves well into the wee hours with replacing dead and wounded horses and their traces, cutting fuses and refilling the caissons with shot, shell and canister so that all would be in readiness for action by dawn.

Soldiers hear hymns and songs of home and wish like fire that this war was over, so they could all go back to their other lives and live as friends once more. Then bugles blare, drummers sound the long roll, and the army stirs itself awake; and even reflective men must turn back into soldiers again. Commands are shouted, battle lines are drawn, blood will surge and all will reach back to heed some long ago and distant inner self that makes war seem glorious, until surely once again it becomes too terrible.

But for now, in this night, the bands have stopped, and there is silence at last. You can close your eyes and make yourself believe that nothing happened here — except for this telltale silence: no whip-poor-wills, no tree frogs, no screech owls, even the silent fireflies are gone.

And in the morning, there will be no birds, no dogs, no roosters, no bleating sheep, no cowbells in the meadow, only pistol shots for wounded horses and the incessant hum of billions of blowflies.

Chapter Seven - Eye of the Storm

I cannot sleep it seems, lest terrors in my dreams
Bring on too soon tomorrow's fight;
I lie here long awake and hear the others make
The little rustling sounds of night.

AS IF OLD THOR DIDN'T GET HIS FILL OF NOISE yesterday, he would come back swinging again today and give it everything he had.

At the first glimmer of light on Friday, the Twelfth Corps commenced with an artillery barrage some distance behind us over towards Culp's Hill. I didn't mind so much, because I had tossed and turned all night anyway. I kept having nightmares about a man with no face.

"What did you do with my face?" he cried, as I shrunk back away from him.

"I didn't do nothing with it!" I screeched.

"You should have held on to it! How would you like it if someone cast *your* face aside like it was nothing?"

"I didn't reckon you'd ever turn up!"

The specter commenced to moan and groan something awful. I sat bolt upright all a-sweat with my heart pounding away and tried without much success to go back to sleep.

Another thing that gnawed at me was persistent thoughts about the battle that was sure to come today. The officers all said this would be the fight that must be won, and the notion of it kept me up. Everybody else seemed to sleep soundly through the night. I had no more than finally drifted off when I was awakened by Lieutenant Haskell sharply tapping me on the bottom of my feet.

"Up Reisie! Today will be a big day, and you should be ready in case General Meade needs you. Get on over there and stand by," said the lieutenant.

Cemetery Ridge was waking up to an oppressive calm and still short on provisions except a hundred rounds of ammunition for every man. Old timers predicted heavy rain, but the moon was still shining bright in the pre-dawn.

"Everything's so quiet this morning," I said, rubbing my eyes. "You wouldn't think a big battle is coming."

"Oh, yes you would," said Lieutenant Haskell. "This is what sailors call the eye of the storm. When you're in the eye, the storm is all around you and there's no way out without going through it one way or another."

The eastern sky was still red as I entered the Leister house. The house had already attracted a small crowd, including Bum Piles. That Bum! I *swear!* I snuck a quick dipper of water from a bucket outside the door and went in and stood in a corner. Bum stepped over and tousled my hair, much to my embarrassment.

General Meade spoke. "Bum, do you have anything more to report about yesterday?"

"Well, Gen'l Meade, soon after I left y'ins, I went 'n got old Rip and picked my way back over there very carefully," Bum gestured towards Seminary Ridge, "and hung around some. I allus brung along some vejabuls to fetch the rebels, and I guess I make such a raggedy-ass sight, I fit right in and ain't seen as no threat to nobody. So I been pretty much free to move among 'em." Bum raised his eyes. "Thus far, that is; they tolerate me, and ain't nobody run me off yet. But if they was to catch on to what I was up to, that'd be the end of *me.*

"Anyways, I don't know what's wrong over there, but gen'lly they seem all out of sorts with themselves. I din't have much time for lissnin' and lip-readin' b'fore all hell broke loose, but as best as I could make out, some of the officers said Lee and Longstreet had a major fuss about offense aginst defense. The frettin' and jawin' took a while, but you can guess which one uvvum won all the arguments." Bum smiled a little. "But by the time they made out what t'do, most of the day was over. Besides, they'd had to wait 'til noon or past for they people to git done comin' in all the way from Chambersburg.

"So after dark, I come back on over and made my way back up the hill and asked around to find out what happened. I'm sure I can't tell you nothin' Gen'l Warren ain't already told you, so stop me anytime y'like; but anyways, they said they fired a shell over Rose's Woods where I seen all them rebels go in that morning. The rebs looked up all at wunst at the shell hissin' over, and our people seen the flash o' they visors or bayonets or such through the leaves and knowed they was in there thick as bees in clover."

Bum took a breath and a drink of water. "Gen'l Warren had sent a man off to get hep from Sickles's Corps, and directly he come back without success. Then Warren, he went off hisself to find Sykes and borry a brigade, and Sykes sent fer Barnes to send one, but no one could find Barnes.

"Then one of Barnes's brigades come up – a Colonel Strong, or Colonel Vincent, I think he was …."

"Colonel Strong Vincent," responded General Meade.

"… Colonel Strong Vincent, then," continued Bum, "And he took it on his ownself to go on up without waiting for orders, and it was well that he did, fer the rebels come out of the woods along Plum Run at that very minute and tried fer all they was worth to take the hill, but they couldn't do it. If he'd o' been a minute later, it'd a been *too* late."

"We surely owe them," said General Hancock.

"Well, they paid dearly for it," said Bum, "but they give out wors'n they got. I seen dead rebels all over the place all the way from the run on up. It was such bad ground to send men over, all them boulders and vines; it almost made you feel sorry for 'em.

"The rebs had sharpshooters down in Devil's Den, and they took to pickin' off officers up on the hill, I'm sorry to say. I heerd tell they got that Colonel Vincent b'fore long. Then some time later they got Gen'l Weed after he come up. Then they picked off Hazlett, the battery captain, when he went to hep Weed. Then O'Rorke come up, and his boys didn't even have time to load and went into line with empty muskets, but they no more'n done that," Bum shook his head, "when they got O'Rorke. His men fired down from the cover of the boulders, and they was well protected and all like that, but the officers, they think they got to stand up there and look brave and expose themselves with they hand in they tunic, which seems right foolish to me." Bum shook his head again. "Blamed poor thing to die for."

"It is grievous about Vincent and Paddy O'Rorke and Weed," said General Meade. "We served together in Fifth Corps."

"I'm sorry to say it is," said General Warren. "Paddy would have headed this army some day."

"Yes, I think he would have," said General Meade.

"He was first in his class in '61, only two years out of West Point."
Now General Hancock shook *his* head.

"So was Hazlett," said General Warren. "It was a remarkable bunch,
'61. Paddy was a couple years older than the others. There are a lot more
of them on this field: Custer, Kilpatrick, Ames, Woodruff, Cushing, Up-
ton, and we are certain to lose some others before this is over."

General Hancock spoke again. "And I regret like hell to tell you that
I lost Ed Cross yesterday and Sam Zook lies mortally wounded this morning. I considered them to be the best brigade commanders in the army."

"I agree," said General Meade.

A lot of sparrows falling these days.

Bum continued. "They say the rebs charged them boys from Maine
five times. The Maine boys ran out of ammanition and had to pick up
what they could from the dead and wounded until they finally run out of
that, too. Then the colonel ordered a bayonet charge, and I guess the rebs
had run out of steam by then, 'cause they was jist whipped and the Maine
boys captured pert near the whole lot – and they done it with empty muskets and just they bayonets!

"But not much wonder. They say them same rebels come twenty-five
mile from Chambersburg that morning, and then were made to do all that
counter-marchin' after they got here. They didn't have no chance to stop
for water and finally sent a couple boys out with all the canteens, but both
uvvum got captured, so the rest went into the fight all lathered up, marched
out and dyin' o' thirst. After five charges in the heat, no wonder they finally
give up."

GENERAL MEADE THANKED BUM FOR HIS REPORT, and Bum said his
goodbyes and promptly left the house. Once again, I marveled at the extent of Bum's knowledge of all that was going on. After Bum left, General
Butterfield said, "How the hell does that old coot always seem to know so
much?"

"Bum Piles is a rare species, a real hen's tooth," said General Meade,
"and he's been invaluable to me. For all his poor appearance, in some ways
he borders on genius. There are few people of any rank or station who

know as much about what's going on as he does. He has amazing skills of observation and deduction. What's more, he's more concerned for his country than he is for himself. He's never asked for a thing except to borrow a horse. He knows what's going on because he wanders all around at the risk of his life, and nobody sees him because he's so plain, he disappears. He's sharp as a tack, has the memory of an elephant and the eye of a chicken hawk." I had been around him long enough to know that this came as an uncommon testimonial from General Meade. It made me proud to know Bum; I almost wanted to tell them he was a friend of my family, Gramma aside.

General Newton spoke. "There's something rather strange about the way the rebels fought these last two days. I can't put my finger on it, but something is missing ... is it old Stonewall? Ewell did a fine job as his replacement until Wednesday when he just seemed to peter out. So many of their brigades have turned in half-assed performances or just couldn't seem to get going. Greene held off Johnson's whole division from Culp's Hill. He had a pretty strong position, but still ...." General Newton looked off somewhere. "Hill went in poorly on Wednesday; Longstreet seems to be dragging his feet, and Jeb Stuart is nowhere to be found.

"Some prisoners claim Stuart's cavalry hasn't reported for days, and Lee is all out of sorts over it. Yesterday, they fought like hell as usual but just couldn't bring it off. Lucky for us something is definitely missing over there."

General Hancock spoke next. "I think Sickles's dumb stunt threw them off balance for one thing. I'm not sure how Lee wanted Longstreet to go in, but I'm sure he didn't mean for him to wait until the best part of the day was almost over. And he surely didn't figure on Sickles being where he was. But why did they let us beat them to that all-important little hill? All too often, they would have snatched it from us, but they dawdled around and then they tried to take it straight on after it was impossible to do so."

General Newton took another turn. "Wright carried our line last evening but had no support and had to withdraw, thank the Good Lord. I know it was hard to see what was going on at that hour, but where was Anderson? Why didn't he support him? Why didn't Wright know he *needed* support and send for it in time to do himself some good? How long does it take to gallop a mile with a message? Two minutes? *Three* minutes? It's almost as if it's in the stars that nothing is working right for them."

"Stars bullshit! Maybe the ones on your shoulder!" snapped General Hancock. "We just whipped their ass this time. Lee didn't manage his battle close enough. He rarely does. It's not his style. But he was mistaken this time. The stakes were just too damn high to let things ride. I agree they haven't been up to snuff, and I think things did get off track somewhere. All the more reason Lee should have seen the need to take command when the day wasn't going right."

General Meade said, "Post mortems are always easier, and this thing is not over by any means. We repulsed them yesterday, but we've not seen the last of them. They've been bringing artillery out up and down the line. Some say it may be to cover a retreat, but I believe such is only wishful thinking. Lee is not done with us yet. I think he aims to hit us just about where we sit." With that, General Meade rode out for an inspection of the line from Ziegler's Grove down to Little Round Top.

As the morning mists lifted from the field, we looked across to see a foreboding sight. From one end of Seminary Ridge to the other, they had rolled their artillery forward onto the plain, well over one hundred strong - ominous, defiant and threatening. The battlefield had become strangely quiet, and we were in doubt as to whether they were making ready to attack or retreat, but surely one or the other.

GENERAL HUNT, HEAD OF ARTILLERY, was about to mount up when several batteries opened on rebel skirmishers out in front of Ziegler's Grove in the direction of the Bliss farm which would change hands some said as many as ten times that day. General Hunt about had a fit.

"Ride up there," he directed a staff officer, "and order Hays's gunners to cease firing! Cease firing, goddamn it! What a waste of ammunition! Remind them that each shell costs the taxpayer $2.67! Shelling a skirmish line is like swatting flies with a sledgehammer. God*damn* it!" The staff officer spurred his horse up the back side of Cemetery Ridge like a shot.

"A goddamn waste for nothing," is the way General Hunt summed up the action. He rode the line instructing his gunners to hold their fire until they had good reason and to concentrate on each enemy battery one at a time and to make every shot count. Good reason would come soon enough.

Then the rebels at the Bliss farm shelled our batteries in front of Second Corps off and on until an hour or so before noon. One shell struck a limber that blew up and set off two caissons in Cushing's battery in a tremendous explosion. In spite of it, Cushing fired on the rebels and blew up one of their caissons in return. Finally, we sent a regiment to go over and burn down the Bliss farm so the rebels couldn't use it to shoot from – a sad thing for the Bliss family, but that ended that.

GENERAL GIBBON'S DIVISION HEADQUARTERS occupied ground that was central to the main line and was just over Cemetery Ridge from General Meade's headquarters. It looked across to the center of the enemy's line, which made it a popular observation point. Thus, it often served as the crossroads gathering place for generals and top brass to pause for coffee and jaw awhile, such as in the present instance.

One by one the generals had departed the session at the Leister house and made their way over Cemetery Ridge to stare across at the enemy through their field glasses. Other generals and officers of lesser rank joined them there. On this particular day, about noon on Friday, there was enough brass milling and strutting around the Second Division coffee pot to "start a spittoon factory," as they say.

Among those present included Generals Butterfield, Warren, Hunt, Hancock, Gibbon, Howard, Newton, Doubleday, Caldwell, Lt. Haskell and two other generals heretofore unknown to me: Brigadier General Alexander Hays, and Brigadier General William Harrow ... and Yours Truly.

I had asked Lieutenant Haskell why no one seemed to warm up to General Butterfield.

"Butterfield has blinders on and they point straight up. He never sees anyone beneath him." he answered. I thought I knew enough about General Meade already that it seemed out of character that he would keep someone like that in such a key position and said so. Lieutenant Haskell answered, "Butterfield was Hooker's man, and that was only five days ago. General Meade will keep him on a little while, because he needs his expertise and knowledge of the army. I didn't say he wasn't smart."

I felt as out of place as somewhere between a stray cat and a pissant in a crowd like that and decided early on to make myself as small as possible and keep my trap shut tight unless spoken to, and even then I might pretend I had lockjaw.

But my young brain was wide-awake, and I strained to remember all the details I could until I *could* write everything down. I have always been blessed with a good memory, and it has proved invaluable throughout my life. I was able to remember a string of numbers a mile long and used to show off with it in school. And, of course, in such distinguished company as this, I was all ears to begin with. Many years later, I read what General Ulysses S. Grant had written about his son's ability to report what he saw:

> "My son accompanied me throughout the campaign and siege, and caused no anxiety either to me or his mother, who was at home. He looked out for himself and was in every battle of the campaign. His age, then not quite thirteen, enabled him to take in all he saw, and to retain a recollection of it that would not be possible in more mature years."

I gathered up as much information as I could from what I heard being said around me. All of it had little impact on my ability to predict what would happen next except to say that it sounded to me like a powerful force had concentrated to whip the rebels and send them packing off south.

THE ARMY SEEMED WELL PREPARED for whatever might come this day. It was now in a defensive posture and under appropriate direction and leadership and awaiting the next move of the enemy. There was little for anyone to do therefore but wait. Consequently, the manner of the generals became casual, conversational. I thought it remarkable that here we were facing a pending attack that could well strike us right where we stood and yet nothing much was being said about it. I guess they all knew they would know what to do when the time came.

I found I couldn't much write and listen at the same time. But if I paid attention and wrote down a reminder word or two, such words would usually bring most of it pretty well to mind later on. "Hunt-Warren-Lincoln" was enough to remind me of the following:

General Warren said to General Hunt, "A congressman's job from his first day is to run for re-election. He must. Other than that, he spends most of his days in Congress taking safety in numbers. If he finds time to do anything of value, we ought to be grateful for it."

"Or at least surprised by it," said General Hunt. "A politician must also learn to speak so that most people will think they hear him say what they want him to say. That way of doing doesn't appeal to me very much, and even though the President is masterful at it, I think much of his message goes over most people's heads."

"I disagree." said General Warren. "The President aims for where their heads ought to be. He speaks in terms that are easy for people to understand and uses his superb persuasiveness to nudge them in the direction he wants them to go. He has keen instincts for just how far he can push a thing before he loses the support of the people. And he is flexible in the details. Except for saving the Union, he is willing to listen to any argument even though it may not be consistent with his own." At least I think that's pretty much what General Warren said, and I did copy some of it down in his exact words.

About then, General Hunt excused himself from the gathering to ride the line again to see to the gun crews and make sure all guns were properly posted and in readiness for what might come.

There were several other conversations going on at the same time:

General Hancock was having one of his own. "I have great respect for Wadsworth," he said. "He could buy and sell the lot of us and have more left over than we'll all see if we live to be a hundred. He could have had any number of jobs that would entitle him to wear a general's stars, yet even though he is past his prime, he prefers to go out there and put his life on the line. He fights because he's a soldier at heart; you can see it in his face. On the other hand, Sickles fights because he loves a scrap — and the uniform helps him strut."

"Isn't Wadsworth a Quaker?" asked General Howard.

"Oh, *hell* no. But I think Meredith is, or *was*," answered Hancock.

"But Quakers are against war," said Newton.

"Well, who the hell's *for* it?" bellowed Hancock.

"Well, obviously somebody must be for it, or all these people wouldn't be here," put in General Hays. "If barbarians threaten your house and home, you sure as hell don't send for the Quakers — Meredith or Wadsworth excepted."

General Gibbon poked the fire and stared into it before speaking. "War is like a monstrous lie. You can't apologize or back down or ever make it right. The only way to be truthful is never to tell the first lie. The only way to avoid war is never to fire the first shot."

"Well, damned if *you* ain't in the wrong business!" said Hancock.

"I'm in the business to end war, not to make it," answered Gibbon.

General Meade, who had just returned from his inspection ride, spoke up. "The answer, Hancock, is that a lot of people were for it, but that was before they knew how bad it would get."

"How *could* anyone know?" said General Howard. "There's never been a war like this one."

"By God, if that's not so," said Hancock. "All the same, this war has been good to some of us. Look at Bobby Lee, he's up four grades in two years, and before the war, it took him thirty years to make Colonel. War is hell, all right, but not for everybody."

"You could say that about a lot of us, Hancock," said General Meade. "You're up *five* grades in two years, yourself."

"I said it has its good side. Anyway, when the men in the ranks go home, we'll all be something less than generals again. Isn't that about what 'brevet' means? Here today and gone tomorrow?" asked General Hancock.

General Hays, said, "Them over there and us over here, both praying and beseeching the Good Lord to carry them to glory and victory. Both claiming Him to be on their side. Yet, both good and bad will fall just as dead, or survive just as mean. If the Good Lord ain't confused, I sure as hell am."

"Come, now, Hays," said General Meade again. "It says in Matthew, *'He maketh His sun to rise on the evil and the good, and sendeth rain on the just and on the unjust.'* God doesn't intervene with reward or punishment every little whipstitch. We have a monumental task before us, and we must make the best use of whatever God gives us to work with."

Heck, even I knew that much.

"'The *Lord helps he who helps himself,'*" General Meade continued. "We've got to win this fight by using everything well that God has provided – our hearts, our minds, our souls and a faith that even reaches above all that. That's what's got us all to here. Don't you agree, Howard?"

General Howard scooted some unburned pieces of wood into the embers with the toe of his boot. "I think there's more to it than that, sir. You'll forgive me, General Meade, when I say I prefer to leave the subject of God's intentions to prayer and to leave understanding His purpose to faith. I have no such compunctions about war and politics, however.

"This army is the best army we've ever had. Lee has come into our country now and has isolated himself physically and psychologically. If we can't stop him now, we never will. He'll be free to roam our countryside. Washington will fall. The President and his cabinet will be arrested and tried as criminals. The country will accrue to the hands of a slave-owning minority, and the ideal of a government run by the people will be gone and forever lost the world over. The institution of slavery will prevail … and obtain until heaven *knows* when.

"We could afford our losses in Virginia, because we could come back home, lick our wounds and fight again another day. In this instance we *are* home. If the enemy gains the upper hand here, he will cut us to pieces. This is the one fight we cannot lose."

"I think that says it all, General Howard," said General Meade.

General Hancock spoke up again. "Well, we can discuss all this 'til Kingdom Come and still not have everyone see it the same way."

"The wonder of this country is that ordinary people are free to struggle to their own ends and improve their lot in life. Abraham Lincoln's struggle made him President, as we all know," said General Warren.

It was General Gibbon's turn again. "Ten thousand poor Mexicans could struggle until Kingdom Come, and none would ever become president of anything. It's more than struggle; it's struggle plus emergence, the right to emerge. The only thing that could stop Lincoln from becoming President was the voters. The only thing that stops you and me from being rich is failure to believe in ourselves and the absence of a good idea. That's the difference."

"Don't forget white skin. You won't get very far if you don't have white skin," said General Howard. (After the war, a college for Negroes and freed slaves was established in Washington and named in honor of General Howard.)

I felt privileged to be present during such fascinating exchanges. Heretofore, most of my experience with adult insight was limited to such gems as "'Bout time to plant taters, ain't it?" – or the one aimed at cutting off conversation or sending children from the room: "Little pitchers have big ears!"

General Meade stood up. "And now, if you will excuse me gentlemen, it's time to return to quarters."

"Me too. Enough of this bullshit. I've got to move on, gentlemen," responded General Hancock, rising from his cracker box. His action triggered the rest of them to do likewise. They all got up and dusted the seats of their pants and began to drift off and return to their duty posts. After they were all out of earshot, General Gibbon turned to Lieutenant Haskell and said, "I'd walk through Hell on hot coals for Hancock any day of the week, as would this whole army, but he can also be a pain in the ass when he's full of bluster, which is most of the time," and turning to me, he said, "Don't you ever repeat that, boy."

"No, *sir!* Not 'til I'm an old man, anyways."

"Well, that's all right; we'll all be gone by then."

The thought troubled me in a way that was new. It was as if, for the first time, I came to the conclusion that no one lived forever. I realized that if war didn't take these men, in time they would all be gone anyway, as would Gramma and Ma and Pa, and me too, someday. I guess I hadn't thought about it like that before and I didn't like the feeling at all. All these strong and brave men were about to stand against a fearful enemy, and no one knew what that enemy would do next if not stopped right here on these very fields I had roamed all my life. Some would die here, but all the rest would die, too – someday. I pondered how so many things were not as important as I once thought, because we would all be gone in the years ahead anyhow.

Take swearing, for instance. I was brought up without swearing in the house, but it's a lot different in the army. Most officers, with the exception of General Hancock, reserved swearing for situations of extreme stress or anger. I had never been around a person who was as free with profanity as General Hancock. The sound of it came as an unpleasantness to my inexperienced ears, and yet it never made sense to me that people got all het up if anyone said words like "hell" and "damn" and, heaven forbid, "*goddamn.*" Yet these self-same people would send their beloved sons out to murder somebody else's beloved sons, call it glory and be a lot more forgiving of it.

I was to hear a lot of profanity during my time with the army. Most of it was never intended as blasphemy but given out under the stress of combat or by those, who, jaded by all they were made to see and endure, had become bereft of the values they had been brought up with. I did notice that the more you heard profanity, the more it lost its power, so that, after a while, it carried no particular punch and sounded just plain stupid.

But in general, I think people make too much of it. I believe if every person that ever lived stood together at one spot on the earth and shouted up curses of every kind imaginable at God for a week, it would certainly detract from their own character, but it wouldn't so much as put a small dent in God. Maybe if we stopped making such a fuss over it, it would disappear altogether.

More important to me is, if 'not a sparrow shall fall that God is not mindful of it,' there's one heck of a lot of people that have some pretty fine answering to do about their part in this war when the time comes. I concluded that God surely doesn't mind if you slip up and say a few bad words but would greatly prefer that everybody would stop this war in its tracks. Once they get going, I don't think there's any way to stop them, like General Gibbon said. Forgive me for saying so, but if God Himself appeared out here on the battlefield and yelled *"STOP!"* I believe they would all just keep on fighting away, except for those who got shot. And in their dying breath, they would get all pious and ask God to forgive them.

Such a way of thinking was apt to be ill received in most quarters – particularly from someone of my tender years – and I never found the right occasion to get advice on the matter. Any words I might come up with to initiate this particular conversation always seemed to get stuck in my throat.

IT HAD BECOME HOT AND STIFLING AGAIN TODAY, and some of the men had set up their shelter halves as best they could along a low stone wall down at the front of the line to eke out a little relief from the summer sun at high noon. Lieutenant Haskell and General Gibbon went off to do things, and left me on my own, so I decided the best thing for me to do was to go make myself handy to General Meade.

A little before noon, I returned from coffee headquarters up on the line and took up my corner in the Leister house 'parlor.' The general dealt with a flurry of staff and couriers coming and going back and forth between headquarters and the battlefield until a little past midday. Some of the horses had been ridden hard all morning and were on their last legs. I busied myself with keeping fresh water on the porch and sweeping out the muddy clods left from a hundred pairs of boots.

After that, I rode with the general back over the ridge to Second Corps, and the first thing that caught my attention was Lieutenant Haskell bent over a huge shallow iron vessel that was bubbling and sending out the most maddening smells of something delicious. He was stirring the contents with a giant spoon.

"General Meade," said General Gibbon, "Lieutenant Haskell has scared us up a couple chickens which he has stewed for dinner. Will you have some, sir?"

"Chickens! Where in thunder did you find chickens? And please don't tell me."

"We'd be proud if you would join us, General. Will you please do so?"

"Well, I really don't have time to sit and jaw, but I can't imagine that I won't pause under the circumstances for a piece of that chicken," allowed the general with a faint smile.

Lieutenant Haskell spooned out to each guest, including me, a piece of the sacrificial birds and some of the potatoes and onions that had been bubbling in the broth and tantalizing all assembled. "It's a shame you went and executed this poor old rooster, Haskell," said General Hancock while making loud sucking noises upon the piece he held between two fingers. "This fellow must've had quite a history. Anything this old has a right to retire in peace and honor."

"Well, not around here, it doesn't, General. That only counts in civilized times," Haskell shot back. "Around here, if it's edible, it gets eaten." About the same time he had come back with the chickens, Lieutenant Haskell had brought along a huge loaf of bread he had rescued from a hog. They caught the poor beast hurrying along with the loaf and took it away from him, dusted it off and cut it to serve with the chicken. The hog got away, lucky it only cost him his bread. "Orderly," said Lieutenant Haskell, "fetch some butter for General Meade."

The generals lollygagged and allowed themselves to grow a bit somnolent in the noonday heat. General Meade issued orders for the provosts (they would later come to be called military police) to return to their units and be ready to serve on the firing line. They would be of greater use there than scouting about for skulkers and skedaddlers whose value was questionable at best. The other generals were swarmed with staff and orderlies coming and going as the hour moved well past noon.

Old Jack, who was sprawled at rest off to one side after enjoying a handout of bones pitched his way after each man got all he could from them, rose bolt upright and sniffed the air. Suddenly, from over on Seminary Ridge, came the report of a cannon. Then, soon after, another.

"That's a signal gun," said Hancock. "I think we'd better eat fast!"

✠ ✠ ✠

Just after one o'clock on the afternoon of July 3, 1863, in the largest cannonade ever heard in the western world, the Confederate artillery opened up and fired continuously for an hour and a half. Upwards of one hundred fifty guns sent no less than fifteen thousand rounds bursting and falling around and about the men defending Cemetery Ridge, an average of three to five rounds per second. We were later told that they could hear the noise in Pittsburgh to the west and Philadelphia to the east, describing a radius of upwards of two hundred miles.

For more than a mile from one end of the line to the other, white puffs of smoke announced the deadly missiles speeding toward us. As the orderly returned with the butter for General Meade, a solid shot cut the poor man in half, making it impossible for me to continue eating. General Hancock rose and announced, "Well, boys, I'd say dinner was over!"

Officers ran about grabbing for the bridle of their horses. General Gibbon's orderly was mangled and killed by a shot while bringing him his horse. The horse galloped off without him and was never seen again.

"Stick with me for now, Reisie," shouted Lieutenant Haskell above the shells now bursting around us. "I think it would be better to stay out of General Meade's way now and make yourself scarce." Well, as long as I had to be where I was, I couldn't think of a better place than with Lieutenant Haskell.

Old Jack disappeared. I guess the noise and commotion were more than he could take. Someone told me he had taken refuge under the Leister house, where he holed up most of the afternoon.

You could look up and follow the projectiles by the hissing sound some of them made, and now and then you could catch a glimpse of the shells as they passed over. Soon, our artillery set in to answering the enemy fire, but it seemed to me as though our guns were not firing nearly as fast as theirs. Someone said General Hunt made our men pick their shots carefully by limiting the batteries to one round every two minutes to conserve ammunition for the assault that was sure to follow. The sharp commands of the gun crews rang out above the din and the stinging smoke. The rebels fired solid shot to disable our guns, and the ground was torn up where they struck as cleanly as a plowed furrow.

The rebels' aim was a little high, and many shells cleared the low crest of Cemetery Ridge and fell among the non-combatants and reserves posted on the low ground around Rock Creek sending hundreds of wagons streaming to the rear in panic. According to General Gibbon, each time a gun is fired, the recoil causes the trail (that part of the gun that sticks out behind like a long tongue) to dig into the earth a little bit, raising the muzzle end and causing it to fire a tiny bit higher each time. Soon, the rebel gunners couldn't see the effects of their fire for the heavy smoke and didn't realize they needed to reset the elevations on their pieces. But now and then, a lucky shot hit a caisson, and the shells and powder exploded with a thunderous, deafening roar, sending shrapnel flying and raining down everywhere and eliciting cheers from the rebels across the way.

One gun crew frantically ran its guns down to the stone wall to fire over the heads of our men crouching there to receive the enemy. The artillerists, stripped to the waist and black as darkies, sweating, some bleeding from their ears, remained at their posts amidst the incoming shells and the clouds of choking smoke.

Soldiers took cover as best they could. There was no rock, however small, that was not sheltering some head pressed up against it. Still, the rain of death took its toll. The spinning razor-sharp pieces of shrapnel could not miss among men packed along the ridgeline. Some were blown apart and died instantly; others had limbs sliced off and lived a little longer. Many lay helpless and bled to death. One foolish young man tried to stop a solid shot bounding down the back side of the ridge with his foot. The shot caught him at the ankle and sent his foot tumbling down the hill ahead of him and left him howling and crying in the dirt.

Strangely enough, in the constancy of the bombardment, the stress, the heat and the humidity, some men were lulled into a torpor and fell asleep. Some old veterans smoked and sat quietly; some continued to play cards while others up on the line laid out cartridges for easy reach. Some had laid out and made ready as many as four loaded muskets with which each man would soon greet the enemy. It being too dangerous for the stretcher bearers to move about, the wounded stayed where they fell and waited in agony for help to come.

AFTER THE POUNDING HAD BEEN GOING ON for the best part of an hour, General Gibbon shouted to Lieutenant Haskell, "Come on, Haskell, let's take a walk!" And to me, he says, "You, too, Reis. Come with us. Let's go out where it's a little quieter!" Well now, amidst all that was going on, I just marveled that General Gibbon would remember my name at all, let alone use it.

General Gibbon was born in Pennsylvania but raised from childhood in North Carolina and still retained that soft, southern accent. He remained loyal to the Union when the war broke out. A fellow officer once said of him, "John Gibbon is the most American of Americans. He has an up and down manner of telling the truth no matter whom it hurts. A tower of strength, he is cool as a steel knife, always unmoved by anything and everything."

The ground out in front was almost unmarked, since there was little there for either side to shoot at. The three of us stepped over the wall and the defenders crouching there and went forward into the field.

"How are you men faring?" asked General Gibbon.

"Oh, just bully, General! We're beginning to like it here."

We walked out directly in front of our lines. I guess the general figured the enemy would make this spot plenty hot soon enough, but for now, it seemed the safest place to be with all the shells whizzing overhead in both directions. It is amazing how many different sounds can come from artillery rounds passing over. I looked back towards Cemetery Ridge, and the entire line from Ziegler's Grove down to George Weikert's house appeared to be consumed by smoke and fire and exploding shells.

I looked up at the brilliant flashes of light as some of them exploded overhead with white puffs of smoke carried away by the wind. At times, and at the proper angle, you could actually see them in their trajectory. Weeks later, Lieutenant Haskell eloquently described the bursting of shells in a long letter to his brother that was made into a book destined to become a classic.

"Their flash was a bright gleam of lightning radiating from a point, giving place in the thousandth part of a second, to a small, white, puffy cloud, like a fleece of the lightest, whitest wool."

There is no description that can come close to what it feels like to be under bombardment. I was scared out of my wits but tried not to show it. The noise hurt like Hades. The sound was so overpowering that before long it seemed to come from within. The earth itself took it up and lifted and vibrated everything with a steady and mounting violence. The sound became something more than sound, beyond anything I'd ever heard before, painful, disabling, and I desperately wanted it to stop. I could feel it and taste it and smell it. I felt angry and hated the rebel guns for this unending assault on my senses.

Further out was a pit where dead horses had been dumped yesterday. Some of the men on the line had sought to take refuge there and General Gibbon sent them back. "You are in the hands of God. No one place is safer than another. Go back to your posts."

"I belong to no church," General Gibbon said to us, "but I have always felt in the hands of God in combat. Whether I am harmed or not is His will, and therefore I have always been willing to go where duty demanded, whatever the danger."

Another hundred yards or so out from where we stopped, I could see under the smoke that had settled low, our skirmishers, crouching like chessmen, waiting for this to pass.

"WELL, GENERAL, ARE WE IN A FIX OR NOT?" asked Lieutenant Haskell.

"I'd say we are, but just for the moment," answered General Gibbon. "I'd like to hold my final word on that opinion at least until sundown – if we're still around to talk about it by then."

"Look around you," said General Gibbon. "This place was so beautiful, and now we're tearing the blazes out of it. War is always tearing things up."

"Yes, it is true," answered Lieutenant Haskell.

"In Virginia, all the fences are gone, and all the trees are gone. After the war, there won't be any way to put up fences to keep the animals out of the crops. If you think that won't be a hardship ...." General Gibbon let the thought hang there for a while.

"I don't know what is left of North Carolina. I can't go back, because everybody there hates me now for being a damnyankee. I don't suppose there's a whole lot left to go home to, anyway. Maybe I'll seek a post out west after this thing is over before they tear that up, too."

"They can't. There's too much of it," offered Lieutenant Haskell.

"They'll find a way. It'll take longer, but they'll find a way. They'll tear the people up, too, the Indians, and the day will come when you won't recognize it," said the general.

"A few people argued until they were blue in the face to keep this war from happening, but all too many on both sides were quick to send the armies out to settle what the politicians could not or would not or did not want to. It was hard to find anybody against the idea, as I recall."

"I'd say that's a fair statement," said Lieutenant Haskell.

The general continued, "Society must take measures to prevent its citizens from invoking violence upon each other, and except in matters of self-defense, violence is condemned. The rules of warfare are just the opposite. Men are praised, decorated and eulogized for bringing that same violence upon the host, whether or not the individual members of that host are guilty of transgressions or not."

Now, General Hancock rode up out of the smoke to our small gathering with aides and couriers flocking around him like moths to a lantern. Major General Winfield Scott Hancock was an imposing figure and carried with him an infusion of spirit that spread throughout the army wherever he went. When he rode the lines, the cheer would go up, "Hancock is here, and we will lick them now!" He was as handsome as you'd want. He wore his hat at a jaunty angle, and the white shirt that peered out from under his uniform was worn clean every day "come hell or high water." He sat tall in the saddle and his commands were direct and decisive. He exuded courage and confidence whether in uniform or not.

"Just what have you boys got going for yourselves out here, a picnic?" he shouted.

"No, no, General. We're just trying to figure out how to improve the world." General Gibbon shouted back. "I came from east Pennsylvania, but I was raised a southerner. I have three brothers somewhere over there wearing Confederate gray. I will fight for the Union, and I will die for the Union, but every now and then, I try to look at things the way I might have if I had stayed down there like my brothers did.

"Their state and the people in it believe that membership in the Union is now, and forever should be, entirely voluntary. Would I not believe it was my state's right to withdraw, if I felt that that membership was no longer in the best interests of its citizens?"

"Forgive me for playing the lawyer here," said Lieutenant Haskell, "but the answer is not that cut and dried, General. We are the *United* States, but we are also, nonetheless, the *several* states. Are we a nation or are we a collection of states? The South has always argued on the side of state sovereignty, state's *rights*. Even the founding fathers held differing opinions on the subject, but that's all right. Differences of opinion are inherent in a free society, and all views need to be heard, because sooner or later, deaf ears will bring big trouble."

"Some states agreed to unite with the understanding that they could leave if it became in their best interest to do so," shouted General Gibbon above the thunder of the guns. "The states now in rebellion claim that it *was*, and we are sometimes hard pressed to make a case to the contrary. Would it not have been better to let the damn South go its way and good riddance? Not an appealing answer, but would it not have been a better solution than the one we are now caught up in?"

"*No!*" answered General Hancock emphatically. "If you expect to make a success of majority rule – and I hold you cannot have a democratic republic without it – you cannot allow a tyranny of factions. Are we not then in danger of being held hostage by any faction we would be hard pressed to do without? What kind of a country is that?

"What about 'We the people, in order to form a more perfect *union?*' Is that what *those* people are doing over there?" The general swung his arm around towards Seminary Ridge. "Forming a more perfect union? I think not, sir!"

I marveled again that out here with war exploding at their elbows, they were discussing almost anything but.

"I would really like to continue talking on this subject, gentlemen," said General Hancock, "but at such time as I am not quite so heavily engaged and do not have to shout every word I say!"

I came to realize after a while what a special bond there was between these men. Sadly, the day would come when death and hard feelings would break this marvelous brotherhood apart. For now, however, I was awestruck to be in their presence and privileged to be witness to these qualities.

Here they sat with tons of shells going over and chewing the fat as if nothing was happening or for that matter was about to happen. It certainly had a salutary effect on my fears and discomforts in the situation.

YESTERDAY, I HAD TOLD LIEUTENANT HASKELL a funny story about my Uncle Reb, for what reason I have forgotten now, but at the time it was apropos of something, and now he insisted I re-tell it. This was no doubt a courtesy to allow me to feel at ease in this distinguished company and had little to do with their interest in hearing my story at such a time as this.

My Uncle Reb worked at a sawmill that lay straight across the river from where he lived, but he had to walk two miles downriver to the nearest bridge and then walk another two miles up the other side to the sawmill. He got the bright idea that he would make himself a small flatboat and pole across, thus saving himself a four-mile walk every morning and every evening.

Well, he did just that. The boat he made was a little bitty thing for a man as big as he was. The morning of its maiden voyage, Uncle Reb had, in his way of making light, worn a small bowtie for the occasion. He was a huge man, and he stepped into his little skiff, struggled to remain vertical, and poled away. Unfortunately for him, he had never thought to give the thing a test run, and his massive weight sunk the tiny vessel, leaving him standing there in water up to his bowtie. He looked up to see an Irishwoman staring down on him from up on the bank. He glowered up at her.

"Mister! What in the name o' heaven would ye be doin' down there standin' in water up to your necktie?" she asked.

"I'm going to work, lady! What the hell does it look like I'm doing?"

"*Ach!* Well, might ye be goin' to work again tomorrow, sor? I'd like to bring me kiddies down to watch."

In telling the story, I think that was the first time I had ever used a swearword in my whole life. Everyone laughed and rose up, signaling the end of our strange little interlude.

About then, the cannonade began to fall off. Even so, the pain of the noise still lingered in the air and filled the void with ominous expectation. General Meade had earlier agreed for the artillery to gradually cease firing so the enemy might be tricked into thinking he had put our guns out of action and to lure him into the open to begin his assault.

And then the field fell silent.

THE DRIFTING SMOKE BEGAN TO CLEAR, and, as if by magic, a massive line of rebels appeared from out of the concealing woods of Seminary Ridge. They arrayed themselves for battle all the way from Pitzer's Woods for a mile or more toward town. Sunlight gleamed on thousands of burnished muskets, and red Confederate battle flags fluttered in a light breeze. The men on Cemetery Ridge looked over in awe at one of the greatest armies ever raised and held their breath.

"Now, the real fun begins," said General Hancock. He turned to the men who had come with him and others who had come up and gathered around. He addressed them. His eyes and theirs glistened as he spoke.

"Gentlemen, this artillery fire will be followed by an infantry assault upon our lines. If we win, the war may soon be over. This battle will be the turning point of the war, and our fine army is about to set the course of this nation for generations to come. No one can tell where any of us will be when this day is over, but before leaving you, I wish to say that I know I speak harshly at times." He struggled gently with the words. "If ... ever at any time ... I have said anything to offend you or hurt the feelings of any one of you, I wish to offer my apology to you now." With that, the general mounted and rode back toward the lines.

Chapter Eight - On God's Side

Young men go forth when cannons roar
To heed the bugle's sound,
Where those who sowed the seeds of war
Are seldom to be found.

THROUGH ALL THAT, AND MIRACLE of miracles, Sally remained tied right where I left her. I had left my two-star pennant sticking up in the saddle hoping it would keep everyone away, and I guess it must have worked. I mounted and raced over to the Leister House where everything was in total chaos and confusion.

Bursting shells had killed all the mounts of General Meade's staff. The bodies of several orderlies and sixteen dead horses littered the yard. Couriers were coming and going in a steady stream, and the general's staff was running about in all directions and looking for mounts. General Butterfield had been struck by a shell fragment and was taken away by ambulance before I got there. I dismounted, and there was still enough noise that it was all I could do to hold Sally from running off and taking me with her.

Two officers were about to come to fisticuffs over the fact that one had shot the other's horse. The first man's horse had been severely wounded, and, in an extreme of excitement and confusion, he had pulled out his pistol to administer a *coup de grace* and shot the other man's perfectly good horse by mistake. At the sight of General Meade riding up, they backed off and calmed down. Some of his staff had collected behind the house for protection, and he chided them for thinking they were any more safe on one side of a "cracker box" than the other.

Several cannonballs that overshot the ridge had hit the house. The little porch roof had been blown away and there was a hole in the roof of the room usually occupied by General Meade. Mrs. Leister's modest little house, barn and property that was never much to start with had been shot up and torn to pieces. Tree limbs were down everywhere and all manner of debris was scattered around. The paltry little implements with which Mrs. Leister worked her garden patch were flung about, trampled and broken.

The general dismounted and paused before going inside. A late solid shot grazed him while he stood in the doorway. General Meade took it in stride as if cannonballs grazed him every day after dinner. A young officer rode up, saluted and spoke to General Meade with breathless sincerity. "With all due respect, General Meade, my exact orders from Provost Marshall General Patrick, if I found you still alive, sir, are to escort you to safer quarters if I have to pry you out of here with a crowbar!"

Somehow, he succeeded and packed off General Meade, snapping and fussing and fuming about it being a bad time to move headquarters. They moved on to a new place a mile or so east. I don't know much about the time it takes to move a headquarters, but this must have been a record, because I no more than blinked, and they were gone. I rode back over the crest of the ridge to Second Corps (thankful that in the confusion no one had tried to take my horse) and told Lieutenant Haskell that the general was moving his headquarters a mile or two east.

THE SCENE ON CEMETERY RIDGE was a dreadful one of death and destruction with broken and burning caissons and wagons strewn everywhere about. The bodies of dozens of dead horses lay scattered and in heaps around the artillery batteries, and the wreckage of the bombardment littered the ridge in all directions. Wounded men were being assisted to the rear, and dead bodies lay all about waiting to be hauled away. Officers everywhere, including Generals Hancock and Gibbon as well as Lieutenant Haskell were shouting orders. General Hunt was riding up and down the ridge line and directing the placement of artillery in anticipation of the rebel assault. Heavy clouds of acrid smoke had returned and hung over everything, covering the terrible scene.

Down by the stone wall, men lay beside the reserves of loaded muskets. Others made ready to load and pass forward a steady stream of muskets so the firepower of our thin line could be sustained without letup.

General Gibbon trained his glasses toward Seminary Ridge and peered through the smoke. "Take a look out there, Haskell. You will never see anything like this again." He lowered his field glasses and handed them over to the lieutenant who put them to his eyes.

"It is a spectacular sight indeed!" said Haskell.

General Gibbon turned to an orderly, "Find General Meade at once and report that the enemy are advancing in great force. Tell him we will need all the help he can send us."

"I never seen the like of it!" I heard a man in the ranks say.

"It's almost beautiful, if you don't think about it," said another.

WE ALL STARED ACROSS AND MARVELED at the magnificent panorama unfolding before us. It was the most fearsome and at the same time the most beautiful thing I ever saw. In all my days, I never saw anything like it again. I knew I would never find the words to describe such a scene anywhere near to what it deserved. I found it hard not to admire something so sublime, even though I knew this massive force would advance within minutes and be dedicated to destroying us, as would we in destroying them.

It was enough to halt the heart of the bravest veteran, and I wondered how many over there in that seemingly solid front faced their ordeal with second thoughts and final prayers. For them, there was in this, their supreme mortal moment, no possibility of turning back, any more than could a man falling from a high place. What madness could have drawn these people together hell bent on their mutual annihilation? Too late for the pondering of imponderables, for that madness had now delivered an immediate and dreadful duty to us all.

General Gibbon had evidently found a horse and was now slowly riding the line encouraging the men to hold their fire, then aim low. "We must hold to the last man," he told them. But each man already knew without being told that all and everything had come down to this moment. Here and now, we must turn them back. Here and now, whoever wins this day determines what course the country will take and whether or not this nation as we know it lives or dies.

The cries began to arise up and down our line.

"Here they come! Here they come!"

"Ready, boys! *Ready!*"

"Remember Fredericksburg!"

Almost imperceptibly the rebel line began to move forward. The sound of their drummers came to us in a soft, murmuring, rhythmic beat, like a subdued growl. There was no rebel yell this time. They were uncharacteristically silent as if to focus on this most desperate measure upon which everything depended.

WHEN THEY WERE ABOUT HALFWAY across the plain, our guns opened on them with shot and shell. When they were nearer still, massed musketry from behind the low stone wall began to pour forth into their ranks a deadly hailstorm of lead.

The Emmitsburg Road runs diagonally between the two opposing ridges, southwest to northeast. A sturdy fence made of huge planks bordered the road on both sides. The rebel line approached at an oblique angle forcing it to cross at a single point along the line of march, much as a wave breaks against the seashore. At another place in the fence, an entire rebel regiment threw its combined weight against it and succeeded in bringing it down on top of some who had already crossed and were lying dead or wounded or had taken cover in the road.

The rebels were now close enough that the smell of them drifted to us. On they came, bent low as if before a great wind. I could see their faces now and saw in them what appeared at first to be fear. Yet it was not ordinary fear. It was an intensity, a monumental stress, a knowing that their hour had come. Unexpectedly, I felt a great pathos for them rise up in me. They seemed like ordinary men, like those I had known and had been taught to respect – men you would see in church or pass on peaceful streets.

The smoke from outgoing rounds and bursting shells combined in dense, drifting clouds, obscuring everything, parting now and then to reveal in a fleeting glance the steady line of men ever closer. Holes appeared where that which had once been men simply disappeared. The holes closed up, were blown open and closed up yet again. Each new rank was blown away, disintegrating, sending arms and legs spinning through the air like war clubs. Everywhere, men were yelling, screaming, cursing … crying, praying, sobbing … dying.

A young general paced back and forth with drawn sword, urging his men to the wall. General Alexander Webb was a brand-new brigadier not yet thirty years old who had been given his brigade the week before. Two of his regiments went forward, and the other two held back much to the general's disgust and humiliation. Finally, he went forward without them. As he stood there with one foot on the wall, he slowly and deliberately lit up a cigar and stared straight into the ranks of the advancing enemy.

Just to my right, the wall stopped in its path and turned east towards the ridgeline. It was just south of that point in the wall where the rebels appeared to be converging directly in front of us!

IN THE MIDST OF ALL THIS, General Hancock came riding the line slowly, appearing and disappearing ghostlike in and out of the smoke. He rode along calmly, and the men took great encouragement from it. It was beyond me how he could make himself such a vulnerable target and not be hit.

A gap had developed just to the left of the position defended by one of Webb's regiments. A colonel ran to General Hancock for permission to take his regiment into the breach just south of a little group of trees and plug the gap. "Yes! Yes! Go *in!* And go in there pretty goddamn quick, sir!" Hancock bellowed above the din. He rode to the left towards some regiments that were pouring a flanking fire into the advancing rebels, fussing and fuming with everyone in his path.

About that time, General Gibbon was struck in the shoulder and fell from his horse. Within minutes, General Hancock was also grievously wounded and lowered from his horse by his staff. As they gathered around him, General Hancock directed them to apply a tourniquet to his leg and twist it with his pistol. His leg bled profusely. "Tighter! Tighter!" yelled the general. "For Christ's sake, don't let me bleed to death!"

One of Webb's reluctant regiments now came down the ridge about halfway to fire over the heads of our men at the wall, and soon joined the others all along the line to pour a deadly fire into the densely packed enemy. Our batteries were using double-shotted canister now, but little by little, the brave artillerymen, who were few in number and totally exposed to enemy fire, were being cut down. Infantrymen on the line left their positions of cover to help serve the guns.

The bombardment had left few of our guns close by in serviceable condition. Those that were left were run by hand down the slope and placed to fire from the wall. Reserve batteries that had been standing by behind Cemetery Ridge were rushed forward to replace those decimated by enemy fire.

Many of the wounded artillerymen remained in the fight. One with his insides torn from him put a pistol to his head and shot himself. I saw the nearest battery commander, who had held his post after being severely wounded, shot through his open mouth and killed as he yelled, *"Fire!"* Others fell among the tangled wreckage of caissons, horses and guns.

Horses were used in many ways, but it seemed to me the worst off were the ones that served the batteries. They were lashed often and rushed forward under desperate circumstances. They were targets for the enemy who sought to disable them. During the bombardment I saw a shell pass through one horse and explode inside another. Some screamed and fell. Others, missing limbs torn off by solid shot or sliced off by shrapnel, struggled to get up and fell again. Still others, wounded in their traces, struggled beside the brave horses that stood their ground. The gun crews at the cemetery had been reluctant to tear up more graves to protect their guns and were being exposed to a murderous fire; after the battle, Lieutenant Haskell counted 71 dead horses of Woodruff's battery alone in an area only fifty yards square.

LIEUTENANT HASKELL HAD GONE OFF for a few minutes and now returned to the field and galloped back and forth in search of General Gibbon or General Hancock. I ran toward him waving my arms for his attention. He spied me, galloped toward me and scooped me up with one arm. I kicked a leg over the saddle behind him and held onto his waist.

"Reis! Where are Gibbon and Hancock?" he shouted.

"They've been shot, sir!" I screamed at him. "I saw them both go down! And they carried them off! I think General Hancock could bleed to death!"

"Hold on tight!" he said. "We are being sorely pressed here and are disposed to act!"

The rebels were firing in earnest now, and balls were hitting all around thick as hail. Although it was a comfort to be with Lieutenant Haskell and have him in front of me, chances were that I had an unknown string of minutes left that might very well run out at any moment. I hoped Ma and Pa and Gramma would learn how I died and be proud of me. God's will be done.

Lieutenant Haskell galloped forward, dropped me off behind an outcropping of rocks near the little group of trees and galloped back to urge the men forward. He spurred to the crest of the ridge, drew his sword and rode among troops who were taking cover there.

"Forward! Forward! This is your purpose now! Who wants to live knowing he failed in the supreme moment of his manhood? *Forward!*" he screamed. "See that thin line at the low stone wall! Those are your *brothers!* Will you leave them to fight alone there?"

Someone yelled that it's a choice between that and certain death. Haskell called out, "Not so! It is *not* certain death. You are no more safe here on this ridge than you would be down at that wall! Many will survive … and *with honor!* Look at *me!* I make a fine target," he reined his horse and raised up in the saddle, "and yet I stand here the only mounted man before the enemy! Look yonder at Webb! He stands at the wall smoking a cigar! He stands there – *unscathed!* It is *not* certain death! *Bugler, sound the advance! Sound the advance! Forward! Forward!*"

The lieutenant began whacking at the reluctant infantrymen with the flat of his sword, and gradually, they began to move. From the ridge, in response to Haskell, a man picked up a battle flag and went forward. The staff was struck and broken and the bearer picked up the stump and went forward again. Men in twos and threes sprang up, and ran toward the wall. Then, as one man, the rest broke and with a loud cheer followed Lieutenant Haskell down to where they too could fire over the heads of the men at the wall. It was an example of leadership that I would never forget.

I looked over and saw a young private a few yards away struggling to force his ramrod into the barrel of his musket, but it would not go in more than a few inches. Evidently, the first cartridge had failed to fire and, unaware of this in the stress of battle, he had added cartridges until he almost filled the barrel. He was swearing and crying in frustration as he tried to no avail to jam the rod in.

There was a dull *thuck!* and a hole the size of a copper appeared in his forehead. His expression was that of a man lost in thought, no pain, no fear – more a blandness. It was not what I would have expected in the face of a dead man, and I thought for an instant that perhaps he was not dead, but dead he was.

GENERAL HUNT APPEARED at the line and began firing his revolver into the mass and screaming, *"See them! See them!"* Even officers were picking up fallen muskets and firing into the enemy host. Somebody picked up a musket and a cartridge box with a handful of cartridges still in it and thrust them at me.

"Here, boy, fetch y'self a little *glory!"*

It was against all my instincts and all I had been raised to believe to fire upon a man. I remember one day after Pa had taught me to shoot I took aim at a bird up high in an old dead tree a couple hundred yards away. I had no expectation of hitting the bird, but I also knew the possibility was there, and I was curious to see if I could do it and anxious to try my skill. I fired. There was an explosion of feathers and the bird's body came spiraling to earth. I was reminded again what Gramma said about falling sparrows.

I felt much regret and was haunted by what I had done. So to shoot a human being was truly unthinkable for me. But would I not fire on someone if it meant life or death for Ma or Pa or Gramma? Yet that was not the case before me; the pressure on me now was of a different kind … an overwhelming pressure, a surge. I was a tiny part of the whole of events that were moving everything in a relentless direction without respect to my own state of mind. And I was angry and embarrassed when I realized I had been crying and discovered I had wet myself yet again. For this alone, I felt angry enough to strike back.

The momentum of the battle now drew me into it. I bit open a cartridge, poured in the powder, rammed in the ball, pulled back the hammer and set the cap. I laid the musket across the rock, pulled the hammer to full cock and pointed it at the approaching enemy. I closed my eyes, and suddenly the gun fired. I don't know if my finger had been tightening of its own accord or whether I simply had come to the edge of conclusion and was disposed to act. I opened my eyes, and as the smoke parted, a young rebel I had noticed before was gone. The possibility that his disappearance was a consequence of what I had just done filled me with remorse.

I began to cry anew and looked about. Others were crying too. Anger rose up within me again, and without thinking, I loaded and fired a second time. Then a third time. All around, everyone was screaming and crying and laughing. Some kept shouting above the tremendous roar of battle, *"Fredericksburg! Fredericksburg!"* Our hair and faces were streaked with sweat and blackened with gunpowder. I added my screams to the multitude. I needed to. It felt good; it felt right.

I fired a fourth time. It had become noticeably easier. Suddenly, in what seemed only a passing of moments, my fingers closed around the last cartridge. I loaded and squeezed the trigger. I had fired them all.

THE REBEL TIDE WAS NOW sweeping up the final rise towards us in a dense cluster of men that must have been twenty ranks deep. As they closed, their rightmost ranks began to bear left and expose their flank to our fire. As they advanced across my front, I took note of one lad in particular.

He was a smooth-faced young rebel on the end of the line, his face streaked with gunpowder, his dark hair plastered to his head. He had no shoes, and the clothes he wore were tattered and pitiful. As he swept along in his determined stride, he stumbled, went down, rose up, stumbled, rose again and went forward. Here he was in a strange and hostile land, far from home, serving his cause and fulfilling his honor as his heart and character demanded of him. I knew at once he would not survive this fight. He would leave this world doing to the best of his ability that which this terrible day required of him. In thinking these thoughts, my mind drifted and my eyes glazed with tears. I rubbed them clear, and when I looked again, he was gone.

Some of the rebels had now reached the wall.

"We've got them now! They're done for! Don't let up on them, boys! *Push them! Push them!* and, by God, they will be *ours!*" cried General Webb.

The mass of men of both sides now convulsed into a dense cloud of smoke and dirt that obscured everything. At this point, no one paid any attention to commands or battlefield order; nothing else mattered except this extreme struggle of destruction and survival.

Amidst the din of battle, a great calm descended over me like a gift from God. I simply became tired of fear. I got weary of the very notion of being afraid anymore. It had worn me out so much I simply let go of it, like something you let slip away because it's become too heavy and hurts too much to hold onto. And in that moment, it was as if I had stepped into another world. Suddenly, I could no longer hear the sounds of battle. Bugles, men's shouts, horses' screams of terror, the ripping of musketry, the reports of cannon all came forth in silence. That I could feel and not hear these sounds somehow seemed comforting, dreamlike, natural.

AS OUR GUNS FIRED THEIR LAST ROUNDS of canister into the face of the enemy, a handful of rebels breached the wall and claimed the two guns just behind it but not for long. The officer leading the charge dashed up to one of the guns, laid his hands on it and claimed it captured. He was immediately hit and fell. All along the line, the rebels took a murderous fire from in front and on both flanks. The brave Pennsylvania regiment held firm at the wall and continued to whittle away at the enemy, reducing their ranks. Beyond the wall, dead rebels had fallen in windrows. Men on both sides kept laughing and crying at the same time, not from fear or joy or sadness but from the agony of extreme stress and emotion.

The rebels were now bunched up in front of the wall in such a mass, they were a certain target for any shot fired from the Union positions. Most could neither retreat nor go forward. They had only the ammunition they brought with them and little of it left. Their officers were down, their colors were down, their buglers were down, and most were stranded without hope, without option and without direction. Some struggled back to the Emmitsburg Road and cleared the fence. The field beyond was streaming with rebels limping and crawling back towards Seminary Ridge.

The Emmitsburg Road came in close on our right. Many rebels had cleared the road but were now pinned down in a shallow swale in front of us. They had no chance of advancing as their charge had faltered and failed, nor could they retire with the fence they had struggled so hard to surmount now between them and the safety of their own lines. As the thinning ranks of their advancing comrades passed over them, those on the ground reached up in their hopelessness to grab their arms and coattails to hold them back from a vain and useless death.

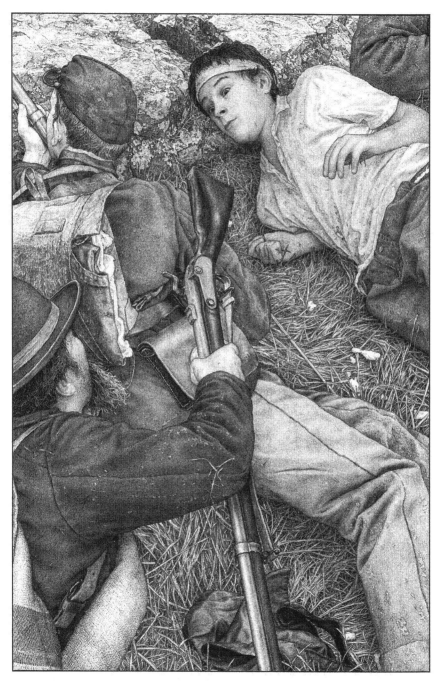

"Here, boy, fetch y'self a little glory!"

Many of our soldiers, having tired of the meaningless slaughter and having witnessed the sublime courage of the opponents now at their mercy, called out across the few yards between them. "In God's name, let's end it now! Come over! Come on over on God's side!" Some stretched forth their hands as if in friendship. Others beckoned, "Come on. Come over!"

Many did. Some waved pitiful little scraps of white cloth. With tears streaming and streaking blackened faces on both sides, men in gray and butternut threw down their muskets and came forward, a few, then many and then hundreds. Some said that almost four thousand Confederates in total surrendered that day. General Meade had returned to the Leister house and rode over the crest of Cemetery Ridge. When he saw so many rebels swarming the crest, he thought there had been a breakthrough.

"No, no, General Meade," shouted Lieutenant Haskell. "They are surrendering! See? They are not armed! We have carried the day, General!"

"You mean, we've turned them *back?*" shouted General Meade. "Praise the Almighty!"

I was cheering like mad with everyone else. Men were still laughing and not realizing they were laughing. It was laughter at the absurdity of being alive. They say pain often disappears under extreme stress, and after a fight like that, you had the urge to hop up and feel yourself all over to make sure everything was still in place and where it should be.

General Hays and some of his aides had gathered up a batch of rebel battle flags and were riding up and down in front of the line dragging these proud but pathetic pieces of cloth in the dirt. General Meade angrily sent word. "Tell Hays to desist! The enemy does not deserve to be humiliated. If you treat an enemy thus, he will someday treat you in kind."

Occasional Confederate artillery rounds were still coming in and falling among the prisoners. It seemed such a mindless cruelty of war, but in the same way as a fight between two people, the rage of battle takes time to subside. General Meade stopped and spoke to the rebel prisoners. Some prisoners flinched and ducked as the rounds hit nearby, but General Meade didn't bat an eye.

A young rebel who had surrendered sank to the ground with his comrades. "I'm done with this damn fight! No more for me. We left home with near nine hunnert men. Agin, we had three hunnert sixty left when we crossed the river. We lost three hunnert here in the last two days and made this charge with only sixty left! Now we are down to *three* – he, thee and me." He pointed to two comrades. "I wouldn't fight no more for Jesus Christ and a host of angels!"

Another exclaimed, "I seen the daggone elephant, all right! I done survived the big one, now, and I shan't go no further." Yet another: "I come all the way from Texas looking for a fight, and by the Almighty, I have made a success of it."

The rebels were astonished to find out how thin our line had been, and some asked if we'd mind if they went back over and tried again. I've heard that when either side takes prisoners, they're often friendly as all get out to one another, maybe because they're so relieved they don't have to fight each other anymore. This would seem to me a sign that most of them didn't want this fight in the first place and given their druthers would like nothing more than to reach out, shake hands, have a drink of whiskey together and go on home. Makes sense to me.

Some of the rebels had a funny way of talking that was hard for me to understand. For example, they'd say, "*ike speckt*," when they meant, "I expect." Or they would say that the coffee was "strong as *Ackee Forty*." I never did find out what that meant. After General Meade departed, I hung back a bit to listen to their banter with the Yankee guards. When a Yankee officer told a batch of them that they didn't seem so bad to him, downright friendly, in fact, one of them responded with just a trace of a smile in his eyes.

"That's the trouble with you Yanks. Y'all don't hate us enough. In truth, suh, we don't feel all that friendly to'ards y'all a'tall one bit. Y'see, weah from East Tennessee, and maybe we just seem friendly to y'all cause we kaanda smaaal ever' time we say a word with a long aaaa in it. Like, 'Haaa, would y'all like a big slaaaace o' apple *paaaa?*' But in truth, we surely do hate y'all through and through, suh. That's whaaa y'all'll never be as good a soldier as we are. Y'all surely have to hate y'all's enemy through and through to be any good at killin'."

It was mid-afternoon with much sun and little water among the men who had suffered the terrible exertion of combat. Lieutenant Haskell said he felt like he had been boiled. His faithful horse, Dick, had been severely wounded today and might have to be put down. Without knowing it, the lieutenant had spurred the horse vigorously. He only realized its condition after the fight was over and was now feeling remorse for pressing it so hard. I had been worried about Old Jack, but here he came now, as glad to see me as I was to see him. After a round of hugs and kisses, we found each other to be as good as ever.

Temperatures rose above ninety degrees, and out on the field, the wounded could be heard praying and begging for water. Tending to the Confederates was hampered by the stupidity of the occasional rebel shelling. Late in the afternoon, some showers broke out, and after dark, heavy rains soaked the field. Patches of moonlight soon gave way to a solid cover of clouds and fog. Piles of dead lay between the lines, and the cries of the wounded would continue mournfully throughout another night. I guess General Hays had a change of heart as he sent details out onto the field with canteens of water for the wounded.

A lot had come together on this field today: angers, faiths, forgiveness, goodbyes, the enormity of an experience every man knew he could never describe, a moment that men would talk about forever – and an overwhelming relief that this battle now seemed to be over. And now, over there across that mile of desolation, the rebels were licking their wounds and aching for us to try something as foolish as what they had just done, while everybody on our side wondered whether or not they had enough fight left in them to try again.

Chapter Nine - Withdrawal

The wounded with no place to hide,
Had crawled among the wheat and died.
And later on their bones were found,
And piled together in the ground.

On Saturday, July 4, the nation's birthday, heavy rains drenched the land for two hours at midday and continued after a short respite.

The men on Cemetery Ridge scanned the western horizon and waited for something to happen. To everyone's relief the day passed quietly without the enemy revealing intentions to renew the fight. The story went around later that a missing hen had held up the departure of the Army of Northern Virginia. It seems that General Lee had a hen that laid an egg for his breakfast every morning. When the army was set to withdraw, the hen was missing. Departure was suspended while the army stopped to look for the general's laying hen. Finally, the hen was found and returned to General Lee, whereupon his army slipped away in the wee hours of Sunday morning and headed southwest on the Fairfield Road.

The Sixth Corps was sent to pursue the enemy, and the cavalry was sent to fret him on his retreat towards Hagerstown. One by one, the other six corps of the Army of the Potomac began to depart on their assigned roads for Frederick to rearm and refit for the next confrontation with Lee's army. Most of them had suffered punishing casualties, and the First and Third would never again operate as the effective fighting units they once were. The following year, they would both be disbanded and the survivors incorporated into other corps.

I stared across at a land I scarcely recognized. Before me was the indescribable carnage of war. More pistol shots sounded here and there from men who had been sent to put the poor wounded horses out of their misery. Aside from these mournful punctuations, a great deafening stillness had spread across the land like a blanket. It was as if all of nature itself were exhausted and all noise and movement had passed from it. The sound of roosters crowing in the morning had been as familiar as my own heartbeat. How strange and foreign was this silence of the morning.

There were no buzzards. In summer, a silent column of buzzards soaring lazily high above was a common sight. On this of all days, there should be thousands of them arrayed for one of the greatest feasts of all time, but even they had rejected so foul a place and would stay away for months.

On the now quiet field, graves dotted the land, and shallow trenches up to a hundred feet long were dug to accommodate the mass of bloated and blackened corpses. Crude pieces of board were marked with names of the dead, if known, for later transfer to more permanent resting places. Throughout the field a somber forest of upended muskets with fixed bayonets stuck in the ground marked graves or still unburied corpses of the fallen.

The rains would persist most of the week. The roads, churned up by man and beast, became impassible muddy ditches. Creeks and small streams overflowed their banks and became roaring torrents. Thousands of wounded that had been laid out in an S-curve of Rock Creek had to be yanked and pulled in agony to higher ground lest they drown, but hundreds did drown anyway before they could be dragged screaming to safety.

So hard were the rains that the blood, filth, waste and corruption of decaying men and animals polluted every spring and stream, turning them into vile and dangerously unfit sources of drinking water. Private wells had been smashed or had dried up. Railroad bridges had been demolished by the enemy, and no water could be brought in by train. In a few days, people of the region and many thousands of wounded faced the terrifying danger of dying of thirst.

At the hospitals set up along Rock Creek, the terrible amputations continued without letup. More than 21,000 wounded men lay in the field or in military hospital tents around Gettysburg. Volunteer surgeons and nurses were on the way from far and wide but would take days to get here. The courageous army surgeons were overwhelmed and worked around the clock. Piles of amputated hands, feet, arms and legs grew into grotesque mountains of rotting flesh and bones until carted off to a common burial. Those who could not be saved were left until last, and received attention often after the need had passed. Said one surgeon, "You do your best to save a man from dying, and if he dies, he dies."

Here and there citizens of the town tentatively ventured forth and appeared on the field, drawn by a morbid curiosity to stare at a carnage monstrous beyond anyone's worst nightmare or to pick among the ghastly residue for souvenirs.

The wagon train of rebel wounded that headed south was seventeen miles long. People all the way to Chambersburg said they could hear it coming for miles and would be haunted forever by the shrieks and moans as the wagons bounced and swayed over rutty roads. This chorus of agony took all day and all night to pass, and still the rebels had to leave 6,000 behind on the battlefield.

I FELT BURSTS OF EXHILARATION come and go that the thing was over. I was stronger for the experience. Not happy, but stronger. Gone was a kind of trust that life was full of good and that good people had little to fear, for there comes a time when innocence must meet the realities of life firsthand and instincts must serve you quickly.

General Meade had ordered the headquarters wagons packed, all but a few critical tents struck and everything made ready for departure to begin soon after the enemy's intentions were known. Within minutes of the report that Lee was gone, the Leister house emptied out and much of the staff was on the road to Frederick in the pouring rain. I took Baltimore Pike out as far as the Schwartz place to pick up Sport at which time I returned Sally with considerable regret. Old Sport looked as good as ever, and I was grateful to see he had fared none the worse. I had a large parsnip for him, which he devoured with enthusiasm but otherwise took our reunion in stride. Now, finally, I was ready and eager to make good on the promise I had made to Pa what seemed like ages ago.

I returned to find the general still on the field but totally engaged in dealing with the movement of his army. I'm sorry to say I found no appropriate opportunity to give or receive any final words.

As I turned my thoughts and attentions toward going home, I thought about how little I had actually been of service to General Meade. I was not happy about it; neither was I ashamed of it, mainly because the army had stayed put most of the time and didn't need my guide services. Time and events had passed quickly; I was with him only a few days. And then it was all over as soon as it began. I hung around partly because I couldn't get home and would get fed and didn't have anywhere better to go – but also because it was an exciting place to be.

I wished there had been a chance to say goodbye to the general but there hadn't been. I knew he had his hands full getting ready for what lay ahead. I also knew that now and then I *had* been of use to him, and it was not without some value that I had held my post through thick and thin regardless of motivations and was always there when he did need me. I knew he knew that, and I always remained proud of it.

The rain came in sheets, and the three of us took to the fields and rode north against the tide of all the units of the army moving south. These were the foot soldiers, the foundation of the army, the infantry – the *children* of the battlefield. Away from the heat of battle, I didn't even feel animosity for the infantry of the enemy for what they were made to do. Perhaps blame, like responsibility, accumulates upward; but are we not also to blame for who we choose to lead us?

As I PONDERED THESE THINGS, Lieutenant Haskell rode up to say goodbye and take time to exchange a few words. His loyalty to General Gibbon required that he make himself available now and help him while he recovered from his wound. Lieutenant Haskell himself had received a mean bruise on his leg yesterday from a ball that struck his scabbard and failed to penetrate the skin, but it was so sore, he had shortened his stirrup and was using it as a sling. He did not dismount.

Rain dripped from his hat and poncho as he spoke to me. "I want you to know, Reis Bramble, that I will always remember you as a friend …."

"Thank you, sir. Me, too." I choked up a wee bit.

"A good friend is to be treasured and never taken for granted," he said and looked me in the eye, "and *'those friends thou hast, and their adoption tried, grapple them unto thy soul with hoops of steel!'*"

Well, now I was choked up. "You sure say some beautiful words, Lieutenant Haskell."

"I agree. The genius who wrote those words was born some 300 years ago," he said. He looked into the distance. "I hope this thing will soon be over, Reisie, so I can go home and return to my law practice. I hear within myself little whispers to go home and raise a family before I let too many more years slip by." He wiped the water from his face with a large bandana.

"That would be nice," I said for want of something better. "I wish you didn't have to fight anymore."

A couple soldiers nearby were packing up and offered us some dregs of coffee they were about to pitch out. I handed him up a tin.

"I'm not so young anymore. I'm at an age that's like when you throw a ball straight up in the air, and it hangs there a moment before it starts back down. When you're young, everything goes upwards. Then it slows down a little, and you reach forty and life hangs there a bit before starting downwards. It's a wonderful time, a time of maturity and a time before old age makes itself known, a time when all your memories are still of youth. Then the ball begins to fall. It's called dying."

"I guess we all will," I said, "but I hope it's a long time coming for both of us."

Lieutenant Haskell took a sip of coffee and winced a bit. "Life is mostly a great yawning stretch, Reisie, filled with that which is neither right nor wrong. Good and bad often accrue to us in unequal measure. For all that, we ourselves decide who we shall be and how it is we see our God." He paused. "For me, God has always been absorption in goodness and good works. There is nothing I have ever found so inwardly rewarding as that small part of my life I let be quietly guided by rightfulness and rectitude."

"Pa says if you talk very much about the good things you do, you can wear them out until there's not much left," I said. "He says there's far more power in a thing if you can keep it between you and the Lord."

"Your Pa is right about that." He continued. "There is an old saying, my young friend, that no one is perfect. There are things I have done that I regret, but there are things that I have not done that I regret even more. Every human being has at least a few moments in his life that have been guided by what is right and such moments are the gems of his character.

"When it all comes down to it, it's not what you have on your shoulder, or how many brass buttons you have, or how many men you command, or how you wear your hat or grow your beard or pose with your hand in your tunic. It's what you do with what you've got that matters. And when you know so many who have fallen, war makes you appreciate the joy of still being alive. It has that value if none other, and he who survives a great struggle is often reborn into a simpler life."

"I will always admire you, sir, for a lot of things," I said, "I guess mainly because of what you did on Friday, but also because you always treated me with kindness and respect — as you do everyone." I babbled a little bit, but I was proud of what I said.

"Thank you, my young friend. Ralph Waldo Emerson said, 'You cannot do a kindness too soon, for you never know how soon it will be too late.' I try to treat every man as if it were the last time I will ever see him, because one day, it will indeed be so."

"They should make you more than a lieutenant. They should make you a general!"

He chuckled. "Thank you, again. If only you were the one giving out promotions! But understand that my loyalty to General Gibbon keeps me in a role that does not justify a higher grade. Sometimes when I get what I wish for, things come with it I didn't expect. I'm in no hurry to leave General Gibbon. I like my work with him."

Lieutenant Haskell took out a pad and wrote for a minute. Then he tore off the sheet, folded it twice and handed it to me.

"Put this in your pocket and keep it dry, and read it on the way home," he said. "And don't be in too much of a hurry to head home just yet. I know you must be anxious to get there, but wait a little longer and make sure all the rebels have cleared out and are far enough down the road."

Then he removed his holster with his Navy Colt revolver and handed it down to me by the barrel. I stared at it in disbelief.

"Oh, I can't do this!" I protested, hoping desperately he would insist.

He didn't say another word but turned his horse and rode off down the Taneytown Road. I stood there and watched him until he was out of sight and felt so proud and rich, I knew I'd never get over the thrill of it. But a great sadness came over me also, because I knew I would never see him again.

I MOUNTED OLD SPORT and made ready to head for home. I had grown a lot in five days and was amazed at how much I had overcome my early terror.

Battlefield terror can cause you to make lavish promises about the future conduct of your life and bring you to beseech God to spare you and deliver you elsewhere, however unlikely you know that to be. In the extreme, you may enter a state of transcendent acceptance where the specter of death is no longer fearful. The world around you slows down, and you feel that a mantle of blessed peacefulness has enclosed you. By and by, as the crisis lifts, you may find your old self returning with a new layer of experience added to its character.

I pondered that I had become, by some measure, a veteran. A man may experience more combat in a single battle than some do in the entire course of a war. The men on the line called it "seeing the elephant," that first exposure to real combat. Those who served in non-combat roles: secure posts, guards, paymasters and battlefield support people behind the lines rarely ever see the elephant. I had doubts I would ever be able to explain these things to anyone and would just have to be satisfied with the whole experience as a sort of advance ticket to maturity.

I had come to admire the officers highly, from Lieutenant Haskell all the way up to General Meade himself. They were mostly decent, God-fearing and God-praising men of the highest courage and character. On the other hand, most of the rebels I had come up against didn't seem all that bad either. I knew there were some bad ones, like the ones who tried to take Sport, but from my limited experience, I couldn't see a whole lot of difference between us and them, and, in other times, I would judge them all to be men of good will, or close to it.

But that being the case, how the Sam Hill did we get into this scrape? A lot of people I've heard say it's Jeff Davis's fault. But is he so powerful that he can order the whole South to war? Besides, he got his job after the rush to war had already been set in motion, so there must be at least a few pioneers that helped get the thing underway. The blame can't be with President Lincoln either, as all agree that all he is trying to do is to keep the country from going to Hades. But what other way can there be to put down a rebellion than this terrible war?

By now, it was mid-afternoon and time to cross the battlefield. I had waited long enough. I headed out onto a field of death, a field strewn with debris of every kind imaginable, including thousands of muskets, many of which, in the desperation of battle, had been jammed up to the muzzle with unfired cartridges.

Anyone still tied to the notion that war is glorious needs only five minutes at the aftermath of a battle to see the terrible toll in lives that lie broken and dead on the field or come filtering back through the wreckage. Unburied corpses lay everywhere, their faces turned black, their bodies grotesquely swollen by the gasses of decay like monstrous stuffed dolls, some bursting, oozing, covered with flies. Some had pockets turned inside out by thieves and scavengers. The smell became overpowering. I was scarcely able to breathe and was compelled to hold a rag to my mouth and nose as I passed through this foul place. A woman who arrived later in the week to help tend the wounded declared that the stench "robbed the battlefield of its glory, the survivors of their victory and the wounded of what little chance of life was left to them."

Some corpses were found as long as months later, in haystacks, in hay mows, in dark corners of barns and cellars, wherever they had crawled to nurse their wounds and die, alone, unknown, missing ... missing from loved ones, missing from life. Other corpses had been rooted up and eaten by hogs or torn apart by dogs ... somebody's son, somebody's brother ... somebody's husband or father, somebody's handsome little boy.

Gone now are the proud, clean, bright-buttoned uniforms of yesterday. Gone is the music, the swagger, the childlike pride. Here on this stained and blighted field, the remains of those who fought each other with savage fervor lay moldering side by side, all passion gone, all anger gone, their weapons trampled into the mud, their accoutrements and possessions and small treasures now past any use. To them, the struggle, the arguments over who was right and who was wrong, even whose side God was really on no longer matter. They lie together in silent honor.

How can it be that we honor such things? But we do.

This then is the glory of war: the burning, stinging, choking agony of twisted and missing limbs, of stumps, of faces gone, of hearts torn out, bellies laid open, of body parts stuck in fences, heads with unseeing eyes. Brains that once held newfound thoughts, recited verse and savored life – splattered, blown to bits. Young lives just begun, cut off, forever unfulfilled.

✞ ✞ ✞

Is IT FOR THIS A MAN IS BROUGHT FORTH of his mother and given life – this child who took her loving hand? Is it for this that he would seek the death of his fellow man? Is it for *this*, then, that a man, even in his final hour, would break a long-held covenant with God?

Back in Washington, when he heard the first reports of the battle, President Lincoln said, "Every life must come and go, but when so many as this are made to go so early, the weakness of man's case on earth is still much in evidence."

Maybe someday I can tell Pa. I would have to think on it a while yet. Even then, it would be a hard thing to find the words to recreate in detail that which I wanted so desperately to forget. How does a twelve-year old boy tell about things so gruesome that he would never dream to think or utter such words at ordinary times? Perhaps I would find resolution simply by deciding not to talk about it at all.

OTHER THOUGHTS AND OBSERVATIONS drifted into my consciousness and lingered there as I rode along.

What is it that causes men to prefer death rather than to be thought a coward? I've thought about it many times, and I've always come away no closer to an answer than before I considered it.

This war is not being fought for gain, or territory or subjugation. This is a war fought to preserve a government created by and answerable to the majority, the principle that a free society derives the ideal to govern from the people themselves. Freedom is the prime commodity of human experience. Duty and commitment to preserve it override all other considerations.

The people here at Gettysburg lost more than belongings or horses or property. They lost in an instant that which they had commonly and forever taken for granted: the assurance that things were always going to go along about the same in life, that prayer and hard work would get you through tough times or that God could be asked to take up the shortfall. When people in the path of war, who had worked hard and led a pious life, were wiped out and left in despair, it would take a long time for some to get their faith in the old ways to come back. Men who heretofore had never known differences of race, religion, nationality and social class were thrown together and confronted with life and death. Some came back torn and broken and forever limited to a lesser life. Thrown together as comrades in arms, they forged a brotherhood that lasted long after the war had passed. Said one volunteer nurse about the character of those she attended, "I have been for a week the only lady in a camp of seven hundred men, and have never been treated with more deference, respect, and kindness … More Christian fortitude was never witnessed than they exhibit. They always say, 'Help my neighbor first, he is worse off.'"

I REMEMBERED THE SLIP OF PAPER Lieutenant Haskell had given me and fetched it out and unfolded it. I shielded it from the rain and read with pride what he had written:

> *To Reis Bramble, Bvt Pvt and Friend – in highest appreciation of his gallant services and contribution to the success of this army at Gettysburg, July 1-3, 1863. With respect and admiration, F. A. Haskell, 1Lt., 2 Div, 2 Corps, U.S. Vols.*

The last few words were a blur due to the fact that both my eyes had sprung major leaks, but I said aloud with quivering lips, "Worth more to me than all the medals in the whole world."

The following year, with everlasting dismay, I read among the casualties, "Haskell, Franklin Aretas, Col., 36th Wisc. Vols., mortally wounded, Cold Harbor, Virginia, June 3, 1864." I was to learn subsequently that, on his first battlefield command, he had been struck in the right temple during a charge after ordering his men to lie down under an intense enemy fire while he remained standing. He had finally achieved field command, and soon thereafter, he was dead. I sobbed unashamedly all day long and every so often for a long time afterwards.

But that came later, and in this moment, I felt blessed, grateful that I was still in one piece, and that Sport and Old Jack had, by some miracle, survived also and that the three of us were headed home.

Chapter Ten - Going Home

The killing all has ended now;
The army marches on.
But who can reconcile somehow
The thousands that are gone?

It had rained pitchforks, and the land was made to pay for it. The roads became canals of thick mud and had been stirred up so bad, "the bottom had gone out." The retiring armies had been forced to take to the fields, and the incessant march of men, beasts, artillery and wagon trains obliterated all evidence of cultivation.

Lead-colored clouds drifted slowly northward and hung so low you could have poked a hole in them with a long stick. The gray haze of earth and sky blended into a landscape without beginning or end. I allowed as how I could sure use one of those rainbows right about now.

Everywhere was death and more death. Everyone had suffered; everyone had lost. I kept thinking of the words from Ecclesiastes, '... *all things come alike to all ....*' As far as I could see, the land was scarred and torn apart. As I passed through the Sherfy place and the fields worked by one of the Spangler families and then on through Pitzer's woods, it seemed that not one square foot had been left untouched – as though every tree was wounded, not even a weed left unbent. Carefully tended fields of corn and grain lay ripped and scarred in sodden ruin.

But I was on my way now, and the pull from inside was great. I was anxious more than ever to get home and put Ma and Pa and Gramma at peace about my welfare. They must be in a terrible stew. Just thinking about home and the gentle succor it offered brought up in me an almost unbearable longing. Imagine. After just *five days!* How must the boys who fought here feel after years away?

I dreaded to think what might have befallen our place and hoped and prayed that somehow we had been far enough off the beaten path to have been spared. Through all my fears and melancholy, Lieutenant Haskell's words came back and echoed over and over, and I took great comfort in them:

"Go home now, and rejoice in your family and a good life. Things may be in a mess for now, but the strength is in you and your folks to make them right again. Always, insofar as the choice is yours to make, take all things in the context of time. If the hurt or anger you feel today will pass tomorrow, let it pass today, also. Learn to let it go in the very moment it rears its head." One of the last things he said to me was, "You have an innate goodness about you; strive to take the high road in all you do."

✞   ✞   ✞

FOR SOME REASON, amusing thoughts kept coming up and dwelling on Aunt Banner and Aunt Fidey, I guess because familial things are comforts that often come to the fore at times like this.

Aunt Banner and Aunt Fidey were sisters well into their eighties and lived together after the rest of their family had died off. They had some strange ways of doing things. They had this bench-legged hound named Shorty they kept chained up in the kitchen, because they were afraid he'd run off. Shorty hated the way his life had turned out, and whenever someone opened the kitchen door, he would take a desperate running shot at it, but the chain always held and yanked him around and he'd fall flat. I learned to open the door and stand back and wait for Aunt Fidey or Aunt Banner to reel him in, because he'd jump up on you and claw at you for dear life, and I hated that.

Uncle Pete had paid them for something with a five-dollar greenback, which promptly disappeared. They turned the place upside down to no avail and concluded that Shorty must have gotten hold of the greenback and eaten it. Well, they watched him closely for days, poked and pulled his droppings apart and sought counsel from everyone who came by. After a long time without results, they gave up, stopped pestering Shorty and assumed that his digestive powers had obliterated all trace of the greenback.

Finally, after everyone was more than worn out hearing the story and after Lord knows how much time had passed – a long, long time, Pa said – Banner thrust her hand down into the corner of her apron pocket where ladies stuff their handkerchiefs and such, and there underneath a handkerchief or two, all wadded up, was the greenback.

Well, Aunt Fidey allowed it was high time Aunt Banner washed that apron, and Shorty was exonerated and allowed to live in peace but limited citizenship status once again. Of course, everyone far and wide had to listen to the new facts of the case all over again, which goes to prove that sometimes the thing you try so hard to find is where it belongs and right there under your nose all the while – and ought to be the first place you look.

I felt I would be thankful for the rest of my life for what I had and now anticipated with great joy that within the hour I would be home and safe once again with those I loved. Then something came along that fetched me clean out of my daydreams.

SOME FOLKS LIVED DOWN THE ROAD a piece, and they had this big dog. He would hide in the bushes, and every time I rode by, he would sense when I was off my guard and make a snarling, snapping lunge at my horse's fetlocks. I would catch his blurred form at the very edge of my vision as he dashed from his hiding place, and it was all I could do to keep the horse under control. He particularly enjoyed lunging at wagons and carriages, and of course everyone hoped he would get tangled up in the wheels and that that would be the end of him.

But on this afternoon, another blurry form came out of the bushes as I passed and caught me in the middle of the daydream about Aunt Banner and thoughts of home. In just the tiniest flash of time, I turned and caught sight of the face of the ugliest, dirtiest rebel I ever did see. He was in the act of swinging a large branch that he gripped by the small end with both hands and swung around in a great arc with all his strength. The branch caught me across the chest and knocked the wind out of me. The blow swept me clean out of the saddle, and I fell hard. I gasped for breath and struggled to my feet.

The rebel grabbed Sport's saddle horn and was fixing to mount up when I grabbed at his pants and pulled for all I was worth. Old Jack joined in and was barking and biting at the rebel's bare feet. He kicked at Old Jack and gave me a backhand that sent me sprawling. I got to my feet and grabbed at him again. I tried desperately to get the pistol Lieutenant Haskell had given me out of my pocket but caught the hammer in the rope that served as my belt. I hadn't even checked to see if it was loaded. He knocked me down again, and this time he sat astride me and held one of those rebel short swords over me. I reached up and grabbed his wrist, but he was too strong, and I couldn't hold him back.

Suddenly there was a loud sickening *thwack!* and the rebel's head was snapped aside and surrounded by a halo of sweat and blood. Blood flew from his mouth. He staggered to his feet to confront Bum Piles, standing there like a guardian angel, holding the business end of his old blunder-buss that he had clubbed the rebel in the face with. The rebel snarled and lunged forward with his sword pointed at Bum's chest. Bum flipped his gun around and fired. There was a great *BOOM!* and I was surprised that the thing worked at all, as I had never known it to be fired before. The rebel was propelled backward and stared down at a big red hole in his mid-dle. He tried to throw his sword at Bum, but it fell from his fingers. Like a tree that's going down and starts out slow, the rebel began to topple for-ward. He spit out a hoarse whisper. *"Damn you ... you damnyankee b...!"*

The last bit of sound came out in flecks of blood. The anger in his face faded into mortal awareness, and all expression left it. He staggered one last small step as if to catch his balance and pitched forward on his face with a hard thump and lay still.

Bum gritted his teeth and paced back and forth and said with great sadness and anger, *"Dang* your hide! I was hopin' t'get through this thing without blood on my hands, but you wouldn't let me! *Dang* you! ... *dang* you all to Hell and back!"

I sat up and gasped at the air in silent heaves until my breath re-turned. I looked over at the dead rebel face down in the dirt and felt ... nothing. I should have been angry or felt sorry for him or *something.* I knew the time might come when the impact of what just happened would stir some kind of emotion in me – perhaps remorse, even. But for now, I was only a little surprised that I felt nothing whatsoever.

My breath returned. "Bum!" I yelled. "Where did *you* come from?"

"Oh, I been comin' up behind you for a spell," he said. "I seen you ridin' along with your head down, like your heart was broke or you was deep in thought. I meant to sneak up on you and give you a quick poke, but this one here beat me to it."

Bum and I stared at the corpse for a long time.

"You know, Reisie, I raised hogs wunst, and hogs is smart. Hogs is smarter than most any other animal I know of. I got quite attached to 'em. I used to talk to 'em and take a stick and scratch they backs and all. Whenever they heerd me a-comin', they'd sidle up to the pigpen and stand there and wait for a scratch. I raised 'em up beautiful and became such friends with 'em, it got so that I couldn't bring myself to slaughter 'em and sold off the whole lot for somebody else to deal with. Well, I still like ham and bacon and side meat just like always, but I have to leave the slaughterin' up to somebody else. I hate it I had to kill that feller there, 'cause I'm not a killing man. This whole war thing and these last few days is a gol'dang evil and an abomination if ever I saw one."

"This is the same kind of rebel I talked out of taking Sport on Wednesday," I told him. "He was pure evil!"

"Don't ever abide evil, Reisie, 'cause if you do, it gits inside you, and it's hard to git rid of. Even now, I don't hate that man over there. I did what I had to, but I don't hate him. I hate the evil that was in him. I hate whatever *put* the evil in him. He wasn't born with it, I don't guess. This is what war does to people."

WE DIDN'T GO DIRECTLY HOME, that is, to *my* home. We took a side trip over to Bum's place. "I ain't been home in five days, m'self, and I want to go by and see to things before I see you on home," said Bum.

Bum's old shack lay tucked away in a secluded hollow a few miles or so from our place. Even before we got to it, I noticed everything was all tracked down, and all the fencing was gone. The closer we got, I expected to see a corner of Bum's house or barn pop into view as we turned the bend in the road. But no corners were showing through the brush as we moved closer. Finally, as we stood before the place where things used to be, it became clear that everything Bum had was completely gone. The shack, the little barn, the chicken coop and corn crib had been consumed by rebel campfires or coffins or whatever other purposes they had been put to. The one thing clear was that it was all gone. Poor old Bum.

"Ever' time I git a little bit ahead, somethin' always happens." He cast his eyes left for a second or two, then right. "Now this." He spit, wiped his eyes with the back of his hand, took off his old hat and smoothed his matted gray hair back, put the hat back on and kicked at the dirt. "Nothin' left but a grease spot." He looked around once more. "A long time ago, fire took the onnee other home I ever had, ... now this. Ain't never had nothin', ... never will. Nothin' from nothin' remains."

We stood there a while in silence, and I felt the tears well up inside me and begin to pour down my cheeks. *'... and from them that hath not, even that which they have shall be taken away ....'* I sniffled and apologized to Bum for my unmanliness.

"It's all right to cry, Reisie, p'ticly these days. Ever'body cries sometime," Bum put his hand on my shoulder. "But life moves on, and if you stop to cry too long, it moves on without you."

"It's a good thing you're older, Bum. I mean doesn't being older make it easier to abide ... I mean it makes it easier than if you were still a kid ... doesn't it?" I asked him.

Bum smiled at me ever so little and said, "I'll tell you something you'll never understand, Reisie, 'til you get old like me, when you're able to look back over things – and that is that you still see out of the same eyes and still feel the same hurts and still have the same thoughts and memories you always did. Life don't get any easier; it don't get any better, and it don't get any worse. Life hurts often and hurts a lot, but you just have to cuss a little and move on. You're always who you are inside, Reisie, and that's that, young or old. There ain't no secret, and there ain't no magic God gives you later that you don't have with you right now. But find it before you let your lifetime pass by. That's the onnee thing being older tells you, knowing what you should've done when you still had the chance.

"One of the biggest mistakes you can make with y'self ... maybe the onnee real one ... is to let life get away from you. Then you wake up old, like me, and wonder who you are and wonder who you was."

"How come you always know so much, Bum?"

"Don't pay no mind to what ever'body else thinks, Reisie. Find out y'self. Them that thinks they knows it all has stopped learnin'.

Don't worry if you don't understand ever' little thing just yet. Leave a little room for faith and magic. And beware o' them that says their way to Heaven is the onnee way. I've thought on God all my life, Reisie, and most of it still remains a mystery. I only know that there's so much more than there is in my poor power to understand, But all you need to do, Reisie, is whatever puts God in your heart, and all else will come right.

"And keep your cool. Save y'self for what really matters," Bum went on. If you can do all that, it'll take you a long ways, and you'll be more growed up than most.

I realized after a while that I was speaking to Bum in a normal tone of voice and that he seemed to hear me just fine. "Bum! How's come you can hear without me shouting?" I asked.

"My hearin's cleared up ever since the big bombardment. I guess it musta knocked somethin' loose," said Bum.

For a long time after the bombardment, most men who were in it shouted at each other in allowance for how their hearing had been impaired. For some, normal hearing never did return, and I believe my own never did come back completely, for I had difficulty hearing the little sounds of tees and dees and esses later on. The one exception was Bum, who, for some strange reason, could hear better than ever.

We both stood there a long while, saying nothing. I tried to change the subject.

"How's old Rip doin'?"

"He doin' fine. He got a whole lotta horse left. Like me."

"You gotta whole lotta *horse* left?" I smiled.

"*Heh, heh,*" Bum chuckled a little, "I mean I gotta whole lotta *me* left."

"Why don't you come stay with us now, Bum?" I offered, Gramma's views notwithstanding. Gramma would have to realize we were all coming back changed from this.

Bum went quiet a bit.

"Boy, I was hopin' they might be a better way and a better time to say this, but I guess they ain't." Bum quit talking and fidgeted with his hat again.

"What, Bum …? Tell me. What?" He kept on fidgeting. "What, *what* …?"

"About your place …" He wouldn't look at me.

"What *about* my place?"

"You're not going to like it, Reisie. It's pert near not there any-more."

"How can it be not *there?*" I could feel alarm welling up inside me.

"Well, they's a lot more than nothin', but a lot less than they was. The rebels carted away everything they could, burned what would burn and trampled the rest into the dirt. Get y'self ready, 'cause you ain't hardly gonna recognize it no more."

GRAMMA GLANCED UP THROUGH HER TEARS from a pan of cress she was picking over and saw a silhouette begin to rise in the road from over the brow of the hill. Soon a man on a horse … then a little man on a big horse … then an *old yeller dog!* … took shape on the horizon! She stared unbelievingly, caught the edge of her chair lest she topple over, and went to her knees. "Oh … oh … oh, my God in Heaven, Almighty! John! Liza! *Come quick!*" Pa said that really perked him up, as he had never heard Gramma say anything like that before in his whole life. Gramma's pan of cress dropped to the porch as she hiked up her skirts and ran up the road to meet us. I don't remember ever seeing Gramma run before. I could see her making the words, "Praise God! Praise God!" over and over as she stumbled and ran towards us.

I slid down off Sport and ran down the road into her outstretched arms, and for a while there, I half expected she would smother me with hugs and kisses.

"Well, 'deed if this don't beat all!" Gramma gasped and shouted, "I had faith you'd come back. I never doubted it for a minute that the Lord would bring you back to us," she panted. "It was *more* than faith. I *knew!* I prayed. I went down deep and waited for the Lord to let me *in!* Then I waited 'til I knew He was ready to give me His attention," Gramma gulped air. "I didn't need to ask Him anything, 'cause He already *knew* what I needed. And then I came to this blessed state where *He* told *me*, and I was reassured, and I *knew!* It wasn't just faith. *I knew!*" Gramma babbled on so, I thought she'd never stop.

Now here came Pa huffing and puffing up the road with Ma about three rods behind. And now, Pa picks me up off my feet and swings me around.

"Pa," I said. "I should have come home like you told me, but I waited too long!"

"I know, son. It worked out just as well that you did. The rebs took Nell and everything else. Now, thanks to you, we still have Sport, and we're sure going to need him to help us put things back the way they were. We'll just have to make do with what we've got left." Pa let me down and hugged me up against him. "And besides, I'm just so gol-darned glad to see you, I couldn't get mad if I wanted to."

"And Ma," I said to her, "I know you didn't want me to go, and I should have listened to you!"

"Oh, my dear boy," she kissed into my ear. "The main thing is that you've come back, and right now, I can forgive you anything!"

We all stood out there in the middle of the muddy road and hugged away for dear life. As if to agree, Old Jack went around the whole caboodle several times and gave everyone a good flapping in the legs with his big old tail. Bum just stood there and took it all in with a big grin. And then, everybody, even Gramma, went over and hugged Bum, much to his discomfort and embarrassment.

I looked around me. Those rich, familiar and comforting fields lay ripped and rutted beyond description from the tread of men, beasts and machines. We knew enough as farmers to keep ourselves and our animals off cultivated fields and away from soft earth soaked by rain. Now everywhere they had been trampled into the mud. And everything else had been picked clean as far as the eye could see.

"They ate us out of house and home," said Pa. "They up and took everything. Bum was right – everything rideable and edible."

"Not my biddies," I asked, hoping for an answer I would like and knowing better. "They didn't take my biddies; not all of them ... did they?" No one answered, but no one had to. I choked up a little; and then

I remembered the things I had seen the last five days and put the thought of biddies out of my mind.

"We begged them to spare our home, but it fell to deaf ears," said Gramma. "There was just too many of them." And then she brightened up and hugged me again. "But you came back, and that's all that matters. We can replace the other things, but we could never replace you!"

I REMEMBERED THE HULLABALOO if the milk cow got into the corn or worse, the garden. Such commotion you never heard. Ma would run out with the broom and chase old Gertie around so much that she caused more damage than if Ma had led her out peaceful. But, oh my land, what a racket! Then Ma would cast around for recriminations and blame everyone in sight whether it made sense or not. One time I hit one of her pineys with a stick I was throwing for Old Jack and knocked the petals off. You'd have thought I hit her personally she went on so. And if a stray dog lifted a leg to one of her hollyhocks or lilies, his life would be over if she caught him. One thing I learned early on was to stay clear of Ma's cultivations.

Now if one dog or one cow or one stick could upset my mother to the degree that she was willing to declare war over it, just imagine the aftermath of a retreating army of many thousands – all of them half starved and willing to take up and eat any animal or vegetable that crossed their path. Add to that tens of thousands more animals and maybe two hundred pieces of artillery with caissons and limbers and wagons. Picture all that traipsing across our place after the heavy rains and you get some idea of what it looked like. I was afraid Ma might never recover from something like that. At least their ambulance train took a different route out the Cashtown Pike.

"I cried, Gramma. I cried a lot," I said. "You'll never know how much I cried! I will never sing before breakfast as long as I live, and I'll never make light of any of your superstitions ever again."

"Well, you won't ever give it a better test than you did, I'll say that!" Gramma smiled at me, and then she took my face in her hands again. "But, oh shoot, Reisie, that's just an old English wives' tale anyway and don't mean nothing. My people were from a long line of Calvinists who never had an ounce of mirth among them. Their faces would have cracked, if they ever *had* smiled. Never hide a merry heart, Reisie, whenever it moves you. Raise up your voice to the Lord, and let it all come out. And just let the Devil take the hind seat!"

We walked down to the house past destruction in all directions. Pa told me that the rebels had used our well after they dried it up to bury their dead. We would need to keep filling it up for years.

Pa showed me the wad of Confederate paper money the rebels had left for food and things taken. I stared at that pathetic, flimsy, poorly printed, rolled up scrip, with its feeble vestige of honor. And I think I hated them more in that moment than I ever did on the battlefield! Them and their *pathetic* Confederacy and the wretchedness of it overwhelmed me, and I broke down at the ridiculousness of this gesture after all I had just witnessed!

And where on earth would we spend it anyway?

I grabbed the pitiful, worthless wad of paper and ran out on the porch and flung it into the air, "Goddamn you! Goddamn all you miserable goddamn rebels! Go rot in Hell!" I screamed. "I wish I could throw all your fine words about your damnable *cause* up in the air with it!" I sat down on the steps and cried my heart out, and somehow, they let me get away with all that cursing. Five days ago, I would have gotten the worst of punishments for it, but now all I got was silence and left alone.

✞ ✞ ✞

BUM CAME TO LIVE WITH US and helped us rebuild and proved to be a wonderful addition to the family. Gramma imposed only a few rules: no spitting in the house, no profanity, no more nostril shots inside *or* out (Bum now carried several large handkerchiefs he privately called his "snot rags"), and that was about it. We all got along fine. We attended church regularly every Sunday now with renewed dedication. Bum took an interest in his appearance for the first time in years and showed up each Sunday morning all shaved and cleaned up for church.

"Well, what *next?*" said Gramma, approvingly, the first time she saw the new Bum. She looked in the mirror and touched up her hair. "I must look a fright." In the past Pa had suggested that Gramma in truth wanted

Bum to think well of her. "Oh, go on with you," she'd say. "I don't give two hoots what he thinks." Could it be that she was now concerned for her appearance *because* of Bum Piles? Now that *would* be a stretch!

A change had come over Gramma. She was sweeter and more gentle than before. It was as if the rebels had captured her sharp tongue and took it south. For the rest of the time we had left together, Gramma's sharpness towards me grew softer, and we treated each other with deeper respect and kindness – not that we ever intended otherwise in the banter that had passed between us, but now there was a difference. She still had her ways, but the hardness of her words … softened, and we found ways to be more expressive of our love for each other, spoken directly or not.

AFTER THE REBELS WITHDREW, the moon which had so brilliantly illuminated the obscenities of the battlefield during those awful days, gave way to days of rain and a new moon that brought with it a world so dark it seemed as though the light had gone out of life itself. But after a while, we picked ourselves up from our depths and with Bum's help returned to the land to work the soil again. The grass came back first; the birds returned and new trees began their long path to maturity. Some distance from the old well, we dug a new one – far enough away that we might never be confronted with the sight and memory of the old one.

We petitioned the government for compensation for our losses to the ravages of war. A little money came eventually and helped us to rebuild. Some things could be restored, but how do you put a price on the eternal loss of things as they were – the stately trees, the magnificent barn built with the loving skills of our ancestors, animal friends that were part of the family? There was something else, something we could never lay claim to, that deepened our sense of loss. It was that connection, that continuity with a past we had taken for granted. We couldn't quite describe this feeling of loss to each other and rarely spoke of it, but it hung over us, and because of it, we understood better what it must have been like for the generations that gave up their roots in Germany and Ireland and all over the world to find a new life in America. They gained the excitement and security and opportunity of a new land, but something irreplaceable had to be left behind: the gentle familiarity and consoling memory of that which was and always would be first home.

I had become some sort of hero among my peers and classmates, although I took no particular pride whatsoever in it and never felt a moment's glory or glamour from a thing that had brought so much suffering to so many. I did take away the valuable lesson that people often don't do the right thing or know what the right thing is.

I had to learn to live with holding my tongue at times when confronted with older people's speculations on what had happened to our land, what war was really like, what it all meant and whether it was worth it, and so forth. In my position of less-than-full citizenship due to age factor, the customs of the day denied me the right to question or criticize my elders. It was just as well, as I didn't really want to talk about it anyway, much less to become ensnared in the fictions and imaginings of those whose views meant so little to me.

For a long time, I had lost my faith in most grown up people. I neither trusted what they said nor what they said they believed anymore. In time, I came to a gentler conclusion: that most people are not inherently mean, or evil, or stupid but that each and all alike contend with life as they see it and as best they can – and are, as all of us are, only pilgrims headed home.

ONE OF THE BEST THINGS to come out of my experience was the reclamation of Bum Piles. He stayed on and looked for Gramma's approval of things he did and changes he made about himself. Now that he had a new lease on life, he took great pains to improve his health and appearance, so much so that he could look downright handsome in the right light. We had room in the big house for Bum to move in with us, which he did to everyone's satisfaction, and he and Gramma enjoyed each other's company for the rest of their days.

Bum could make or do just about anything. In ways that were most useful and practical and even tender, he could be quite creative. When he found out that Gramma favored applesauce cake with currants and black walnuts, every now and then he would surprise her with one of his own creation. Gramma allowed that it was the best applesauce cake – if not *any* cake – she had ever tasted.

When spring came round again, he showed me how to find stick worms and water worms that proved irresistible to trout, and I caught more than ever. He mixed compost and manure and applied it to Ma's garden and helped tend it. The garden prospered and became a wonder to behold.

One day, I asked Bum, "Did you ever think in all your born days that things would turn out the way they have?"

"Sometimes things'll work out for the best if you just let 'em be," he said.

Some time ago, Pa had referred to Bum as one "of the least among us." I had to disagree with Pa's assessment; to me, he was closer to being the *most* among us.

ONE SUNDAY MORNING that first fall, not too long after we laid in what harvest we could, Bum came downstairs all dressed up in a brand new frock coat, a new bowler hat, shoes all shined and ready for church. I never did find out where he got the clothes, but he just about sparkled. Again, Gramma was made aware of the inadequacy of her own appearance.

"Why, land sakes. There you go again! I must look a fright!" said Gramma. "You do put a body to shame, Bum."

Did I just hear what I thought I heard? That I would live to see the day!

"You know, I'll never cease being grateful to you, Bum, for bringing our dear boy home safe." Gramma smiled at him with an uncharacteristic tenderness that I'd never seen aimed at Bum before and placed her hand lightly on his forearm. I was having a conniption inside and struggled not to let on.

"Well, it's all been worth it just to hear you say that like that, Miz Bramble. I reckon it must be an ill wind that don't blow *nobody* no good. As for Reisie, well, he come almost the whole way all by his ownself, and he had an awful lot to contend with, and he still has more to tell you about when the time is better," said Bum. "I onnee hepped him some that last little bit."

"Bum sure has a lot to tell us about, too, someday." I offered my two cents.

Then Gramma said, as if she had a thought that had never crossed her mind before, "I don't think I ever told you my first name, Bum." She looked up at him. "It's Carrie."

"I know'd it all along, somehow." Bum smiled.

"Really? Well, I wish you would call me Carrie then from now on."

"I will then," he nodded.

"And what is your real name, anyway, Bum? I'd like to start calling you by your real name. I expect anything might be better than 'Bum.'"

Bum cocked his eyes to the side and looked back at her kind of sheepish like. "Seymour," he said. He looked down. "It's Seymour … Piles." He looked up again, "… Seymour Piles."

The warm smile never left her face as she let that sink in a second or two. "Aha," she said softly, "Well … in that case … I think I'd just as lief stay with 'Bum'."

AFTER WORDS

An awful game is war, not just the blood and gore,
When orphans weep and widows keep
A vigil at the door.
A soldier falls in pain to never rise again,
To those he leaves and she who grieves
Forever is the game.

THE WAR

SOMEWHERE AMONG ALL THE REASONS why wars are fought, there is surely the one that says that war, as seen from a distance and away from the horrible realities of the battlefield, bears a mystical and irresistible attraction for most men. The drawing of the sword stirs the imagination of every man from childhood and feeds an ancient fire strongly felt but little understood beyond an urgent call to action. Whereas to advocate an alternative path - that is, to think deeply into the causes and consequences of war and seek answers to seemingly unsolvable problems by peaceful means, often goes down in failure and is likely to provide little compensating glory or reward in any case.

A man once said there is no such thing as an inevitable war, that if war came, it would be from a failure of human wisdom. From all I had ever heard, this war had been on its way for a long time. No one seemed to be willing or able to head it off. I guess no one *person* ever could, which means that it takes a lot of people to avoid a war and therefore, I guess you could say it takes a lot of people to start one.

Some people said the war was fought to free the slaves, and the national stress caused by slavery certainly helped make it inescapable. Emancipation was indeed an outcome of this long and bloody war, but at the outset, the South saw the war as a fight for independence and state sovereignty, and the North saw it as a fight to put down the rebellion of a section of the country against the central government.

Although much has been said about how alike the two sections were, Pa always said that North and South were as different as night and day. He said the South was like the turtle, whereas the North was like the chameleon. The turtle stopped changing because it didn't see any need nor have any desire to change, and the chameleon was a different color every time you look at it.

IN THE VAST AREA of a million square miles east of the Mississippi where most people lived at mid-century, the North and South had been engaged in a perpetual quarrel over state versus federal governance and had been drifting further and further apart ever since the Revolution. Southern society favored the rich and powerful to the exclusion of everyone else. So why on earth would those in power want to change anything? Men that were born lucky made immense fortunes planting cotton and lived in fine houses, drank fine liquor, rode fine horses, courted fine ladies beneath the live oaks. What a wonderful world – except that almost four out of ten people who lived in the South were not so lucky. Four million people were held in perpetual bondage and forced to carry the endless burden of hard labor that produced the wealth accumulated by their masters.

While the South chose to remain forever suspended in time, the North, with twice the population and twice the number of states, was running off in all directions. Factories were being built to mass produce inventions that would change the world. Telegraph wires were going up, railroad tracks were being laid; roads and canals were being carved into the landscape at a frenetic pace. Ordinary people found jobs, earned money, bought new things. Mass immigrations of hungry men and women poured in from Europe desperately seeking a way to make a living. The South became alarmed by this estranged and prosperous yet unrefined new world unfolding alongside and saw it as a dangerous and intolerable threat to the status quo of southern life. They persuaded themselves that salvation lay in secession – breaking away and forming a new country where they could keep things the way they were and the way they wanted them.

NO ONE UNDERSTOOD better than Abraham Lincoln that the United States held the promise of a great nation and that the war was not a fight for territory. There was no such thing as "our land" or "their land," but that all the land belonged to all the people, he said. He believed if this experiment in representative democracy – the people's right and ability to govern themselves – failed, this noble idea would be lost for generations in a world yet to come, perhaps forever. In his almost magical ability to envision what the nation could become, Lincoln dedicated his life to holding it together and thus setting an enslaved people on a long path to equality as well.

THE BATTLE

BESIDES THE TOWN ITSELF, the actual battleground at Gettysburg covers several areas of perhaps less than ten square miles in total and varies from sweeping plain to dense and rocky hills and woods. The battle began around eight o'clock in the morning of Wednesday, July 1 and ended late Friday afternoon on July 3.

With Robert E. Lee staking the fate of the Confederacy on the outcome, this battle was among the most desperately fought of the war. Seasoned veterans said that the fighting, particularly on the Second Day in and around The Wheatfield, was the most violent and ferocious of their experience. In only a few hours, total casualties may have exceeded *twenty thousand*, almost as many as the battle of Antietam, the bloodiest day of the war, which was fought not for hours but all day long.

Many regiments and their towns and communities back home suffered unimaginable losses. Casualty rates among some units at Gettysburg such as the First Minnesota, the 26th North Carolina and the 24th Michigan were greater than any of the war.

Some say that Gettysburg was Meade's best battle and Lee's worst. They say Robert E. Lee was accustomed to winning his battles, but this time was different. Lee expected morale in the Union army to be low. He found it to be just the opposite. His decision on the Third Day to send his men across almost a mile of open terrain to attack Meade's fortified line has been called by some a gamble. It was not. It was a calculated risk, and fate decrees that no one wins all calculated risks.

Lee, whose men had never failed him, believed in the invincibility of his army and lost. On top of everything, he had been off his game and ill with dysentery. His misfortunes were multiplied by the fact that he was without the crucial eyes of his cavalry, which had been missing for days. All three of his corps commanders turned in uncharacteristically flawed or mediocre performances. Loyal to the death, the men in the ranks gave Lee their best fight as they had done every other time. This time, it would not be enough.

THE FORTUNES OF THE CONFEDERACY peaked at Gettysburg. In a military sense, their army had known remarkable success until then, and southern hopes ran high. There were shortages and privations throughout the south, and, of course, the crushing tragedies of the battlefield struck every home. But before Gettysburg, there was widespread faith that the Confederate cause would prevail and that they would yet emerge victorious and build for themselves a new nation. As one hard-liner put it, "This will mark the end of the damnyankees tellin' us what to do and when to do it!

But with the loss at Gettysburg, the legendary initiative of Robert E. Lee would pass to Union hands, never to return to a southern army. The next day, July 4, Vicksburg fell, splitting off Arkansas, Texas and most of Louisiana, leaving all of the Mississippi River under Federal control and foreboding ruin the Confederacy.

AFTER

MUCH WAS SAID AT THE TIME and has been said since about General Meade's failure to follow up his success with a vigorous pursuit of Lee's army. Critics saw this as the best opportunity since Antietam to defeat Lee and put an end to a horrific war. In fairness to General Meade, who could claim the first real success following a long series of failures by his predecessors, several factors need to be recognized.

In the urgency to overtake Lee's Army of Northern Virginia before the battle, all seven corps of the Army of the Potomac had been pressed into a march of many miles beginning near Fredericksburg, Virginia, some units making an incredible thirty miles and more in a day. The men poured onto the battlefield ravenously hungry, thirsty and exhausted. The two sides had pounded each other with intensity for three days. Ammunition of every kind was low or depleted. Animals, wagons, artillery, caissons, small arms and other materials were in critical need of replacement. The men were desperate for food and rest, and the army was in dire need to be refitted and re-supplied. Torrential rains persisted for days after the battle.

Roads became impassible, slowing everything down and making effective pursuit and maneuver next to impossible.

The case could be made that Lee faced similar constraints and worse. However, an army in retreat has no choice but to run. Lee was all but out of artillery ammunition, short on all other materials and far from home and resupply. He had lost the battle and had no alternative except to risk everything on a rapid escape. Meade, a cautious man, faced a clever and resourceful enemy and was loath to confront him with less than a viable army and risk the signal accomplishment of his success. No one could be exactly certain of Robert E. Lee's plans, but he was as dangerous in defense as a wounded tiger.

Meade finally caught up with Lee near Falling Water on the Potomac nine days after the Battle of Gettysburg and prepared to attack the following morning. But the swollen river had dropped just enough to allow Lee to slip safely across during the night and continue fighting for another twenty-one months.

I WOULD ALWAYS REMEMBER GENERAL MEADE as a consummately decent and honorable man, one who could be depended upon at times when sacrifice and duty of the highest order were urgent and immediate. I remained forever grateful to him and to the others for driving the rebels from our home and held General Meade to be one of the great unheralded heroes of the Civil War.

Meade's performance has been called by some a paradigm for an ordinary man who did his best. But when it came to steadfastness, fortitude, devotion to duty, courage and the ability to manage his army, Meade was anything but ordinary. And this Army of the Potomac, that Meade was given to work with only three days before the battle opened, had come to Gettysburg seasoned, determined, well led and aching to whip Lee's ass.

THE SOLDIER

HEROES OF ALL KINDS abounded at Gettysburg. John Buford and his tireless cavalry desperately held the field against all odds on the First Day while the rest of the army came up. Brigadier George Sears Greene, age 61, saved the day at Culp's Hill and kept the Union right secure all night long and into the Second Day against a superior rebel force. Nineteen-year-old battery commander Lt. Bayard Wilkeson was hit by an artillery round that left his leg hanging by shreds, and while still on horseback, cut it loose with his pocket knife before falling dead on the plains north of town. The young battery commanders and classmates barely out of West Point, Alonzo Cushing, George Woodruff and Charles Hazlett, held their posts to the death. A nameless thin line of heroes held on at the Low Stone Wall against Lee's desperate charge on the Third Day and changed the course of history. And still thousands of others went bravely forward into the jaws of death.

Toward the end of the war, after witnessing almost four years of horrific savagery, a young Confederate veteran officer lay in the trenches outside Petersburg one night. He said,

> "As we lay there watching the bright stars, many a soldier asked himself the question: What is this all about? Why is it that 200,000 men of one blood and one tongue, believing as one man in the fatherhood of God and the universal brotherhood of man, should in the nineteenth century of the Christian era be thus armed with all the improved appliances of modern warfare and seeking one another's lives? We could settle our differences by compromising, and all be at home in ten days."

FOR A WHILE, I HATED ALL REBELS. I hated them for coming here. I hated them for making me hate them. As I grew older and perhaps wiser, I came to believe that the men on both sides indeed were, "more to be pitied than censured." That they were wrong by any true Christian or any other moral ethic goes without saying; that they went forth and did their duty as required with uncommon valor goes without question. They faced enormous social and cultural pressures to serve the gods of war at a time when it was universally regarded as a right and manly thing to do. The courage required to endure intense social rejection by refusing to fight was greater and far less common than was the courage to go along.

In later years, when I heard old men taking counsel among themselves and extolling the glories of the battlefield, I was able to separate those who had survived the terrible experience of combat from the ones simply making use of what they had heard others say. I found that the quieter they were, likely the more intense had been their experience. The real combat veteran – from the unnamed lonely lad who walks his post at midnight and waits for war to come in the morning to someone's mutilated son who lies out among the corpses and begs for water – understands that living war firsthand is beyond words and remains silent while others prattle on.

Once, one of the old timers offered for the millionth time the contention that the rebels gave us no choice and that war had been inevitable and necessary to save the Union. An old soldier with his right arm gone from the shoulder, who customarily sat quietly among them, offered this observation: "Maybe so, but the war was hard on all of us and one helluva way to solve the problem."

✞   ✞   ✞

IN RECENT TIMES, I CAME UPON a photograph of an assembly of important people at the second inauguration of President Lincoln. It occurred to me not without some sorrow that all of those important people were dead now, and that every one, for all his pride and fame and fortune, was powerless to affect anything at all. I was saddened by the thought that each of them had carried forward and into the current generation no more than the most cursory scrap of his memory, as will be true for all of us.

For such as they, all pride and praises, all aspirations and trappings of office now lie among the fading pages of history. And, in the cold, impersonal light of each succeeding generation, those who were once loved are loved less, and those who were once hated, are hated less; and those who rose up and ruled and were exalted will surely be, by the passing of years, forgotten altogether. I am old now and given to reflecting on things past. And so it seems to me that that part of the world that is yet without man's presence is better off left that way; because for all his triumphs, man is still to me an absurdity – except for what he leaves behind in the transcendence of his art, music, literature and ideas.

Buford, Brig. Gen. John, Cavalry Corps, I Div, Commanding, 37, born March 4, 1826, Woodford County, KY – West Point, 1848; saw much frontier service with the dragoons in Texas, New Mexico, Kansas and Utah before the Civil War. Strong, dedicated, superb soldier; some said the best horseman in the Union cavalry; so badly wounded at Second Manassas, he was reported dead. At Gettysburg, his dismounted and greatly outnumbered troopers held the thin line with their Sharps breech-loading carbines until First Corps could reach the field. Stricken with typhoid fever in the autumn of 1863, General Buford died in Washington, DC, on December 16, some said from the exhaustion of non-stop service.

Butterfield, Maj. Gen. Daniel Adams, Headquarters Chief of Staff, 31, born October 31, 1831, Utica, NY – Credited with having composed the bugle call that became known as "Taps." Staff officer; intelligent, able, but obsequious and not trusted or highly regarded among peers. General Butterfield had a rather distinguished post-war career in various enterprises. Died July 17, 1901, Cold Spring, NY.

Caldwell, Brig. Gen. John Curtis, I Div, 2 Corps, Commanding, 30, born April 17, 1833, Lowell, VT – Volunteer; Modest and approachable and well-liked by his men, General Caldwell handled his brigades on the battlefield at Gettysburg with courage and skill on July 2. He practiced law in Maine after the war and held numerous state and Federal appointments. Died August 31, 1912, Calais, ME.

Cutler, Brig. Gen. Lysander, 2 Brig., I Div, I Corps, 56, born February 16, 1807, Worcester County, MA – Volunteer, first colonel of famed 6th Wisconsin; wounded at Second Manassas, his brigade fired the first volley in the battle of Gettysburg. His health ruined by wounds, exposure and hard campaigning, he asked to be relieved of field command in August 1864. Died July 30, 1866, Milwaukee, WI,

Dawes, Lt. Col. Rufus Robinson, 6th Wisconsin, I Brig, I Div, I Corps, 24, born July 4, 1838, Malta, OH, – Volunteer, courageous leadership at railroad cut on First Day; survived war, said to be only one of 1,058 in 6th Wisconsin during war to come out without a scratch. Brevet promotion to brigadier general 1864. Later, distinguished congressman from Ohio, orator and civic leader. Successful in lumber and railroad business. Son, Charles, was U.S. vice president under Calvin Coolidge and wrote the music to the song, "All in the Game." Died August 2. 1899, Marietta, OH.

Doubleday, Brig. Gen. Abner, 3 Div, I Corps, Commanding, 44, born June 26, 1819, Ballston Spa, NY, West Point, 1842. Inaccurately associated with the invention of baseball. Aimed first gun at Confederates at Ft. Sumter. He obtained a patent on the San Francisco cable car that still runs there. Temporary commander of First Corps after Reynold's death. Died January 26, 1893; buried at Arlington National Cemetery.

Gibbon, Brig. Gen. John, 2 Div, 2 Corps, Commanding, 36, born April 20, 1827, Philadelphia, PA – West Point, 1847; born in Pennsylvania but raised in North Carolina, General Gibbon remained loyal to the Union. Before the war, he served as best man at the wedding of Confederate Maj. Gen. Daniel Harvey Hill to the sister-in-law of Stonewall Jackson. He had three brothers at Gettysburg; all were Confederates. He developed the famous Iron Brigade. Noted on the battlefield for his level-headedness and cold courage, he was respected by all. Severely wounded at Gettysburg on the Third Day. Thirteen years after Gettysburg, Gibbon's command was first to find and bury the bodies of the 7th Cavalry (George Armstrong Custer) after the Battle of the Little Big Horn on the Montana plains. Died February 6, 1896 in Baltimore and is buried in Arlington National Cemetery.

Hancock, Maj. Gen. Winfield Scott, 2 Corps, Commanding, 39, born February 14, 1824, Montgomery Square (Norristown), PA – West Point, 1844; captain of quartermaster in the sleepy little town of Los Angeles, California, at the outbreak of the war. Profane and full of bluster, he became a fearless and effective leader on the battlefield and a favorite of the men in the ranks. In the final hours at Gettysburg, he received a severe wound that would trouble him for the rest of his life. General Hancock ran for president in 1880 and lost to James Garfield (also a Union general and later assassinated) by fewer than 10,000 popular votes, the slimmest popular vote margin in U.S. history. Of all the high accolades, including being cited by Congress, his epitaph was perhaps best expressed by a staff member who said, "One felt safe when near him." Died February 9, 1886, at Governors Island, NY.

Haskell, Lt. Franklin Aretas, Aide to General Gibbon, 34, born July 13, 1828, Tunbridge, VT – Moved to Wisconsin and entered service there; exceptional staff officer. With Gibbon and Hancock wounded, he rallied Union troops to repulse Confederate assault on the Third Day at Gettysburg. He wrote a 136-page letter to his brother in the days following the battle that would become a classic document. General Gibbon said that he, "… did more than any other one man to repulse Pickett's assault … and he did the part of a general there." Later promoted to colonel commanding the 36th Wisconsin, he was mortally wounded at Cold Harbor, VA, June 3, 1864.

Hays, Brig. Gen. Alexander, 3 Div, 2 Corps, Commanding, 43, born July 8, 1819, Franklin, PA – West Point, 1844; big, strong, red-haired and hot-headed; fearless in battle, admired by his men for his courage under fire; good friend of Ulysses S. Grant. General Hays's men held the line on the right in the repulse of Pickett's Charge on the Third Day. Killed in action in the Wilderness, May 5, 1864.

Howard, Maj. Gen. Oliver Otis, II Corps, Commanding, 32, born November 8, 1830, Leeds, ME – Bowdoin College 1850; West Point, 1854, 4th in class; lost his right arm at Seven Pines; bad luck seemed to be a feature of his career. Under his command, the Eleventh Corps performed poorly at Chancellorsville and at Gettysburg according to many, but he was nevertheless voted the thanks of Congress. Included in the ups and downs of his post-war career, he was a founding member of Howard University in Washington, DC, and saw service in Indian country in the 1870s and 1880s. In 1893, he received the Medal of Honor for his bravery at Seven Pines. Died October 26, 1909 in Burlington, VT.

Hunt, Brig. Gen. Henry Jackson, Chief of Artillery, 43, born September 14, 1819, Detroit, MI – West Point, 1839; he revised, with others, the system of light artillery tactics used throughout the war. Conscientious, dedicated and able, Hunt served in artillery training and command. Seventy-seven guns under his direction blunted Pickett's Charge on the Third Day at Gettysburg. Died February 11, 1889 at Washington, DC.

Meade, Maj. Gen. George Gordon, Army of the Potomac, Commanding, 47, born December 31, 1815, Cadiz, Spain (his father was in Spain on business) — West Point, 1835; civil and topographical engineer, served with distinction throughout the war; wounded twice; appointed to command three days before Gettysburg to the relief of his subordinates who had suffered the misfortunes of his predecessors. Modest, steadfast, courageous, loyal and effective, General Meade retained command of the Army of the Potomac under U. S. Grant through Lee's surrender at Appomattox in April 1865. Died November 6, 1872, Philadelphia, PA.

Newton, Maj. Gen. John, I Corps, Commanding, 40, born August 25, 1822, Norfolk, VA — West Point, 1842. Second in his class, he was, like George Thomas, a Virginian who remained loyal to the Union. He was involved in a controversial affair to have Gen. Ambrose Burnside removed from command following the disaster at Fredericksburg. Appointed by Meade over Doubleday to command First Corps upon the death of Reynolds at Gettysburg. He later served with distinction under Gen. William T. Sherman. Died May 1, 1895, New York, NY.

Pierce, Matilda "Tillie", **born** March 11, 1848, Tillie was fifteen years old at the time of the battle. She lived with her family on Baltimore Street in the town of Gettysburg and fled the first day's fighting to the Jacob Weikert farm several miles south where it was hoped she would be safe. Ironically, the Weikert farm was near much of the Second Day's actions. Many wounded were taken there where young Tillie witnessed the horrors of battle wounds and amputations and was pressed into nursing service of exceptional magnitude. Tillie married Horace Alleman in 1871 and moved to Selinsgrove, PA. She would later write a successful book on her experiences entitled, *At Gettysburg: Or What a Girl Saw and Heard at the Battle.* Tillie died March 15, 1914 and is buried in Trinity Lutheran Cemetery, Selinsgrove.

Reynolds, Maj. Gen. John Fulton, I Corps, Commanding, 42, born September 20. 1820, Lancaster, PA – Career soldier. West Point, 1841; considered by many to be the best general in the Union army, he turned down Lincoln's offer of command because non-interference from Washington could not be guaranteed. Killed in action on July 1, 1863. He had been secretly engaged to a young woman he met on ship while sailing from California who entered a convent after his death.

Rowley, Brig. Gen Thomas Algeo, 3 Brig., I Div, I Corps, 54, born October 5, 1808, Pittsburgh, PA – Volunteer captain in Mexican War; commissioned Colonel of Volunteers on April 25, 1861. Upon the death of Reynolds, Doubleday acceded to temporary command of First Corps and Rowley replaced Doubleday in command of the 3rd Division. While inebriated, he apparently believed he had been given command of the entire First Corps. Court-martialed in 1864 for drunkenness, he was restored to duty in Pittsburgh. Died May 14, 1892, Pittsburgh, PA.

Sickles, Maj. Gen. Daniel Edgar, 3 Corps, Commanding, 43, born October 20, 1819, New York, NY – Volunteer; Tammany Hall war Democrat, he was appointed brigadier general by President Lincoln as one measure to build an essential coalition of disparate Union political factions. Headstrong, vain, volatile and argumentative, he was courageous in battle and dedicated to his men; lost a leg at Gettysburg on July 2. Before the war, he served in the U.S. House from 1857 to 1861 and shot his wife's lover (the son of Francis Scott Key) in Lafayette Park across from the White House in 1859, then forgave his wife and took her back. Defended by Edwin M. Stanton, the future Secretary of War, he pleaded not guilty by reason of temporary insanity and the "unwritten law" for the first time in American jurisprudence and was acquitted. Appointed minister to Spain after the war by U. S. Grant, he became intimate friends with Isabella, former queen of Spain. He served another term in Congress in 1893-95 and died confused and cantankerous on May 3, 1914 at age 94 in New York, NY, and is buried in Arlington National Cemetery.

Sykes, Maj. Gen. George, 5 Corps, Command-ing, 40, born October 9, 1822, Dover, DE – West Point, 1842; acceded to command of Fifth Corps on June 28 following appointment of Meade to army command. Methodical and the least colorful of the corps commanders at Gettysburg, he was small and thin and ap-peared stiff and crusty but was mannerly, cour-teous and likeable. After an exhausting march General Sykes arrived and deployed his various units very effectively at Gettysburg where needs were most critical along the wide front left in shambles by Sickles's Third Corps' rout. Died February 8, 1880, Brownsville, TX.

Warren, Brig. Gen. Gouverneur Kemble, Chief of Engineers, 33, born January 8, 1830, Cold Spring, NY – West Point, 1850, second in class; Gen. Warren is best known for ral-lying Union troops to occupy Little Round Top on the Second Day saving the Union left and perhaps the army. Acceded to command of the Fifth Corps, he was unfairly relieved of command a week before the end of the war by Philip Sheridan, ending his career. He was exonerated by a court of inquiry in 1879. After the war, General Warren made a number of signal engineering accomplishments including a rail-road bridge across the Mississippi. Died August 8, 1882, Newport, RI.

Webb, Brig. Gen. Alexander Stewart, 2 Brig., 2 Div, 2 Corps, 28, born February 15, 1835, New York, NY – West Point, 1855; born into a prominent New York newspaper family, General Webb was appointed to command the 2nd Brigade only a week before he found himself the focus of Pickett's Charge at the center of the Union line. He bravely urged his brigade to stand fast and repulse the Confederate charge. He was wounded at the "bloody angle" and was later awarded the Medal of Honor for his gallantry on July 3. He was gravely wounded in May of 1864 at Spotsylvania and returned in January as chief of staff to General Meade. In 1870, General Webb requested discharge to accept the presidency of the College of the City of New York where he served for 33 years. Died February 12, 1911, at Riverdale, NY, and is buried at West Point.

Weed, Brig. Gen. Stephen Hinsdale, 3 Brig, 2 Div, 5 Corps, 31, born November 17, 1831, Potsdam, NY – West Point, 1854. Before the war, he served as an artillery officer on the frontier; at Gettysburg, his men used sheer muscle power to drag three artillery pieces onto Little Round Top. The 140th New York Regiment of Gen. Weed's brigade command was rushed into the line to save the day after Vincent's brigade began to give way on the right in the late afternoon of the Second Day. Shortly after, General Weed was mortally wounded by a Confederate sharpshooter in Devil's Den.

Early, Maj. Gen. Jubal Anderson, Early's Division, Ewell's Corps, Commanding, 47, born November 3, 1816, Franklin County, VA – West Point, 1837; Early took part in all the engagements of the Army of Northern Virginia from 1862 through 1864; irascible, argumentative and difficult, he was nevertheless a brave and fearless fighter. Sent to threaten Washington in July 1864, his attack on Ft. Stevens was observed by President Lincoln from the parapets marking the only time an American President has been under fire by an enemy force. An unrepentant rebel to the end of his life, he engaged in an unseemly controversy with James Longstreet after the war. Died on March 2, 1894, at Lynchburg, VA.

Ewell, Lt. Gen. Richard Stoddert, Second Corps, Commanding, 46, born February 8, 1817, Washington, DC – West Point, 1840; short, bald, eccentric, generous, self-effacing and profane, Ewell was a brave and dependable fighter and was loved by his men, who called him "Old Bald Head." He lost a leg at Second Manassas, and as a trusted subordinate of Stonewall Jackson, was chosen to succeed him upon Jackson's death. He married the wealthy widow, Lizinka Brown, whom he customarily introduced as, "My wife, Mrs. Brown." In the two weeks prior to Gettysburg, Ewell performed "flawlessly." At Gettysburg, Ewell's Second Corps faltered at the end of a successful First Day, and Ewell was held by many to have contributed to the Confederate loss for failure to exploit his early advantage, with which he tended to agree. He was captured at Saylor's Creek, Virginia, three days before Lee's surrender at Appomatox. Died January 28, 1872, Spring Hill, TN.

Heth, Maj. Gen. Henry, Heth's Division, Hill's Corps, Commanding, 37, born December 16, 1825, Chesterfield County, VA – West Point, 1847 at the bottom of his class. A distant relative of Robert E. Lee, Heth was said to be the only officer in the Army of Northern Virginia whom Lee addressed by his first name. Heth had the distinction of setting off the Battle of Gettysburg when he took his division to town to look for shoes and to confront any Yankees there. He did so contrary to Lee's orders but with Hill's acquiescence. He was wounded early and out of action most of the day. Died September 27, 1899, in Washington, DC, and is buried in Hollywood Cemetery, Richmond, VA.

Hill, Lt. Gen. Ambrose Powell, Third Corps, Commanding, 37, born November 9, 1825, Culpeper, VA – West Point, 1847; saw gallant service throughout the war from Seven Days battles through Petersburg. "Little Powell" was fearless and impetuous and was reputed by some to wear a red shirt into battle. Promoted to lieutenant general and given command of the new Third Corps after Chancellorsville. In failing health, Hill never performed as well in corps command as he had done so magnificently as a major general. Hill had once been in love with the same woman as Union Gen. George McClellan whom she later married. His health mysteriously continued to decline, and he was killed by a Union straggler on April 2, 1865 near Petersburg, a week before Lee's surrender. He is buried in Richmond.

Lee, General Robert Edward, Army of Northern Virginia, Commanding; 56, born January 19, 1807, Westmoreland County, VA – West Point, 1829, second in class. He was one of only two individuals in the history of the academy to graduate without a single demerit. Courageous, audacious, clever and steadfast in his cause, he was at all times a courteous and proper Virginia gentleman. Son of Lighthorse Harry Lee, a Revolutionary War hero who died penniless, he enjoyed a long and illustrious career of gallant service. Cited for bravery for deeds in the Mexican War and throughout his career, Lee declined the offer of command of all Union forces at the outbreak of the Civil War. Replacing the wounded Joseph E. Johnston in June 1862, he became the best-known figure in the war on either side and rose to virtual god-like status throughout the South. Lee succeeded in defeating every Union general arrayed against him in the year preceding Gettysburg. After the war, he was appointed president of Washington College that now also bears his name. Died October 12, 1870, Lexington, VA.

Longstreet, Lt. Gen. James, First Corps, Commanding; 42, born January 8, 1821, Edgefield District, GA – West Point, 1842; "Old Pete," referred to by Lee as "my old war horse." Served with gallantry in the Mexican War and fought in every battle of the Army of Northern Virginia from Bull Run to Appomattox, except for detachment to the western theater in late 1863 and for a few months after being wounded in the Wilderness, June 1864; strong, stolid, powerful battlefield fighter. Disagreeing with Lee over Second and Third days' tactics at Gettysburg, Longstreet's performance was sluggish and half-hearted. Many in the South blamed him for losing the war at Gettysburg. Others believe had Lee followed his advice, Gettysburg might have been won. Gen. Longstreet was further excoriated in the South for switching to the Republican Party after the war, and controversy followed him to the end. Died January 2, 1904, at Gainesville, GA.

Pickett, Maj. Gen. George Edward, Pickett's Division, Longstreet's Corps, 38, born January 28, 1825, Richmond, VA – West Point, 1846, last in his class; brevetted twice for gallantry in Mexico, he served in Texas 1849-55 and Washington territory 1856-61. Notable for defiance of the British in the San Juan Island Affair. Wounded at Gaines's Mill. The famous charge on the Third Day at Gettysburg bears his name, although his division comprised only about one-third of the units engaged. Inclined to be vain, insouciant, overdressed and perfumed, he was unjustly relieved of command by Lee shortly before the surrender at Appomattox. Died July 30, 1875, Norfolk, VA.

AUTHOR'S NOTES

Most of the people depicted in this book really lived. All military officers named were real, for example. Ma, Pa, Gramma and Reis, are fictional, as are brother Jed, Mrs. Broderbundt, Mrs. McGrath and Mrs. Carlisle. Tillie Pierce, George Sandoe, Jenny Wade, Billy Bayly, Mrs. Harriet Bayly, Albertus McCreary and the McCreary family were real people.

The values, idioms and idiosyncrasies expressed herein are modeled after those of my ancestors. Gramma's character and personality are a blend of my grandmother and my mother, and much of what Gramma says is taken from childhood memories of both.

The main character, Chester Reis Bramble, derives his name from the surnames of my maternal great-grandparents, Eliza Reis and John Bramble. Their daughter, Carrie Lee Bramble, was my grandmother, whose only son was named Chester and whose daughter, Eva Mae Johnson, was my mother.

The names of Aunt Banner, Aunt Fidey, Uncle Pete and Uncle Reb were the names of actual relatives who harken back to another era and another context.

The character of Bum Piles is a special case and derives from a tale told me by master storyteller Bud Parker up in my log cabin one evening many years ago about an old West Virginian of a bygone era who carried that intriguing name. I found Bud's portrayal of Bum's character irresistible for use in this story.

Sport and Nell were two plow horses from my childhood.

At this writing, I have just passed my seventy-ninth birthday, old enough to have experienced firsthand such things as tending farm animals, raising crops, hog-butchering, henhouses, corncribs, buckboards, coal-oil lamps, straw-filled tick mattresses, thundermugs, deerskin rugs, gathering wild nuts and berries, dipping drinking water from a spring, riding atop old Sport to fields to be plowed and running the hills with Skippy, my sidekick and faithful companion for eighteen years. I hold many other memories of a life of struggle and denial that are nevertheless filled with a richness and a directness to the land itself, and I would not have missed it for all the trinkets and distractions of the modern world.

ACKNOWLEDGEMENTS

To a host of good friends who gave service as readers and nitpickers: Carole Jones, Nelson Robinson, Ted Coffey, Mary Margaret Martin and Kelly Siegel Ritchie; to my niece Dede Snook, her husband Eric and boys, Adam, Daniel and David for their inspiration and for the hospitality of their sparkling Pennsylvania farm; to my ninth-grade English teacher, Miss Margaret Workman, for imparting a love for the language and a lifelong facility with its peculiarities; and to Leslie Parrish for her talented editing, essential advice and keen eye and for her long and precious hours ...

To Fred and Fran Lorenzo for generously allowing us to use the image of their lovely restored country home as a model for the family home in the book. I remember with delight the day I found it right where my imagination and good luck said it should be ...

To my small platoon of junior readers whom I enlisted to temper my manuscript with a freshness and brightness that might help bring young readers to read about to the history that surrounds them without boring them to death. They are:

C. S. Taylor Burke IV, Christine Tarullo, Julianne Tarullo, Diana Vose ... and most especially to my devoted young friend, Michelle Vereb, for her diligence in reading the whole thing from Page One to the end and for her hundreds and hundreds of notations and advices of a quality much beyond her twelve years at that time ...

To my son Bob, for his kind and gentle recommendations. Thanks also for my web site and blog design (see www.singbeforebreakfast.com) ...

And most especially to my son, Doug, the most skillful editor I know, for his lovely, original art of which I am very proud; for his patient, meticulous search for typos, anomalies and repetitions that had disappeared before my eyes; for his deep interest and assistance in the creation of this book and for being so qualified and so informed in the history of the Civil War as to provide invaluable critique and authentication.

To each and all alike, thanks from a grateful heart.

Made in the USA
Lexington, KY
28 October 2013